WOMEN ATTACHED: THE DAILY LIVES OF WOMEN WITH YOUNG CHILDREN

WOMEN
ATTACHED
THE DAILY LIVES OF WOMEN WITH YOUNG CHILDREN

Jacqueline Tivers

ST. MARTIN'S PRESS
New York

©1985 Jacqueline Tivers
All rights reserved. For information, write:
Scholarly & Reference Division,
St. Martin's Press, Inc., 175 Fifth Avenue, New York, NY 10010
First published in the United States of America in 1985

Library of Congress Cataloging-in-Publication Data

Tivers, Jacqueline.
  Women attached.

    Bibliography: p. 272.
    Includes index.
    1. Women – England – Merton (London) – Time management.
  2. Time management surveys – England – Merton (London)
  3. Mother and child.   I. Title.
  HQ1600.L6T58   1985   331.4'4   85-18439
  ISBN 0-312-88726-4

CONTENTS

FIGURES AND MAPS

Figures

Maps

TABLES

TABLES

TABLES

ACKNOWLEDGEMENTS

For advice and constructive criticism of my research
work during my period of registration as a Ph.D
student, I owe thanks to Barrie Morgan and Tony
Warnes (both of the Department of Geography, King's
College London). To Professor R.J. Irving and
colleagues in the Home Economics Department, University of Surrey, I owe a debt of thanks for encouraging me to complete the research project and
providing me with the time and resources necessary
to do so. The work was supported financially by the
Social Science Research Council.

The final form of the questionnaire used in
this study owes a great deal to the advice of John
Hall (Polytechnic of North London) and Alan Marsh
(O.P.C.S.), while John Utting (National Children's
Bureau) helped me in the construction of the
sampling procedure. Advice concerning questions on
mobility came from Mayer Hillman and Anne Whalley
(of Political and Economic Planning - now, the
Policy Studies Institute). The coding and analysis
of the time budget data was discussed at length with
both Ian Cullen (Bartlett School of Architecture,
University College London) and Peter Jones
(Transport Studies Unit, University of Oxford).

Assistance with the provision of 'environmental'
data and the results of previous local studies came
from the Planning Department of the London Borough
of Merton and from Dave Johnston of the Social
Services Department. Amongst others who have helped
me more generally with the development of the
research, I would like to thank Sophie Bowlby, Glenn
Hurley, Suzanne Mackenzie, Linda McDowell and Laurie
Pickup.

Thanks are also due to my twelve interviewers
who worked conscientiously with minimal supervision.
A special note of thanks should be recorded to

ACKNOWLEDGEMENTS

my 400 survey respondents, without whom the study would not have been possible.

Finally, thanks to my husband, Mike Day, for his support and to the children - Mark, Katie and John - without whom I would never have understood the special problems faced by women with young children.

For my parents

Chapter 1

INTRODUCTION

'We might ...be forgiven for thinking that women
simply do not exist in the spatial world'. (Women and
Geography Study Group of the IBG, 1984,19). However,
the traditional 'invisibility' of women within social
science research and teaching, based on implicit
assumptions of conventional gender-role differentiation, has not been without challenge in the last
few years. The growing subject area of 'women's
studies' has been a major force in showing up both
the gender inequities present in modern society and
the gender-blindness of many academic writers.
    Geography as a discipline has emerged very late
in the list of study areas subjected to feminist
analyses. In Britain most geographical material
relating to gender issues has appeared within the
last five years (see, for example, Tivers, 1978; IBG
Women and Geography Working Party, 1981; Bowlby et
al., 1982; Drake and Horton, 1983; McDowell, 1983;
McDowell and Bowlby, 1983; Momsen and Townsend
(eds.), 1984; Women and Geography Study Group of the
IBG, 1984). Despite the recent proliferation of
publications, it is clearly apparent that traditional
human geography (the type that is taught to most
undergraduates) remains largely unaffected by feminist critiques.
    The research project discussed in this book had
its origins in an era which pre-dated the above-
mentioned studies. The results of earlier geographical research in North America were slowly becoming
available but it was necessary to draw mainly on
sociological literature in the formulation of the
research model.
    Even within the disciplines of sociology and
psychology very few empirical studies had been
reported dealing with the special problems of women
with young children (the important work of Gavron

(1966) being a notable exception here). Certainly, within geography, the study of this population sub-group was a new departure. However, it had become clear in the project formulation stage that it was impossible to make meaningful sense of the structure of daily lives and activities of women without taking into account the nature and impact of constraints on such activities. By selecting women with young children to be the focus of research attention, it became easier to identify and discuss general constraints on women's behaviour, since they are most clearly visible at this stage of a woman's life cycle. Thus, one aim of the research project was to relate empirical findings to the existing social science literature dealing with constraints on activities.

The study of the daily lives of women with young children, however, is a valid and useful research effort in its own right, quite apart from any theor-etical discussion of social roles. Women have so often not been accorded the importance in research that their numerical significance would suggest but have instead been considered marginal to any 'serious' study. This book is an attempt to redress the balance slightly in favour of women's activities and specifically focuses on a group of women who have only rarely been the subject of research interest. It is unashamedly an empirical study, although it is important to stress at the outset that the collect-ion and use of empirical data does not imply any rejection of alternative paths to truth. On the other hand, it is the author's view that social theory should be subjected to empirical verification, in so far as this is reasonably possible. Although a questionnaire survey can only provide data relating to a particular point in time and a particular loca-tion, even cross-sectional data of this type can be useful in providing a bench mark against which to check the progress of hypothesised social change.

It is probably unnecessary to justify the study of activity patterns per se as a valid and useful focus in human geography. With Smith (1977,5), we would assert that, 'For human geography to be relevant to the needs of a society, whatever its form, it must focus directly on the type of problem faced by people in their everyday lives.' Hayford (1974,2) goes further in stating that, 'The study of geography is concerned ultimately with an understanding of the means by which people overcome the constraints of time and space.' Whether or not this latter view is accepted, it is certainly true that increasing

interest has been shown by geographers in the study
of activities. This can be seen mainly as the
result of the recent emphases in geography: firstly,
on process rather than on spatial patterns; secondly,
on a behavioural level of analysis and thirdly, on
questions of the 'quality of life' and 'social
justice'.

It is essential to define at the outset what is
meant by the term 'activity pattern'. Hemmens (1970,
53) provides an all-encompassing definition of
'activities' as being '...simply...the things people
do - the what, when and where of their regular
routine.' This study will use a similar broad
definition but will consider only weekday (daytime)
activities (when women are in the position of having
sole responsibility for their children) and, like
Hemmens' study, will focus entirely on out-of-home
activities. By disregarding domestic activities, it
should not be concluded that in-home activities are
considered to be less important than extra-domestic
ones. In fact, as will be demonstrated later (see
Chapter 2), for women with young children it is in-
home activities which assume dominance in the overall
activity pattern. The exclusive study of out-of-home
activities must, therefore, be justified. The justification rests on two criteria; in the first place,
the study of out-of-home activities permits the
consideration of a <u>spatial</u> as well as a temporal
dimension and it is <u>this</u> spatial, or spatio-temporal,
dimension which is of chief interest to geographers.
In the second place, the study of extra-domestic
activities inevitably by implication throws light on
the importance of in-home activities and the patterns
formed around them.

Having accepted a broad definition of out-of-
home activities, it becomes a straightforward matter
to define the term 'activity pattern'. Simply, an
'activity pattern' can be considered a logical ordering of activities, both in time and space. The use
of the term implies the existence of some sort of
rational structuring by the individual. Like Cullen
<u>et al</u>., (1972,284), 'We do not comment on the ration-
<u>ality</u> of...behaviour for we would contend that all
behaviour is to some degree purposeful and that the
assessment of rationality by an observer is a dubious
process which must be subject to a variety of
cultural, ideological, and personal biases... Thus,
although we do not see behaviour as consistently
rational and well informed in the classical econom-
ist's sense, we see it as containing highly organised
episodes which give structure and pattern to the

whole stream of behaviour.'

Since this study concerns the activity patterns
of women with young children, it is necessary briefly
to explain the latter term. The term 'women' was
chosen deliberately rather than the term 'mothers' or
that of 'housewives', since the latter contain implicit assumptions which this study sought to avoid.
'Young children' as a descriptive term does, unfortunately, vary slightly in different parts of the
study. The intention was to consider women with
children of pre-school age. Official statistics and
previous research results (quoted in this thesis)
refer to pre-school children as those under the age
of five years. However, in the context of the
empirical study, it was necessary to alter this definition slightly. Most children in the London borough of Merton (the survey area) commence full-time
schooling before their fifth birthday. Since the
empirical study was concerned with the activities of
women with children under the age of full-time schooling, the population for the survey was more restricted than the population considered in previous research. However, the difference is slight.

Structure of the Book

Having considered the aims and terms of reference of
the research, the present chapter goes on to consider
previous research on the subject of activity
patterns, concluding with a discussion of the
conceptual approach of this study. The background
literature on constraints is introduced in Chapters
2 and 3; the nature of these constraints is firstly
discussed and then the impact of the constraints on
activity patterns. Each chapter is concluded by a
consideration of the question of linking theoretical
work with the generation of empirical variables.

Following on from the discussion of constraints
on activities, Chapter 4 presents a detailed research
model and briefly outlines the methodology of the
empirical study. The following five chapters present
an analysis of the data collected with reference to
the various research hypotheses; Chapter 5 looks at
the situation of respondents with respect to paid
employment; Chapter 6 considers their non-employment
activities (here designated broadly as 'unpaid work'
and 'leisure' activities); Chapter 7 discusses
questions of mobility and the local orientation of
women's lives; Chapter 8 considers the provision of
child-care facilities in the study area and respondents attitudes to and, use of, these; finally,

Chapter 9 attempts an interpretation of the 'quality of life' experienced by women with young children.

In conclusion, Chapter 10 summarises the findings of the research study, both from the review of previous literature and from the empirical survey. Relating the findings to broader social theory, various possibilities for the future are outlined and considered.

Approaches to the Study of Activity Patterns

The purpose of this section is to outline the different approaches to the study of activities which have been taken by researchers; these fall basically under three headings: time-budget, spatial behaviour and time-geographic approaches. The major strengths and weaknesses of each type of approach will be discussed. Finally, the approach adopted by this study will be presented.

1. The time-budget approach

Modern studies of activity patterns derive from a foundation in time-budget research. The latter, according to Anderson (1971,354) '...developed out of 19th century studies of urban life and poverty (for example, Engels, 1892), and was later influenced by 'time-and-motion' studies.' In the Western world, the chief application of time-budget research has been in the general area of leisure studies and questions about the 'quality of life' (excellent summaries of this work are given in Hedges, 1974 and Gutenschwager, 1973). As a definition, '...the term time-budget is used loosely to describe any research study that obtains a detailed, and usually quantitative account of the way in which people spend their time' (Hedges, 1974,35). As a result, 'The time-budget statement is an average or typical account of aggregated individual activity systems' (Gutenschwager, 1973,379). The normal method of data collection is the use of diaries, administered to a sample population, in which all activities are listed for a required period of time - often the preceding day or week.

While time-budgets alone can be used to give a very useful description of activities undertaken by populations as a whole, or sub-groups within them, a spatial dimension is also necessary for the analysis of activity patterns. The inclusion of a spatial variable in time-budget studies is a relatively recent development despite the fact that 'Researchers

involved in time-budget studies have...long felt the
need to broaden the scope of their investigations by
including the spatial or locational aspect of everyday activities in their observation' (Szalai,1972,4).
The resulting 'space-time budget' studies have been
undertaken by social scientists primarily in the
context of planning decisions (Macmurray, 1971,196;
Bullock et al., 1974,45).

The space-time budget approach is described by
Thrift (1976a,5) as deriving '...from empirical
observations which are in the final analysis just
time-budgets with a spatial location tacked on.' Because of this, the area of study has been by no means
the exclusive domain of geographers. The primary
emphasis rests on the use of time as a resource in
the urban context and spatial pattern only becomes
important as the outcome of time allocation procedures. Thus, Ullman (1974,134) notes the substitution
of time units for space in the perceptual measurement
of distance, for example, in the definition of a
place as being 'ten minutes away'.

The researcher whose name is most consistently
associated with a space-time budget approach is F.S.
Chapin. In essence, Chapin's approach can be described as the use of activity choices as a way of
viewing the ordering and structuring of cities
(Hemmens, 1970,56). Major surveys have been undertaken in the United States by Chapin and his
associates, using the technique of recall of previous
day's activities by members of sample households (for
example, see Chapin and Hightower, 1965; Chapin and
Logan, 1969; Brail and Chapin, 1973). There is a
basic continuum in their activity classification
between 'obligatory' and 'discretionary' activities.
Activities are aggregated into 30 categories, while
respondents are also aggregated into classes of
people in order to test the assumption that members
of these classes have different life-styles which
involve different activity patterns (Chapin and
Logan, 1969,311). In fact, Chapin suggests that a
metropolitan area may be viewed as being made up of
relatively few 'activity systems', which are related
to particular life-styles and characteristics of
spatial location (Chapin and Logan, 1969,312).

Although Chapin does not by any means exclude
the importance of various constraints (for example,
of income, life cycle stage and access to opportunities) in influencing activity patterns, he sees the
chief role of such constraints as being the context
within which motivations and preferences are framed.
In other words, he sees activity patterns as examples

of expressed demand and, fundamentally, as the outcome of choice processes.

A similar stance has been adopted by other
researchers. Hemmens (1970,55), for example, writes
that 'Our analysis of out-of-home activity patterns
is being conducted within a framework which views all
of the daily activities of an individual as a linked
sequence of activity choices.' He admits that
activity patterns are influenced by existing land use
patterns and transportation systems and that distance
is important in inhibiting interaction but, as in
Chapin's work, constraints are seen primarily as
implicit assumptions in the formation of choice
rather than as the chief determinants of activity
patterns. Hemmens' study is based on transportation
survey data, which explicitly exclude non-motorised
trips and, therefore, give a rather biased overall
picture of total activity patterns. (The same
problem arises with a number of other activity
studies - see, for example, Wheeler and Stutz, 1971
and Forrest, 1974; also Eliot-Hurst, 1969).

The work of Hitchcock (1972) has also been
closely connected with Chapin's research objectives
but Hitchcock emphasises the importance of choice
mechanisms even more strongly since he is dealing
only with non-work activities which, in Chapin's
terminology, are very largely 'discretionary' in
nature. Chapin's idea of describing the city in
terms of activity systems which are related to
different life styles is taken up by Banz (1976) who
discusses the use of life-style mapping as a planning
tool. He suggests that time-budget studies could be
used to derive data on life-styles, which would
provide a relevant input into planning models.

The most extensive study which has been undertaken, involving the use of space-time budgets, is
the study of daily activities in twelve countries
directed by Szalai (1972). A huge data file, of
150,000 cases, presented enormous problems of
analysis but it did facilitate the comparison of
patterns of everyday life in the different countries
for the first time. Substantial similarities in
activity patterns were revealed by the study. In
particular, Robinson et al., (1972,119;121) record
that 'The plight of the employed woman pervades all
of our time-budget records...substantial inequalities in the division of labor by sex remain every-
where.'

Other studies have come to similar conclusions:
'There is probably no other social phenomenon in
which time-budget research has produced such

unambiguous, well-documented and dramatic insights
into social reality as the sexual division of labour'
(Szalai, 1975,388). Vickery (1977,45) notes that, if
anything, the amount of time spent by women on household tasks tends to be underestimated in time-budget
research. Certainly, their dominant pattern of
activity based on child care and household work is
very clearly evident in time-budget studies (for
example, British Broadcasting Corporation, 1978) as
is their relative lack of 'free time', (Wigan and
Morris, 1979,7-9).

There are obvious advantages in the use of a
time-budget approach to activity patterns. In the
first place, the simplicity of the data recording
procedure should be noted. Secondly, '...space-time
diaries...record behaviour patterns which are not
directly observable because of their spatial and
temporal extent' (Anderson, 1971,359); thirdly and
'Equally important is the fact that the identity of
individuals over time is preserved' (Anderson, 1971,
359).

The methodological problems posed by the use of
space-time budgets in research are however formidable. These are listed by Hedges (1974,39) in the
following categories: 1) the collection of valid
data, 2) the classification of activities and time
uses, 3) the analysis of data collected and 4) the
conclusions to be drawn from the patterns of activity
displayed. Regarding the first of these categories
of problems, Scheuch (1972,69) notes that 'It is...
very hard to collect answers that correspond to
reality with at least some degree of accuracy. Representing the expenditure of time is one of those
subject matters where the reliability and validity of
data are extremely sensitive to details in the manner
of data collection.' With studies extending over
more than one day's activities, there is always a
danger that the recall of activities may be biased in
favour of certain types of activity. On the other
hand, the self-administration of data collection by
the use of diaries may encourage an artificially high
level of activities overall, since people make a more
concerted effort 'to do things' as they are under
study (Hedges, 1974,42). A related problem, which is
also difficult to handle, is the question of the ty-
picality of the data collected. It is usually necessary to supplement the straightforward time allocation material with questionnaire information on
irregular and infrequent activities although, even
then, the problems of seasonal variability remain
(Anderson, 1971,356-357).

The second major group of problems involved in space-time budget research concerns the classification of collected data. The trouble with human activity (from the time-budget researcher's point of view) is that much of it is messy and indeterminate' (Hedges, 1974,40). People often do more than one thing at a time and while it is possible (and may be necessary) either to deal with such activities in terms of primary and secondary importance, or to eliminate multiple activity periods from the analysis, this may serve to distort the pattern of activities considerably, '...particularly in the case of wives and above all mothers of young children, for whom the ability to do many things at once is a necessary condition of existence.' (Hedges, 1974,40).

The analysis of space-time budget data again presents problems. Although sophisticated computer facilities now exist to handle multi-dimensional data, in general dimensions have been collapsed and data extracted from the total information to be used in separate analyses (Thrift, 1976b,122). Anderson (1971,358) lists the various ways in which such 'simplication procedures' have been carried out. In particular, there has been a tendency to concentrate mainly on <u>time</u> allocation to activities, while the spatial dimension is formalised into very limited categories, such as 'at home', 'at work', 'at a restaurant' and so on. There has also been a neglect of the sequencing of activities, mainly due to the problems of data analysis: thus '...discussions have ignored the fact that any event in an individual's day is part of a sequence of interdependent events and that the decisions governing these events must, therefore, also be interdependent, owing to the necessity of continuity of action in both time and space' (Cullen <u>et al.</u>, 1972,281). (It will be shown later that this is one problem which is explicitly considered in the time-geographic approach to the study of activity patterns.)

The problems of inferring conclusions from the analysis of space-time budget information form the final group of problems mentioned by Hedges (1974, 39). It is important to remember that the results of time-budget studies tell us nothing about the relative importance placed on different activities by individuals, nor do they indicate the motivations which underly the activities observed. Consequently, the interpretation of time-budget information must also depend on the use of supplementary interview information (Gutenschwager, 1973,380).

2. The Spatial behaviour approach

Parallel to the interest in activity patterns as the outcome of time-allocation procedures, there has been developed (primarily by geographers) an interest in activities as aspects of spatial behaviour. The two approaches are to a certain extent related in that they both rely heavily on choice theory. Thus, Chapin (see Chapin and Logan, 1969,306) relates his study of time-oriented activity patterns to the 'revealed preference' idea of spatial behaviour; he states specifically that activity choices show what people actually want and therefore what should be planned for.

In general, however, spatial behaviour studies have tended to ignore the importance of a time dimension, at least explicitly. Instead, the emphasis has been on the relationship between activity patterns and urban spatial structure (a relationship which is, of course, also considered in time-budget studies but which does not form the chief focus of attention). The activities of an individual are seen as taking place within an 'activity space', '...defined as the subset of all urban locations with which the individual has direct contact as the result of day-to-day activities' (Horton and Reynolds, 1971,37). Conclusions are drawn concerning the importance of the learning process and choice mechanisms in spatial behaviour. The main difference between the space-time budget approach and the spatial behaviour approach, therefore, lies in the fact that whereas the former places emphasis on activity patterns, the latter focuses on activity spaces. It is, however, clear that the spatial approach is equally dependent upon the notion of choice among various activities and, therefore, upon theory developed in psychology (for example, see Higgs, 1975).

Particularly influential in behavioural geography has been the notion of 'revealed space preferences'. This concept, introduced by Rushton (1969), links overt spatial behaviour to the structure of preferences. In summary, Rushton views spatial behaviour as the outcome of a search among alternative spatial opportunities and says that preferences for certain alternatives account for observed spatial behaviour (Pirie, 1976,947). Specifically, he says that 'Spatial behaviour, exactly as any other behaviour, is determined by preferences only' (Rushton, 1969,400). It is, as mentioned before, in this 'revealed preference' idea

that spatial behaviour studies most closely accord
with studies using a time-budget approach. In both
cases there is an overwhelming emphasis on choice
mechanisms and on activity patterns as the outcome
of preference structures.

Although framing his work within the same
context of activity choices, Eyles (1971,244) states
that 'The concept of revealed preference does not go
far enough, since if an individual does not have the
opportunity to behave in a certain way his preference for this cannot be revealed.' He, therefore,
introduces the idea of 'repressed preferences',
which represent '...those opportunities or courses
of action perceived as impossible to activate, given
the individual's present social position' (Eyles,
1971,244). A radical change in access to resources
is required in order for such preferences to be
activated. Eyles, therefore, does recognise the
importance of constraints on activity patterns but
his principal emphasis remains on the relationship
between preferences and overt spatial behaviour.

3. The time-geographic approach

As Anderson (1971,363) points out, '...depend-
ing on the relative emphasis given to 'positive' and
'negative' determinants, we may make a crude distinction between 'choice' and 'constraint' oriented
approaches to behaviour.' The approaches so far
considered - namely, the space-time budget and
spatial behaviour approaches - are clearly choice-
oriented, despite their recognition of the existence
of environmental and personal constraints on
activity patterns. Observed behaviour is thought of
primarily as reflecting values and motivations but,
'If highly constrained situations are not recognised
as such, observed behaviour may be interpreted mis-
leadingly as what people "choose" rather than "are
forced" to do' (Anderson, 1971,363). Pirie (1976,
949) reminds us that '...the dimensions of choice in
spatial contexts are probably not as great as is
often thought, and the application of choice frame-
works to the analysis of spatial behaviour will not
always be well advised.' He concludes his critique
of 'choice' approaches to the study of behaviour by
stressing that 'Hobson's choice, after all, is no
choice, and on many occasions spatial behaviour is
rigidly circumscribed' (Pirie, 1976,953 - see also,
Gray, 1975; Duncan, 1976; Pahl, 1975).

The most comprehensive approach to the study of
constraints on activity patterns is undoubtedly that

initiated by Hägerstrand in Sweden. This is
described by some (c.f. Thrift, 1976a) as the 'time-
geographic' approach. Superficially, since
activities are considered in terms of time and space
use, there are parallels with the space-time budget
approach, already referred to. The emphasis here on
constraints, however, serves to distinguish the two
perspectives. Collection of time use data would show
only behaviour already adapted to the constraints and
limitations of the setting ... What people cannot do
is just as important as what they are able to do,
and often more revealing' (Thrift, 1976a,25). As in
work involving space-time budgets, there is a heavy
emphasis on questions of the 'quality of life', which
Hägerstrand (1970,7) describes as involving '...the
fate of the individual human being in an increasingly
complicated environment.' He stresses that the time-
geographic approach is a 'point of view' rather than
a research technique and this emphasis is reiterated
by Thrift and Pred (1981,277) when they state that
time-geography is '...a way of thinking about the
world at large as well as the events and experiences,
or content, of one's own life.' It focuses on
individuals and their movements in time-space which
Hägerstrand denotes as 'paths'.
     Hägerstrand (1970,12-16) identifies three inter-
acting groups of constraints: 1) capability
constraints are '...those which limit the activities
of the individual because of his biological
construction and/or the tools he can command,' and
include principally the need for sleep and the
ability to move around, these determining the size of
daily 'prisms', 2) coupling constraints, operating
within the capability constraints, '...define where,
when and for how long the individual has to join
other individuals, tools and materials in order to
produce, consume and transact, so controlling the
individual's path inside the daily 'prism', and 3)
authority constraints refer to limitations and
control of access, occurring at different levels to
produce hierarchies of 'space-time domains'.
     Summarising the importance of constraints in
determining access and hence the 'quality of life',
Hägerstrand (1970,19) stresses that '...access
involves much more than the simple juxtaposition of
supplies in regions of arbitrary size. It involves
a time-space location which really allows the life-
path to make the required detours.' Certain
activities are more 'fixed' in time and space than
others and these serve to demarcate the size of
possible prisms. (There is a connection here with

the classification of activities into 'obligatory'
and 'discretionary' types by Chapin.) In contrast to
the spatial behaviour approach, 'The decision of
where to shop at three o'clock in the afternoon is no
longer taken in the context of a purely theoretical
action space surrounding the individual's residence
but is taken in terms of a highly specific time-space
prism anchored between the individual's location at
that time and his next forecast commitment' (Cullen
et al., 1972,283-284).
       The time-geographic approach, developed at the
University of Lund, has been used by a number of
Swedish writers in their studies of activity patterns,
although much of the material produced remains
entirely in the Swedish language and is, therefore,of
limited use to English-speaking geographers. The
scope of this work is, however, excellently portrayed
in Carlstein, Parkes and Thrift (eds.)(1979,Vol.2),
and is also discussed by Godkin and Emker (1976). Of
particular relevance to the present research study is
the model of constraints on spatial behaviour
developed by Öberg (1976,18). This model takes into
account both 'human resources' and 'environmental
resources' as determinants of activities but the
chief concentration is placed on problems of physical
access to services.
       Besides the great volume of work based on
Hägerstrand's original formulation of time-geography,
produced both in Sweden and by other researchers in
Britain and elsewhere (see, for example, Wigan and
Morris, 1979; Miller, 1982), the idea of viewing
activities in a time-geographic framework has also
been developed in other related studies. An example
is the work of Cullen in London on the structure of
activity patterns. This differs in some respects
from Hägerstrand's model. Cullen et al., (1972,284)
describe their work as being based on '...an
empirical study of activity patterns...', its
objectives having been '...limited simply to finding
out more about the way in which the individual's
time-space decisions are structured.' Rather than
dividing activities into two simple classes: fixed
and unfixed, they attempt to assess the importance of
activities in terms of priority ratings and the
degree of flexibility associated with them. They
suggest (1972,287) that people have a habit of
structuring their days in a fairly standardised form,
regardless of the lack of direct constraints but
since they only see constraints as being 'imposed
externally' (1972,285) by the economic, physical and
institutional environment, they may, in fact, be

overlooking the existence of social constraints which are tending to structure behaviour patterns.

Like the work of Cullen and his associates in London, the survey by Bullock et al., (1974) in Reading uses fairly standard time-budget information as the input to a model which is structured in terms of time and space restrictions on activity patterns. The empirical information is hence taken as the starting point for modelling, rather than the end result of the research process as in the case of space-time budget research. The chief interest here is in the forecasting of probable activity patterns on an aggregate scale to aid in the planning process. The modelling of travel demands is one aim of a research study based on time-geographic principles carried out by Jones et al., (1983) in Oxford. Respondents were also asked to evaluate the effects on daily life patterns of various policy changes using an activity simulator.

The Conceptual Approach of this Study

As has been shown, many studies lay great emphasis on choice mechanisms in determining activity patterns but, as Anderson (1971,362-363) reminds us, 'The limits of free choice are generally wider for the more wealthy and spatially mobile, and narrower for the poor, the old, those with young children, those without a car, and so on.' For the study of the latter groups of people (including women with young children) a constraint-oriented approach provides a particularly useful framework within which to view activity patterns. However, most work so far undertaken within the time-geographic framework, although using the individual as the focus of analysis, has tended to aggregate individuals into households (for example, Hägerstrand's and Martensson's work on family diaries - see Thrift, 1976a,13-15). Studies of individual household members are less common. In particular, there have been very few studies of the activity patterns of women. Palm and Pred (1974,36), in discussing this point, stress that, 'Although students of the urban scene...have concerned themselves with so-called "spatial injustice," the problems which face women in their efforts to accommodate the myriad of roles and responsibilities they must fulfil during their daily lives have been largely ignored.' However, there are two interesting recent examples of the application of time-geography to the study of women's activities. Hanson and Hanson (1980) concern themselves with urban activity

patterns in Uppsala, Sweden, while Miller's (1982)
study applies a simulation model to consider
women's access problems in Nineteenth Century
American suburbs.
   Women with young children form one major group
within society which is severely constrained in terms
of activity patterns. In Hägerstrand's terminology,
they are subject to many 'authority' constraints
since they have very little power in society; they
are tied to the needs of their children by 'coupling'
constraints and they are subject to difficulties in
movement. Hägerstrand (1970,21) stresses that all
constraints on activities should be classified in
time-space terms but, while this may provide a useful
overall perspective on the nature of constraints, it
is not the only relevant means of classification. In
particular, it has been suggested by Rose (1977,45)
that '...the Hägerstrand model appears to over-
emphasise the time dimension, sometimes at the
expense of the spatial dimensions,' and that time
itself may be difficult to define objectively.
Personally experienced time may, in fact, act as the
greatest time constraint on activity patterns (Rose,
1977,44).
   While the constraints which operate on women
with young children could be grouped according to
Hägerstrand's classification, there appear to be good
reasons for not doing so. In the first place,
Hägerstrand emphasises, in particular, the environmental constraints on activities (Thrift, 1976a,5 - and
see also Öberg, 1976) whereas the presence of young
children is itself certainly one of the most
important (if not the most important) constraints on
women. This constraint would not seem to be
adequately considered merely within the time-space
notion of a 'coupling' constraint. The depth of the
gender-role constraint (see Chapter 2) seems much
greater than the simple idea of having to be at
certain places at certain times in order to attend to
the needs of children. Similarly, social class norms
of behaviour could be considered as 'authority'
constraints but again the subjective importance of
such constraints is not adequately dealt with in the
established terminology. In the second place and
following Rose's (1977,45) point, the importance of
time in the classification of constraints may be
overstressed in the case of women with young
children. Of course, there are fixed points in the
day when certain activities must take place - notably
the feeding of children and their collection from
school - and, of course, economically-active mothers

are extremely subject to time-limitations on
activities, but it is contended here that the
average, housebound woman with young children
(particularly if they are all under school age) is
not particularly subject to time constraints on her
activities. The chief problem may be getting through
the lonely, isolated hours without adult company and
the 'invention' of activities to pass the time,
rather than the problem of time constraints.

Methodologically, the present study can be
clearly placed within a 'constraint' rather than a
'choice' approach. Thus it owes more to the ideas of
the time-geographic school than to the space-time
budget or spatial behaviour approaches. However,
like the work of Cullen and Bullock, already referred
to, the study will use empirical space-time budget
information as the data source (seeking to avoid the
worst of the problems presented by this approach,
mentioned earlier) and will not model hypothetical
situations using normative data, as Hägerstrand has
done. The principle aim of the study is to produce
an accurate picture of the importance of different
constraints on the out-of-home activity patterns of
women with young children. An intuitive classification of constraints is therefore suggested and
resulting hypotheses tested using space-time budget
and questionnaire data empirically derived. Actual
behaviour patterns in time-space will, therefore, be
studied in terms of the hypothesised constraints.
The weekday (daytime) pattern of activities and
constraints is the subject under consideration since
it is felt that women are most severely constrained
in their activities when they are solely responsible
for their children.

Unlike the work by the Swedish geographers, this
study does not place greatest emphasis on physical,
environmental constraints or activities but instead
seeks to explore the more complex field of societal
constraints. It may justifiably be argued that the
dominating influence on the behaviour patterns of
individuals is the existing structure of society
based on specific class and gender relations.
Physical constraints, on the other hand, are here
viewed largely as 'relational elements' with
activity patterns, since with the latter they are all
the products of the way in which society is structured and organised. Thus, they cannot be treated in
a simplistic manner as causal constraints (through
regression modelling, for example) but their inter-
relationships with activity patterns are of no less
interest because of this. The discussion of

background literature concerning specific types of
constraints on activities follows in Chapters 2 and
3, before the presentation of the detailed research
model and the description of methodology in Chapter
4.

Chapter 2

FOCUS ON CONSTRAINTS I - SOCIETAL CONSTRAINTS

In considering the constraints operating on the
activity patterns of women with young children, it is
first necessary to look critically at the ways in
which society is structured. Physical constraints -
of mobility and service provision - may have an
immediate impact on behaviour patterns but they are
themselves, with activities, simply the spatial
patterns produced by the social processes at work in
society. Similarly, 'Characteristics (of people) do
not explain the causes of behaviour; rather, they
are clues to socially created and culturally defined
roles, choices and demands. A causal analysis must
trace them back to the larger, social, economic and
political systems which determine the situations in
which roles are played and the cultural content of
choices and demands, as well as the opportunities for
their achievement' (Gans, 1962,641).
    Specifically, in this chapter, two dominant
aspects of societal structure will be considered in
terms of their influence on activity patterns:
gender and socio-economic structures. The roles
which individuals play in relation to these
structures are conditioned by the ideologies, or
ways of thought, evident in society. In turn, 'Every
idea, every element of ideology, is derived from and
reflects some objective reality, some real aspect of
the material world,' (Carnforth, 1963,80). Thus, an
ideology can be understood as a partial view of
reality, based initially on an objective fact but
building on this to form a general system of beliefs.
So far as this study is concerned, the most important
ideology to be considered is that which leads to the
existence of gender-roles. Gender-role ideology is
that body of belief, based originally on the objective fact of biological sex roles in reproduction but
expanded to include cultural roles, which conditions

the differentiation of roles of men and women so
clearly visible in society. This belief system and
its results, in terms of women's accepted role and
subsequent activity patterns, will be taken as the
first subject of this chapter.

From here, the discussion will move on to
consider socio-economic structures. It is quite
clear from a consideration of relevant literature
that there are societal 'forces' other than the
gender-role structure of society which act as
constraints, or influencing factors, on activity
patterns. These 'forces' can be grouped under the
heading of 'socio-economic constraints'. Together,
they reflect the ideology which gives each individual
within society a 'position' or 'status' relative to
other individuals or groups.

A constantly recurring theme in the newly-
developing literature on the position of women is
the debate concerning the fundamental basis of discrimination against women. Many writers, especially
those who would call themselves Marxists, identify
the causes of women's oppression within the class
structure of capitalist society. To these writers it
is the working classes which are oppressed and women
as a part of the proletariat. They would specify the
nuclear family as the site of women's subjugation and
stress the importance of the maintenance of traditional family roles in the interests of labour
power reproduction. Thus, gender relations in this
view are merely one aspect of the structuring of
society along class lines.

Hunt (1980,1) asserts, however, that, 'What marks
out Capitalism is not the subjection of women as such
since this pre-dates Capitalism, but the privatis-
ation of domestic labour and the exclusion of women
from social labour, which serves to reproduce the
subjection of women in a specifically capitalist
form.' It is apparent from cross-cultural studies
that, while the specific form of gender-differentiation varies from one society to another, the
existence of such differentiation is in all times and
places clearly visible, even in situations where
considerable progress has been made towards equality
(see Lane, 1983). Many writers have, therefore,
stressed the prior importance of gender-roles, over
and above socio-economic structures, in determining
the position of women and, hence, their activity
patterns. The present author is included in this
number. This does not, however, mean that income and
class differences are not important in influencing
activities. At the same time it is evident that

strong inter-connections do exist between the maintenance of gender-role ideology on the one hand and
the needs of capital for labour power reproduction on
the other. The assumption upon which this study is
based is that the existence of gender-roles operates
as the major constraint on the activities of women
with young children. However, the degree to which
this constraint actually influences activity patterns
is largely determined by the socio-economic position
of the individual woman.

The Gender-Role Constraint

1. The nature of the constraint

a) The position of women and the female gender role

Differentiation of roles on the basis of sex has
obviously always been significant and remains so.
The supreme example of this is the exclusive female
attribute of biological motherhood. However, it is
not this biological role which society values; if
this were the case then, as Oakley (1974b,196)
reminds us, the attitude of society to unmarried
mothers would be quite different from that which in
fact pertains. What is valued is the cultural
motherhood image, encapsulated within the traditional
family structure. 'In Western culture today, motherhood is the chief occupation for which females are
reared. It is a major component of the feminine
gender role as taught to a female child...What she
learns to value is not her inherent and quite un-
challengeable capacity to give birth to children, but
the multitude of servicing activities she must
perform for them: not the absolute value of her
biological womanhood, but the relative value of her
culturally learnt ability to "take care" of children'
(Oakley, 1974b,190;193). In the industrial, modern
world women are confined to the domestic sphere, not
on the grounds of sex-differentiation of roles but
on the grounds of gender-differentiation. 'The
desire for motherhood is culturally induced and the
ability to mother is learnt' (Oakley, 1974b,201).
The heavy emphasis in society on the social role
of mother has been noted, in America, by Lopata
(1971,182), who points out that society places almost
total responsibility for the rearing of children on
mothers. 'The father is usually not held accountable
for what happens to the children...' (Lopata, 1971,
183-184). The same theme recurs again and again in
the literature on family relationships in the Western

world. Along with the positive biological role of
childbirth and feeding of the very young, goes the
cultural role of child care and responsibility for
children. The functional basis of such gender-
differentiation is rarely explored or questioned but
such a situation is obviously of great benefit to
men. Oakley (1974b,197) reminds us that, 'Many of the
protestations about the glory of motherhood are
uttered by men, and it may be speculated that women
speak with the same voice because they have assimil-
ated the attitude of men.'
      Sullerot (1971,88) explains that concepts of the
'female role' are rigid and unchanging in pattern
'... because people insist on describing woman as the
cornerstone of the family, the guardian of tradition
and the defender of social stability.' It is this
concentration on the family role of the woman and,
especially on her role as a mother, which largely
determines her position in society. Galbraith
(1974), for example, has referred to housewives as a
'crypto-servant' class. However, Mitchell (1966,11)
reminds us that there is nothing inevitable about the
form or role of the family any more than there is
about the character or role of women. Anthropolog-
ical studies abound which demonstrate the differing
character of the family and woman's role in it in
different societies (for example, those quoted by
Hayford, 1974 and Mitchell, 1971). Many writers, in
particular, point to the clear division in types of
family structure between pre-industrial and industrial societies. Apps (1975,7) states that 'All
activities were once household activities,' and
Hayford (1974,3) explains that before the Industrial
Revolution women were central to the functional
organisation of society, as each family was relatively independent economically. The new productive
relationships brought into being by industrialisation
and the development of separate public and private
spheres of activity caused women to lose their
centrality in society and emphasised their restrict-
ion to the domestic sphere, now devoid of the status
it had once enjoyed (Hayford, 1974,12; - see also,
Wekerle et al., 1980,8).

b)   The care of children

      Apps (1975,11-12), speaking of policies on child
care, asserts that '...resistance to transfer of any
part of this activity (from the domestic sphere) has
been maintained largely through the promulgation and
reinforcement of attitudes concerning motherhood and

the needs of children...' Early studies of maternal
deprivation were focused on groups of children such
as war-time evacuees, separated from their mothers
(and fathers) for months or even years at a time, or
the children of one-parent families, for whom personal problems were compounded by financial difficulties, or long-term hospitalised children. To take the
results of such studies and generalise them to cover
the total population of children is inexcusable, both
academically and ethically. Nevertheless, this has
been the case, with the result that all children not
cared for by their mothers tend to be considered as
maternally deprived and, therefore, potential problem-
children or even delinquents. In contrast, a recent
analysis of data from the Child Health and Education
Study showed that 'Analysis of behavioural deviance
in children did not suggest that maternal employment
was associated in any systematic way with increased
rates of behavioural deviance. If anything, children
of employed mothers were <u>less</u> likely to be deviant'
(Osborn, 1983,65).
     It cannot be too strongly stated, despite the
large number of studies relating to child care, that
where alternative care is provided for young children, '...no evidence has been found of physical neglect nor of intellectual or emotional damage to
children...' (Thompson and Finlayson, 1963,150) as a
direct result of lack of full-time maternal care (see
also Jephcott, 1962,149). On the contrary, many
studies suggest that children may be positively
harmed by excessive maternal care or over-protection.
Mitchell (1966,32), for example, states that '...the
attempt to focus women's existence exclusively on
bringing up children, is manifestly harmful to children.' In addition, '...the quality of physical environment for child care in the traditional family is
subject...to the inequities of earned income distribution and to individual earner discretion...' (Apps,
1975,13).
     If continual maternal involvement is bad for the
child, then it is equally bad for the mother to be
constantly in the company of her children. Myrdal
and Klein (1956,135) note that '...the habitual sharing of women's lives with those of their children far
too often brings mothers down from the level of mat-
urity which should be their own to that of their
children.' In addition and, perhaps,even more seriously, a constant involvement in her children's
lives when they are young may make it impossible for
the mother to release them from her care as they grow
older. This syndrome of maternal over-possessiveness

is described by Oakley (1974b,220) as the problem of
'...the position of women in society as a whole,
their dependent position in the family, the cultural
expectation that the maternal role should be the most
important one for all women, that makes the exagger-
ated wish to possess one's child an entirely reasonable reaction. Deprived and oppressed, women see in
motherhood their only source of pleasure, reward and
fulfilment...'

c)   Maternity - the great leveller

    Oakley (1974b,197) makes the point that matern-
ity is a great leveller; most women, whether middle
class graduates or members of the working class, see
themselves primarily as wives and mothers. This is
perhaps one of the most interesting facets of the
whole issue, since class differences in attitudes are
usually considered to be of enormous importance in
every sphere of life. The 'traditional' marriage
with its clear-cut role-differentiation is often considered a specifically working class phenomenon.
Studies of working class areas, such as the famous
one by Young and Willmott in East London (1957), picture a society controlled by rigid class and sex
norms of behaviour. Dennis et al., reflect on the
causes of such role-differentiation in a mining community, basing their diagnosis on the differential employment opportunities available to men and women
but they also agree that, 'The pure economic fact of
man's being the breadwinner for his family is reinforced by the custom of family life, the division
of responsibility and duties in the household, and
the growth of an institutional life and an ideology
which accentuate the confinement of the mother to the
home. "Woman's place is in the home" is a very definite and firm principle of thought and action in
Ashton' (Dennis et al., 1956,174). That the existence of differential employment opportunities in
working class areas is not the reason for maintaining
traditional family relationships, is clearly pointed
out by Pahl (1977) in a letter to 'The Times'. He
notes that, 'The position of females in some inner
city job markets is stronger than males who have few
or no skills,' and suggests that policies to encourage men to take on domestic duties so that their
wives could work would be '...more relevant than mis-
guided attempts to train unskilled male workers for
jobs which are not available or highly subsidized.'
He admits, however, that 'Changing...social attitudes
may be almost as hard as returning to the small

factory age.'
    In contrast, middle class attitudes to marriage
and family roles have often been considered more
'enlightened'. Young and Willmott (1973) go so far
as to designate the new type of (largely middle
class) marriage as 'symmetrical', their definition of
'symmetry' implying that '...there should be no mono-
polies for either sex in any sphere. Women should
have as much right as men to seek, and to gain fulfilment out of the home as in it' (Young and Willmott, 1973,275). However, most research evidence
shows the middle class woman to be just as tied to
the conventional wife/mother role as her working
class counterpart. Above all, there is the psychological tie of the mother-child link, which is predominantly the result of societal reinforcement of gen-
der-rather than sex-roles within society. Gavron
found that the presence or absence of available help
with the children made little difference to the
middle class mothers whom she interviewed; the overwhelming majority felt that they ought to be with
their children (Gavron, 1966,69;110). In this attitude, the middle class housewives did not differ significantly from the working class sample.
    In addition, there are other factors which may
tie the middle class wife and mother more firmly to
an exclusively domestic role than her working class
counterpart. Middle class husbands tend to be more
mobile, work less predictable hours and more often
require their wives to be social assets as well as
minders of home and children. Thompson and Finlayson
(1963,165) come to this conclusion: '...it seems that
wives with higher educational qualifications, whose
husbands' work often necessitates migration, have to
face the greatest difficulties both in finding work
which will utilize their qualifications, and in making suitable arrangements for the care of children.'
The problems faced by the wives of relocated husbands
have also been studied by Burtenshaw (1973). It is
an implicit and unquestioned assumption in work of
this nature that the wife's interests are very much
secondary to those of her husband and that it is his
career which should determine family life-style and
mobility. Especially is this true of the managerial
class, studied by the Pahls (1971) and by Young and
Willmott (1973). The latter state (1973,260) that
the managers' wives whom they interviewed were expected to be available at short notice for social occasions and for this reason 90 per cent of them were
entirely confined to home duties, compared with only
50 per cent of the wives of other men in the sample

(see also, Finch, 1983,88-93). However, although it
is true that the gender role constraint is as dominant for middle class as for working class women, the
ways in which the constraint affects actual activities (especially social activities) differ according
to the socio-economic standing of the women. Thus,
for example, a woman in a high income household may
have a living-in nanny to take part-time care of the
children and so free her for more varied social activities during the daytime, even though her husband's
position constrains her ability to work outside the
home. The gender-role constraint, although still
present, may be less irksome for middle class, higher
income mothers; access to a car, in particular, may
widen activity patterns without in any way changing
the dominance of the overriding constraint.

d)   Housework

The 'housework' part of the traditional wife/
housewife/mother role set is generally considered,
both by women themselves and by society at large, to
be inferior to the job of being a mother. However,
'The equation of femaleness with housewifery is
basic to the structure of modern society, and to the
ideology of gender-roles which pervades it...not
only is the housewife role specifically a feminine
role, it is also women's major occupational role
today...' (Oakley, 1974a,29). Oakley (1974b,1) lists
what she considers to be the characteristic features
of the housewife role in modern industrialised
society: a) its exclusive allocation to women, b)
its association with economic dependence, c) its
status as non-work and d) its priority over other
roles for women. The first of these characteristics
remains true, despite the increased sharing of
domestic tasks by husbands; the chief responsibility
for the running of the household remains with the
woman. A recent study (Jowell and Airey, 1984,133-
134) found that families remained far from
'symmetrical' in their allocation of household tasks.
In particular '...households with young children were
relatively inegalitarian.'
     The second characteristic - association with
economic dependence - is related to the third;
because housework is not considered to be 'real'
work, the housewife receives no payment directly for
her work and therefore occupies a position of
economic dependence. 'This central contradiction -
housework is work, housework is not work - appears as
a constant theme in the analysis of the housewife's

situation' (Oakley, 1974b,4). Oakley herself bases
her thesis on the fact that housework is work and
therefore that housewives should be accorded the
status of other workers. The same view is held by
many writers (for example, Bell and Healey, 1973,
160). However, it is certainly true that women in
general do not regard the housewife role as a work
role. Gavron (1966,147) makes the point that the
housewives in her sample did not feel themselves to
be at work. This point relates to the fourth characteristic of the housewife role as described by Oakley
(1974b,1) - its priority over other roles for women.
'The addition of paid work to the housewife's
activities does not mean she is no longer a housewife' (Oakley, 1974a,38). The position of economic
dependence and the status of being a 'non-worker'
remains, even when the housewife also works outside
the home; such is the primacy of the housewife role
in the value-system of society.

e)   The mental health of women with young children

One final characteristic of the housewife role
should be mentioned - that is, its isolating nature.
An international time-budget survey came to this
conclusion: 'The normal housewife in our samples
spends almost twice as many of her waking hours alone
as her employed husband...Too little is known about
the social psychology of loneliness to make any very
strong assertions about the effects of this amount
of solitude' (Robinson et al., 1972,140). Enforced
loneliness, which as Oakley (1974a,88) states is
'...an occupational hazard for the modern housewife
...' is one of the biggest problems which must be
challenged in order to improve the life chances of
women. (An excellent account of the isolation of
housework is given in Rothblatt et al., 1979, chapter
2).
Watts (1980) summarises the problems of women
with young children: '...by the standards of the man-
made society, new mothers who give up their jobs to
stay at home and look after their children also give
up status, money, independence and identity. They
are often isolated and lonely, and they have a lot of
hard, monotonous and unpaid work to do.' In rather
more polemical terms, Kenny (1977) states that '...
the profile of an urban mother in a modern flat is
now that of a frustrated and depressed person, with
little support from family, or friends, swallowing
Valium just to keep going.' Significantly, she
continues: '...what is striking about this picture is

that it is a contrast to everything we have been led
to believe about motherhood.'
    This latter point echoes the essential contrad-
iction which faces women with young children and
which for many can precipitate problems of identity
and loss of emotional well-being, or even, in extreme
cases,severe psychiatric disturbance. Motherhood
has been elevated to an idealistic pinnacle, such
that almost every woman feels 'unfulfilled' unless
she produces children. But the reality of being a
mother is a totally different experience, as Watts
recounts in the terms quoted above. Harper and
Richards (1979,135) refer to the 'alienation' of
housewives, noting that this is a word normally used
to describe a situation of paid labour but arguing
that it is equally appropriate in the case of young
mothers, few of whom have really 'chosen' their role.
    The role of housewife and mother is seen to be
frustrating, lacking in prestige, unstructured and
invisible, inescapable and ill-defined (Gove and
Tudor, 1973). Gove (1972,34), considering the higher
incidence of mental illness among women than men,
stresses that,'It is the roles confronting married
men and women and not some other factor such as women
being biologically more susceptible to mental illness'. It is fashionable to describe the emotional
problems of young mothers in purely clinical terms,
as aspects of 'post-natal depression'. This is a
subject researched in depth by Oakley (1980), who
sees the experience of childbirth as only one element
in the loss of mental health: 'It may be neatly
labelled post-natal, but it is simply a heightened
form of the unconscious depression which is the
natural daily state of many women' (Watts, 1980,
referring to Oakley, 1980). In other words, the
varying occurrence of depression (like childcare itself) is the result of gender, rather than sex,
differences.
    There is certainly well-documented evidence to
show that women with young children suffer higher
rates of depressive illness (Richman, 1976). Brown
et al., (1975) indicate the special vulnerability of
working class mothers to depression, in opposition to
the views of Becker (1964) who considered that middle
class women would be more '...vulnerable to feelings
of disappointment with attendant feelings of guilt,
low self-esteem and depression' (Becker, 1964, quoted
in Brown and Harris, 1978). In his community survey
in Camberwell, South London, Brown found 25 per cent
of working class women, but only 5 per cent of middle
class women to be psychologically disturbed. A second

sample in Camberwell showed a figure of 42 per cent suffering from depressive illness amongst working class women with children aged six or less. One explanatory variable suggested for this situation is the greater ability of middle class women to lead interesting lives in the present and look forward to a more satisfying future. Richman, (1976,75) notes that,'In general depressed women appear to have less material and social resources than comparable groups of non-depressed women', and suggests that financial and housing difficulties (especially flat-living) may be particularly stressful. Clearly, loss of mental health, while being a characteristic of women with young children as a group (compared to other groups in society), is, in reality, more closely associated with particular members of that group (see also, Melville, 1983; Osborn, 1983). Brown et al., (1975, 248) conclude that some '...women in our society have a significantly greater than average risk of suffering from depressive conditions. To the extent that the unequal distribution of such risk is the result of more widely recognised inequalities within our society, and our findings certainly point in this direction, we believe that it constitutes a major social injustice'.

2. The influence of the constraint on activity
    patterns

'Women have felt limited by roles which are prescribed for them by society. These roles, which have certain spatial and temporal characteristics in themselves, create spatial and temporal limitations on both the occupational and leisure-time options open to women' (Palm and Pred, 1974,1). The influence of the gender-role constraint on the activities of women with young children is all-encompassing. Their whole lives revolve around the care required by their children and, therefore, this constraint can be seen as the most important of all constraints in limiting their activity patterns.

a) Paid employment

Women with young children may be divided into two groups with respect to the gender-role constraint - those in paid employment outside the home and those who are full-time housewives. For the latter group, the role constraint is complete, since only activities which can take place in the company of children are possible but, on the other hand, time

limitations are probably less important (as
considered in Chapter 1). For those in some form of
extra-domestic employment, the constraint of
continuous physical child care is obviously modified,
but there is still a 'coupling' time-space
constraint, which limits job possibilities and at the
same time reduces opportunities for other activities
outside the home (see Palm and Pred, 1974,21).
     Because of the lack of child care facilities
(itself the result of the policy that young children
should spend their time with their mothers, see
Chapter 3, section b) together with the emphasis
placed on domestic responsibility, most mothers work
only part-time and, therefore, are not able to obtain
jobs with a high status and salary (see Fig.1).
They tend to select jobs with convenient hours or
locations, jobs which they can integrate easily with
domestic work and child care (Coverman, 1983,624).
'Consistently in all developed capitalist societies,
women are the part-time workers, women are the home-
workers, women are heavily-concentrated in very few
industries, women are paid less, women have borne the
brunt of unemployment' (Smith, 1978,12). In many
cases paid employment means simply a reinforcement
of the domestic role (in the form of house-cleaning
jobs or child-minding) or the home production of
goods for sale, such employment bringing neither
good wages nor the compensation of adult companionship (see Hakim, 1980). 'Is it surprising that so
many women regard their jobs as peripheral to their
real responsibilities, and themselves as peripheral
to the work force?' (Walters, 1977), since '...the
existence of part-time "paid" work is premised on
women's primary role within the family and, therefore, reinforces the sexual division of labour which
means that women have the prime responsibility for
the home and children' (Bland et al., 1978,70).
There are indeed '...multiple disadvantages
associated with part-time work' (Hurstfield, 1978,
77).
     A survey by Hillman et al., (1976,85) found that
three-quarters of the women interviewed who were not
working intended to return to work and for 88 per
cent of women with pre-school children, their
children's age was the major reason for not working.
Of part-time workers who were interviewed, three-
quarters stated that the presence of children was the
reason why they did not work full-time. Gavron
(1966,69) found that the beginning of full-time
schooling was clearly seen as a turning point in
women's lives. Regardless of social class or

Figure 1:   Influence of the gender-role constraint on women's employment

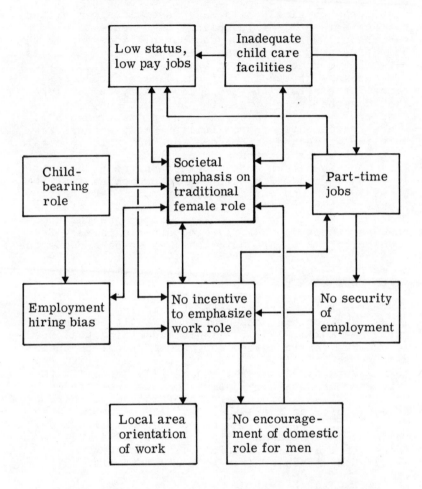

education, only a very few of her interviewees did
not intend to return to work when their children
were all at school. However, '...in many cases,
children do not cease to present problems of care...'
(Rapoport and Rapoport, 1975,214) after they begin to
attend school and there remain the problems of
arranging child care for after-school hours and
holidays.
        If a woman does manage to find suitable employ-
ment and child care facilities, this doesn't
necessarily lead to the sort of 'symmetrical' family
arrangement discussed by Young and Willmott (1973).
'Research shows that if a wife takes employment, her
role does not automatically take on the power and
authority conventionally associated with the
husband's role in marriage' (Oakley, 1974b,237). The
same point is made by almost all writers in the
field. Chapin and Logan (1969,325) state that '...
even when the factor of sex is controlled for employment status, women carry a much greater share of
household and family-related tasks than do the men.'
The international (and inter-class) survey referred
to earlier says 'The plight of the employed woman
pervades all of our time-budget records...The major
portion of (men's) contribution remains with the more
peripheral household care activities, and women in
the household, whether employed or unemployed,
shoulder almost all of the housework burden'
(Robinson et al., 1972,119;124; see also Noordhoek
and Smith, 1971,46; Coverman, 1983,625). As Hanson
and Hanson (1980,299) found from an empirical study
of activity patterns in Sweden, '...rather than being
a catalyst for role shifts within the household, a
woman's participation in the labor force, brings
changes in only her own space-time budgeting'.

b)   Social interaction

        For activities apart from outside employment,
women are normally accompanied by their children and
their activity patterns are thereby constrained.
Mention is made in Chapter 3 of the mobility problems
of women with young children and the consequent usage
of local services and facilities. However, the local
activities of women may also reflect in another way
the nature of the gender-role constraint. Many
writers make the point that shopping expeditions, in
particular, are undertaken as much for social reasons
as for their more obvious purpose (see Bruce, 1974,
281; Brail and Chapin, 1973,172-173; Mann, 1965,162;
Hillman, 1970,21; Bracey, 1964,121; Jones et al.,

1983,77-78). For a woman, largely confined to home in the daytime by young children, 'Her shopping expeditions are her "excursions into the world" and for this reason she tends to expand them in a manner which to non-housewives is often difficult to understand' (Myrdal and Klein, 1956,148). The same is probably true of park-visiting activity, which may also serve as a means for social interaction among such women.

Both the need for social interaction with friends and relatives and the actual patterns of home visiting which result from the satisfying of this need are the result of the gender-role constraint. The traditional role of women determines to a large extent the location of the friends which are visited: 'Women generally find their female friends nearby, especially if they are mothers and are restricted in their movements' (Gans, 1961a,138). Tied to the immediate neighbourhood by the difficulties (both of time and mobility) generated by the presence of young children, women inevitably visit only proximate neighbours and relatives during weekdays. For those without close friends and kin living locally, extreme loneliness may be the result of the gender-role constraint. This situation is especially evident on new housing estates (both private and council), where families have re-located almost without exception in relation to the husband's work location (Bracey, 1964,38) or status expectancy. For the wife, throughout the day tied to a strange area (which was moreover selected without the primary consideration of her requirements), home visiting activity may be severely restricted by the absence of potential contacts.

Even in established areas, the gender-role constraint may still be very important in restricting home visiting activity for women with young children. Interestingly, Gavron (1966,98) found that working class women were much more home-centred in their activities and visited friends far less frequently than middle class women: 'This serves to indicate how middle class wives were able to maintain a fair degree of independence outside their roles as mothers during the period when the children were young, while the working class wives were not.' This conclusion might seem surprising in view of the traditional picture of working class areas sustaining high levels of social interaction and in view of the greater expectancy of motherhood as the chief life role by working class women, thus allowing a realistic prior knowledge of possible activities under those

conditions. But, as Gavron (1966,81) points out,
'The working class mother who sees motherhood as
inevitable is in fact less prepared for the ties of
children and is less able to cope with the isolation
that follows.'
       A further interesting result emerges from a
number of studies of home visiting activity; that
is, that '...the more young children a mother has,
the more intense her visiting activity...is likely to
be' (Carey and Mapes, 1972,63 - see also, Lopata,
1971,283). Having a child and being subsequently
'tied' to home represents probably the greatest
change in life style ever undergone by a woman. It
takes time to establish new social links to replace
those relied upon formerly and it seems reasonable
to suppose,therefore,that the longer a woman has been
a mother and the greater number of children she has,
the more likely it is that a pattern of home visiting
activity will have been developed by her. In
addition, dissatisfaction with the restrictive
traditional 'female' role and consequent involvement
in other social roles would seem to be a more likely
characteristic of women in the later, rather than the
early, child-rearing period. The empirical finding
that women with more children have more developed
home visiting activity patterns, therefore,appears to
be explicable in terms of the gender-role constraints
of society and the lessening of the impact of these
constraints over time in the individual woman's
experience.
       It seems likely that activities involving social
interaction are emphasised by women with young
children because of their inability to take part in
other outside activities. Hall and Perry (1974,17),
in their survey of leisure in two industrial cities,
found that young women respondents were markedly less
satisfied with their leisure opportunities than were
other respondents, reflecting the importance of the
gender-role constraint. The presence of young
children has been identified in a number of recreation surveys as a major constraint on out-of-home
recreation activity (see, for example, Sessoms, 1963;
Angrist, 1967; Bollman et al., 1975). However, the
heavy emphasis placed by society on the 'female' role
of women may in any case mean that opportunities are
not provided to fulfil the recreational and social
needs of women. In many instances, the leisure
facilities in an area are all oriented towards evening and weekend use by men (Dennis et al., 1956,202).
(A comprehensive review of the whole field of
research concerning women and leisure has recently

been produced by Talbot, 1979.)

Socio-Economic Constraints I - Income

1. The nature of the constraint

a) Definitions of terms

The use of the term 'income', considered as a socio-economic constraint on activity patterns, is here taken to imply not only direct financial assets but also the wider notion of 'access to resources' - 'resources' being defined loosely as all those attributes which are sought after by groups within society and which act as the bases of life styles and activity patterns. Car ownership could, of course, be considered as one aspect of 'income', since the possession of a car permits a wider mobility. Both Eyles (1974) and Tulpule (1974), in their respective surveys, found a strong relationship between car ownership and money income, although Hillman et al., (1976,138) note that '...the areal variations in car ownership, two-car ownership and thus car availability are certainly not wholly due to variations in income...' Eyles (1974), in particular, found that households with young children, regardless of money income, were in general subject to low levels of car ownership. The question of access to private transport is considered in more detail in relation to mobility issues, in Chapter 3.

In considering the lack of access to resources as a major constraint on activity patterns, one is inevitably led to an examination of existing patterns of income inequality and their importance in influencing the 'life chances' of individuals (Pahl, 1975, 204). It is important, however, firstly to stress the semantic difference between 'inequality' and 'relative deprivation'. Many studies use the term 'deprivation' to imply an absence of resources (of some type) in an area or group, as compared to others more fortunate (for example, Davidson, 1976). This usage of the term is consistent with that employed in government reports, for example, the 1967 Plowden Report on primary education, which first introduced the idea of 'positive discrimination' in the provision of educational resources in favour of areas suffering from 'multiple social deprivation' (Hardy, 1973,81).

The more specific term, 'relative deprivation', must however be defined more exactly. Runciman, in a leading work in the field, says that, 'Relative

deprivation should always be understood to mean a
sense of deprivation; a person who is "relatively"
deprived need not be "objectively" deprived in the
more usual sense that he is demonstrably lacking
something' (Runciman, 1972,12). The same point is
stressed by Birrell (1972,317): 'Relative deprivation arises when discrepancies between conditions
enjoyed by different groups are recognised.' He
goes on to say: 'A comparative reference group is the
group whose situation a person contrasts with his
own' (Birrell, 1972,318). The two notions of
'relative deprivation' and 'reference group' are
inseparable. 'Dissatisfaction with the system of
privileges and rewards in a society is never felt in
an even proportion to the degree of inequality by
which its various members are subject,' (Runciman,
1972,3), because those in greatest need do not
compare themselves directly with those who are most
well-off; their 'comparative reference group' (a
notion taken from the discipline of social psychology) is of a more modest stature. There is no
necessary correlation between felt needs and real
needs (Knox, 1975,7).
    The term, 'relative deprivation', therefore,
refers to people's attitudes to their own conditions
of life. The term, 'inequality',on the other hand,
refers to an objective characteristic of resource
supply situations. Inequality and relative deprivation may increase commensurately, as is suggested by
Miller and Roby (1970,210) in their forecast of the
future of American society but, on the other hand, a
negative relationship between the two is equally
possible. Runciman suggests, for example, that
increasing equality may lead to an increase in
relative deprivation. He notes the '...tendency for
overt discontent to be relatively rare in stable
hardship and to rise alike in frequency, magnitude
and intensity as opportunity is seen to increase'
(Runciman, 1972,24).
    Objective measures of inequality have tradition-
ally been based on economic prosperity (Knox, 1975,5)
but recently there has also been a growing interest
in the subject of variations in social well-being
(see, for example, Smith, 1973; Knox, 1975).
Patterns of inequality identified by both economic
and social studies have been subject to analysis in
terms of a theoretic distribution under conditions
'of social justice'. Harvey (1975,97) states that,
'The concept of social justice is not an all-
inclusive one in which we encapsulate our vision of
the good society. It is rather more limited.

Justice is essentially to be thought of as a
principle (or set of principles) for resolving
conflicting claims.'

b) Social inequality

The literature on basically aspatial aspects of
inequality and deprivation is vast. It includes the
whole subject of class inequalities emphasised by
Marx and by later writers and, in particular, the
question of disparities of income and wealth. The
vexed question of whether objective social inequalities are in fact increasing or decreasing in Britain
at the present time occupies the attention of a
number of writers. Willmott (1973) maintains that,
despite an improvement in the social status of manual
workers, an increase in their political power and
general rises in standards of living, there has been
little change in the distribution of income and
wealth within society as a whole, nor does he forsee
any reduction in inequalities this century. In
contrast, Eversley's (1973) statistical evidence
appears to support the idea that incomes and wealth
are becoming more equal. A recent government report
on the subject (Royal Commission on the Distribution
of Income and Wealth, 1975) in part supports both of
these points of view. It shows that in the period
from 1949 to 1973 there was a decline in the percentage share of total personal income for the top 5 per
cent of people but that the position of all other
groups remained virtually unchanged.
Relative deprivation, in social terms, has been
studied by Runciman (1972). His conclusion that,
'The denial of equal opportunity begins in infancy
...' (Runciman, 1972,347) but that people are in
general slow and reluctant to change, supports his
general thesis that the level of relative deprivation
in Britain is low and certainly far lower than the
objective disparities would suggest. However, he
warns that,'We must beware of confusing acquiescence
with contentment: the impossibility of remedy can
inhibit action without inhibiting the sense of
grievance' (Runciman, 1972,30).
Marxists would argue that an increase in
relative deprivation (through class identification)
should lead to a lessening of inequality (through a
fundamental change in political, social and economic
structure). In their view it is the capitalist
system of production which is to blame for inequalities in society, which are functional to the system.
The only alternative is the overthrow of capitalism

and the substitution of a method of production and a
way of life designed around principles of equality
and social justice (Peet, 1975,565). Pahl, for one,
is less sure of such an outcome: '...to achieve many
of the goals of those who usher in the new order, a
more altruistic or socially responsive human nature
must be postulated: without this there is likely to
be replacement of one sort of system of inequality by
another' (Pahl, 1975,5). Pahl stresses the importance of 'social gatekeepers' in allocating and
controlling resources (Pahl, 1975,201) and suggests
that these are equally important in socialist as in
capitalist systems (Pahl, 1975,284).

One major focus of study by Marxists and non-
Marxists alike has been the problem of poverty,
especially in an urban setting. The existence of a
Welfare State in Britain has led to the widespread
impression that poverty has been abolished and many
writers are at pains to establish that this is not so
(for example, Simmie, 1974,93; Runciman, 1972).
Like inequality, Peet asserts that the existence of
poverty is vital to the normal operation of capitalist society (Peet, 1975,565) and therefore cannot be
eradicated without revolutionary social and economic
change. A more moderate socialist approach would see
the possibility of action to combat poverty within
the existing political system but would still
involve a major attack on the distribution of
financial resources within society.

Runciman (1972,307) suggests the use of three
criteria for the testing of a 'just' situation.
After redistribution, inequalities in wealth there-
after should be based on need, merit and contribution
to the common good. A perfectly equal distribution
is never possible but the important point is that
'...all social inequalities require to be justified
...' (Runciman, 1972,310). The means for achieving
this state of social justice is, of course,the major
problem inherent in the concept. Marxists, like Peet
(1975,570), would say that,'True social equality can
be achieved only by changing the generating forces of
inequality.' In other words, it is the capitalist
system which stands between the poor and social
justice. Harvey (1975,110) elaborates on this point:
'...programmes which seek to alter distribution
without altering the capitalist market structure
within which income and wealth are generated and
distributed, are doomed to failure.' But there are
also writers who see the possibility of moving towards a more just society; Eversley (1973), for
example, states that 'British society has made

considerable progress in the right direction in the last fifty years, despite some claims to the contrary.'

2. The influence of the constraint on activity patterns

a) The influence of poverty

It is clear that major inequalities do exist within society in terms of access to resources. Individual households, therefore, differ widely in their use of resources and subsequent activity patterns. The nature and problems of poverty have already been considered and it is evident that those who are trapped in the 'sub-culture of poverty' face the greatest constraint on their activities. Moreover, it is very likely that the women members of impoverished families will bear the greatest burden of the income constraint, since women throughout society have a lower access to resources of power and status than men (in Hägerstrand's terminology, they are more subject to 'authority' constraints.).

In particular, women with young children in such a situation will be very restricted in their activities. Lack of sufficient family income will preclude the use of paid child-minding facilities (even if these are available locally) in order for them to earn a wage as well as their husbands. There will be a heavy emphasis on walking to various facilities such as shops, not only for reasons of convenience and neighbourhood identification (as determined by a mobility constraint - see Chapter 3) but also because the cost of public transport makes this travel mode possible relatively infrequently (MIL Research Ltd., 1976,25). The cost of fares may also severely restrict home visiting patterns, if relatives live at a considerable distance (Young and Willmott, 1957, III).

b) Availability of resources

It is perhaps an obvious point, but one nevertheless that should be emphasised, that people can only participate in activities when the necessary resources for participation are available to them. Thus, for example, activities which entail the payment of a sum of money in entry fees are not available to those who cannot afford them. It has been shown (Hall and Perry, 1974,20) that, in the case of recreation and leisure activities, for example, an increase in the amount of disposable income available can be directly correlated with an increase in activity. The same point has been made by Sessoms (1963) and by Brail and Chapin (1973,182) writing of the American situation.

However, access to resources may be as important as a subjective constraint as it is as an objective constraint. It has been noted in the preceding section that levels of relative deprivation are in general low - people do not perceive that other groups in society have a much greater access to resources than they have. Consequently, activities which are perceived as being beyond their immediate resources are simply not considered as potential activities.

For women with young children, a subjective income constraint may be the more important factor in determining activity patterns. Thus, if it is felt that a certain activity cannot be afforded, the activity will not be undertaken, regardless of the actual amount of money available. In addition, a low level of information may reinforce the income constraint. For example, if a woman has no sure way of comparing shop prices locally and at a distant centre, she may decline to use public transport to reach the centre for shopping purposes on the grounds of the high cost of fares but in doing so she may in fact be paying far more by using more expensive, local shops. This stress on the subjective elements of the income constraint should not, however, be allowed to mask the very important objective differentials in access to resources which vitally influence the character of activity patterns.

Socio-Economic Constraints II - Social Class

1. The nature of the constraint

a) Class norms of behaviour

Social class, as an independent variable, has long been considered a primary determinant of human behaviour patterns. The idea that people identify with others of the same social standing and so create groups in society whose existence is emphasised by the growth of cultural norms of behaviour is a major focus of the sociological study of society. It is important to stress existing differences between social classes since, as Weber (1964a,64) says '...so much of our analysis treats space-related behaviour as though populations and space were both homogeneous

...' This is despite the fact that, at the behavioural level of study, 'The differences (in activity
patterns) among individuals are extensive and are not
easily explainable in terms of social groups and
characteristics' (Chapin and Logan, 1969,329). It is
argued here that these differences are due to the
differential effects of other constraints, which interact with the social class constraint, rather than
to the lack of importance of social class as an
independent variable.
    The study of class differences in life style,
from Marx onwards, has been closely connected with a
concern for inequalities of wealth and status (see
the previous section). While liberals have urged a
decrease in social class polarity (and there is some
evidence that this has, in fact, occurred in recent
years - see Eversley, 1973 and Willmott, 1973),
Marxists have called for increased class identification, in order to overthrow the existing social
structure. Despite the different attitudes towards
the question of social class differences, there is a
general agreement that class differences remain
important and that activity patterns are at least
partly shaped by class norms of behaviour.

b)   Empirical definition of social class

    However, when considering the nature of the
social class constraint as it operates on women with
young children, it is important to stress the precise
terms of reference which are being used. Empirical
studies of the behaviour patterns of households, or
individuals within them, tend to use the social class
of the 'head of household' as the explanatory refer-
ent. Almost always, the head of household is a man
and even where it is the activities of the housewife
or children which are under consideration and not
those of the household head, it is the occupational
standing of the husband and father which is used as
the social class input to the analysis (Oakley,
1974a,37). It is not therefore surprising that
'social class' does not appear to be a uniformly
important predictive variable when the activities of
women are the subject of the investigation.
    Oakley (1974a, 9-10) makes the vital point that,
'Apart from the question of wealth, married women
have personal resources of education and sometimes
occupational training: many are also employed during
their marriages and are in receipt of income and
status from this source. The assumption that women's
own resources become inoperative on marriage means

that abrupt alterations to the class structure are liable to occur every time someone gets married. An occupationally based class categorization of married women would put many in a different class from their husbands.' In particular, as Chapman (1976,13) notes, 'It seems accurate to say...that few women actually possess middle class status in their own right - rather, that they enjoy it on loan through their attachments to middle class men.'

There are, however, certain problems involved in the substitution of the wife's social class for that of her husband in analysing activity patterns. In the first place, women's occupations are heavily concentrated in a very limited number of socio-economic groups - these are primarily of the 'Inter-mediate' or 'Junior Non-manual' type (school teachers, nurses, secretaries, clerks) or the 'Un-skilled Manual' or 'Personal Service' type (factory assembly workers, domestic servants). Socio-economic classification, as constructed by the Registrar General and commonly used in social science research to indicate social class (see Reid, 1977,15-18), was designed to categorise the wide variety of <u>men's</u> occupations and tends not to discriminate adequately between the occupations of women. It would, of course, be possible to use some other system of occupational classification (as, for example, in Martin and Roberts, 1984) but this would make compar-ison with previous literature on class differentiat-ion much more difficult.

The second reason why it is difficult to use women's own occupations as the basis for their social class classification is the problem of deciding which occupation to classify. Women who are in paid employment when their children are very young tend to occupy jobs of a lower 'status' than those they held before the birth of their children (see Elias and Main, 1982). This is primarily the result of the gender role constraint on activities. It is also true that the majority of women with young children do not participate in any form of paid employment - they are full-time housewives - and as such are difficult to fit into any social class categorisat-ion. Obviously, both these problems could be over-come by using the last full-time occupation before the birth of any children as the basis for classifi-cation, although the problem of the classification system itself would still remain. However, as discussed above, the gender-role constraint operates as a long-term influence on activity patterns and it is very probable that even previous occupational

'status' may not accurately reflect the social class
orientation of a woman. Substitute measures such as
education level may in fact prove more reliable
indicators of class than socio-economic group in this
case, although these, too, may be partly determined by
differences in family roles.

It is hardly surprising, therefore, that in
social science literature women are assumed to
possess the social class attributed to their
husbands. The fact that this 'borrowed' social class
does often seem to be important in differentiating
between women itself reflects the importance of
gender role differentiation in society and the
dominance of male values and attitudes.

2. The influence of the constraint on activity
    patterns

a) Differences between classes

However 'social class' is defined, it seems
clear that class norms of behaviour are significantly
related to activity patterns. For possible differences between social classes in the ways in which
they are influenced by constraints of distance and
gender-role, see Chapter 3 and the first section of
this chapter, respectively. Here, social class will
be considered in terms of actual family structure
and its influence on patterns of social interaction
will be the main focus of attention.

The majority of studies dealing with the life-
styles of different classes have stressed differences
in marriage relationships and family structures.
Obversely, studies confirming differences in marriage
roles and social networks seem merely to be emphasising the importance of class differences. Thus, for
example, although Bott (1957) asserts that variations
in conjugal roles are related to the form of social
networks and not directly to the influence of class
differences, Bell and Healey (1973,167) '...consider
that in making conjugal roles dependent on networks,
Bott was simply employing a manageable unit of
analysis rather than the most valuable unit, which
was class and the normative systems derived from
class.' Although family roles generally have been
shown to be more rigid in the case of working class
families, it is interesting to note that Gavron
(1966,89) found equally close relationships between
husbands and wives in working class as in middle
class families. This finding, she asserts, is the
result of recent changes in attitude towards

traditional family structure.

b) Home visiting activity

The influence of social class (and consequent differences in marriage relationships) on home visiting and social interaction has been much considered in the literature. Lopata (1971,233), for example, found in her study of housewives that middle class women made more formal visiting arrangements, whereas working class women tended to favour a more spontaneous type of interaction which often did not include actual home visiting. Class differences appear to be re-inforced by exclusivity of social interaction: 'The most general finding (from previous studies) is that individuals prefer to interact socially with those of like socio-economic status' and, obversely, 'The individual is constrained in his social travel by perceived social barriers in the form of status levels...' (Wheeler and Stutz, 1971,373;385). Gans (1961a,137) reminds us that these perceived status levels may not necessarily correlate strictly with objective class differences; as he says, 'Social relationships are not based on census data, but on subjectively experienced definitions of homogeneity and heterogeneity which terminate in judgments of compatibility or incompatibility'. Nevertheless, attitudes (for example, towards child rearing) which tend to be class-based, must be sufficiently similar before a relationship can develop (Gans, 1961a,138). Gans (1961b,177) shows that a mere mixing of different class people in a residential area will not necessarily stimulate social interaction; in fact, it may quite often have the opposite effect. In arguing in favour of homogeneity at the block level, Gans formally recognises the dominance of intra-class social relationships.

In Britain, most 'community' studies have dealt with social relationships in working class areas. Most famous of these studies is probably that by Young and Willmott (1957) in East London. Like its American counterparts, this study stresses the dominance of the extended family, close kinship networks and the informality of visiting in a working class area. The study of a mining community by Dennis et al., (1956) describes a similar situation, emphasising the constant informal visiting between housewives and their relatives and neighbours. British studies have also drawn comparisons between traditional, urban working class areas and new, suburban council estates. Young and Willmott (1957),

for example, found that at 'Greenleigh' there was
much less contact with relatives than in Bethnal
Green and further that, 'The relatives of Bethnal
Green have not...been replaced by the neighbours of
Greenleigh. The newcomers are surrounded by
strangers instead of kin. Their lives outside the
family are no longer centred on people; their lives
are centred on the house' (Young and Willmott, 1957,
127). Toomey (1970,259) summarises the findings of
these studies: 'The longstandingness of the
"traditional" working class communities and the
physical proximity of kin and neighbours within them,
it is claimed, have combined to produce an inter-
meshing of social bonds which give formidable power
to the social controls of community life and these,
in turn, have served to strengthen and conserve the
norms and values of "traditional" working class life.
The new estates, it has been argued, tend to lack
these kinship bonds and, therefore, have developed a
more "home-centred" pattern of life focussed upon the
nuclear family...'
   Toomey questions the value of such findings on
the grounds that age of the population has not been
controlled for. In his study, which compares samples
similar in age, occupational status and family life-
cycle stage, he found no evidence of major differences between the two types of working class area
(Toomey, 1970,266). It appears then that the younger
generation of the working class may not live the sort
of life style that is characterised by the early
British studies (and even by current studies in
America). Gavron (1966) suggests that changed
conditions in society since the 1950s have encouraged
the development of different attitudes among the
present generation of young people. Of her working
class sample of 'housebound' housewives in London,
she asserts, '...it may be said that the younger
generation (and this study points in this direction)
have genuinely shifted their pattern of living from a
neighbourhood centred life to a family centred life'
(Gavron, 1966,93). Despite the physically close
presence of extended family members, she found the
dominant focus of interest for these women to be the
nuclear family. Neighbourly visits also tended to be
less important than expected in a 'traditional' working class area. 25 per cent of her sample had no
real friends at all and a further 40 per cent had
only one or two friends to visit during the day
(Gavron, 1966,89).
   The focus on the nuclear family and the lack of
emphasis on 'community' life and informal home

visiting does not, therefore, seem to be class-based
any longer. It is as characteristic of the younger
generation of the working class as it is of the
middle class. Carey and Mapes (1972), for example,
in their study of social activity on new housing
estates, failed to find a significant relationship
between home visiting and social class. If anything,
recent studies appear to show that middle class
housewives now socialise more than their working
class counterparts with both neighbours and
relatives. Gavron (1966,97) found that, 'A great
difference between the working and middle class wives
was in the number and pattern of friendships.' 67
per cent of her middle class sample (as compared with
35 per cent of the working class wives) regularly
visited a large number of friends, while none of the
middle class housewives admitted to having no friends
at all and only a tiny minority (4 per cent) did not
take part in any home visiting activity during the
daytime. Gavron stresses that the middle class
housewives in general promoted far better neighbourly
relations than the working class wives,' in contrast
to the findings of previous studies. Bell (1970)
also stresses the importance of the extended family
to middle class women. The evidence with respect to
class differences in social interaction and particularly in home visiting patterns appears rather
inconclusive. The hypotheses concerning these
patterns must, therefore, remain open to empirical
testing.

c)   Other activities

     Other forms of activity, however, appear still
to be largely class-biased. Perhaps the best example
here is involvement in adult education. Jary (1973,
269), for example, states that, 'Adult education...is
markedly incongruent with working class life.' However, it is important to remember that in this case,
class norms of behaviour may well be reinforced by
the presence of other constraints on participation -
in particular, the constraint of distance and
mobility. There is also evidence to suggest that,
despite apparent differences in recreation activities
between social classes (Sessoms, 1963), actual
activity patterns may be the result more of differences in the supply of resources than of any difference in demand for those resources (see Cicchetti,
1971,22; Lindsay and Ogle, 1972,19). Similarly,
differences exist between classes in terms of
shopping behaviour and the use of local facilities,

but these differences can to some extent be attributed to differential levels of mobility and income as between classes. The differential use of libraries and other 'cultural' facilities and the membership of social organisations are more clearly class-biased forms of activity.

Socio-Economic Constraints, III - Type of Area

1. The nature of the constraint

The area where people live is obviously a physical entity and the physical environment affects activity patterns in terms of the provision of opportunity (see Chapter 3). Here, however, we are concerned with 'type of area' as an aspect of socio-economic structure. Webber (1964a,63) uses the term in this way in his discussion of working class areas and it is worthwhile quoting his argument at some length: 'The physical place becomes an extension of one's ego. The outer worlds of neighbourhood-based peer groups, neighbourhood-based family, and the physical neighbourhood place itself, seem to become internalised as inseparable aspects of one's inner perceptions of self. In the highly personalised life of the working class neighbourhood, where one's experiences are largely limited to social contacts with others who are but minutes away, the physical space and the physical buildings become reified as aspects of the social group. One's conception of himself and of his place in society is thus subtly merged with his conceptions of the spatially limited territory of limited social interaction.' Webber stresses here that the physical and social environments become inter-related only in working class areas; his general thesis is that the coincidence of neighbourhood and community does not occur among the so-called higher social classes. However, even he has to admit (1964a,66) that,'...the least place-bound cosmopolite behaves as an extreme localite when playing-out some of his roles,' while for middle class wives, the immediate locality remains the 'community' focus.

It seems valid, therefore, to consider the type of area in which women live as a potentially important independent influence on their activity patterns, regardless of their personal social class position. However, many of the characteristics of an area obviously relate to the social class and income of the residents - in particular, the size and density of the dwellings. Mode of tenure of housing

is also partly related to income, although it is also
related to permanence of occupation of the housing,
which is itself another factor making up the total
character of an area. The quality of housing is also
important, a factor which is related both to the
income of the residents and to the age of the
dwellings, as is the predominant age and life-cycle
stage of the residents and the degree of homogeneity
or heterogeneity in population composition. Together, these various characteristics contribute to
the specific nature of different residential areas
and the development of normative modes of behaviour.
In turn, the type of area may act as a constraint on
activity patterns which fall outside of this normative framework. 'What affects people, then, is not
the raw physical environment, but the social and
economic environment in which that physical environment is used.' (Gans, 1972,373).

2.   The influence of the constraint on activity
     patterns

     The clearest evidence of the influence of type
of area as a constraint on the activity patterns of
women with young children derives from studies of
home visiting activities. Forrest (1974,303), for
example, stresses the importance of owner-occupier
status and consequent stability of residence as a
factor in determining the extent of social interaction in an area. Lopata (1971,294) and Gavron
(1966,98) both note the greater intensity of visiting
activity among house-dwellers than among flat-
dwellers; presumably the type of housing in this
case is very highly correlated with mode of tenure.
The extent of permanence of residence in an area is
obviously very likely to affect the level of visiting
activity. In America, residential mobility is
generally high and Muller (1976,16) makes the point
that it is the more permanent location of residence
in the working class suburbs which gives these areas
a tighter local cohesion and higher level of social
interaction than the less permanently occupied
middle class suburbs. In Britain, residence is
generally characterised more by immobility than by
mobility (Morgan, 1976) and such a class-based
differential is unlikely to be observed. Finally,
the size of house and land plots may be important in
affecting the extent of visiting activity. Large
houses and gardens inevitably lead to minimal casual
contact with neighbours and possibly, therefore, to a
greater concentration on individual privacy and less

home visiting activity than would be the case with
terraced housing, for example. Hillman et al.,
(1973,9), writing of the woman with pre-school
children, state that,'The type of housing occupied
and its density affect her opportunities for seeing
neighbours or contacting friends, which provide a
welcome change from child-rearing.' On the other
hand, people may prefer space and privacy to high
density and forced sociability (Willis, 1969,304):
it is those who can afford to choose who are least
affected by the constraint of type of area, as indeed
they are also less influenced by most other
constraints on activity patterns (see Harper and
Richards, 1979,164).

Studies of the visiting patterns of mothers of
young children have pointed out the propensity of
these women to interact socially with others in a
similar situation and have implied that a conscious
choice is made in this direction (for example, Gans,
1961a,137; Athanasiou and Yoshioka, 1973,55; Carey
and Mapes, 1972,15). Thus it is commonly found that
friendships are established 'through the children'.
However, the opposite conclusion is equally possible
- namely, that since women with young children are
the only people (of a roughly equivalent age) likely
to be available for interaction during the daytime,
other women are constrained in their choice of
possible acquaintances. Carey and Mapes (1972,63),
in their study of the social activity of housewives
on new housing estates, admit that '...visiting with
estate members develops because they happen to be
conveniently situated during the period of child-
rearing when the housewife has more time for visiting
generally.' Choice of friends is far more likely to
be based on age-group similarity and may, therefore,
be fortuitously correlated with life-cycle stage.

Other forms of activity which make up the total
life-style of women with young children may also be
restricted by the prevailing character and derived
behavioural norms of the local area. That these
norms of behaviour are not precisely the same thing
as class norms might most clearly be seen in a
socially heterogeneous area which, despite internal
differences in life-style based on class, still
maintains an overall 'community' structure which
influences the activity patterns of its residents.
This is as clearly seen in a temporary rooming area,
where social interaction is severely restricted by
common consent, as it is in an area of immobile
owner-occupiers, where set patterns of behaviour have
developed over the years and experimentation or

deviance is shunned.

Problems of Defining Variables

The importance of societal constraints as influences
on activity patterns has been stressed in the preceding sections of this chapter and some empirical
findings have been quoted. However, much of the
literature in this area necessarily focuses at a
theoretical, rather than an empirical, level. In
particular, there have been very few practical
research studies dealing with the position of women
and the influence of gender-role differentiation.
Part of the reason for the lack of quantitative
empirical work must surely be the problem of defining
suitable variables for study. Much of the information which one seeks to collect is essentially qualitative in nature.

Although it may be obvious to the researcher
that the influence of gender-roles permeates all
societal structures, it is less easy to prove this
quantitatively, especially using a one-off, cross-
sectional questionnaire study. By selecting a sample
of women with young children, it is here assumed that
all respondents are subject to the effects of gender
role differentiation. It then becomes possible to
look more closely at variations within the group, in
the way that the constraint is perceived and felt.
Thus, this study uses variables such as reasons for
activities and attitude scores, together with
objective data concerning the number and age of young
children, type of outside child care used and so on,
in order to consider the differential impact on
activity patterns resulting from the gender role
constraint.

In dealing with socio-economic constraints it is
somewhat easier to select appropriate illustrative
variables if only because previous research in the
area is much better-developed. However, it has to be
admitted that the variables chosen for study may only
scratch the surface of the underlying problem. Thus,
for example, the previously-mentioned interpretation
of 'income' as 'availability of resources', although
useful theoretically, is almost impossible to handle
empirically; so we fall back on the more easily
obtained 'household income' variable as an approxim-
ation of true 'income'. Similarly, 'social class'
has to be seen in terms of socio-economic group or
terminal education age because these variables may
be explored in a questionnaire survey.

Essentially pragmatic decisions have, therefore,

been made concerning the choice of variables to illustrate the presence of societal constraints on activities in this study. However, this is necessary if theoretical and empirical work is to be linked together, thereby enhancing the development of social theory.

Chapter 3

FOCUS ON CONSTRAINTS II - PHYSICAL CONSTRAINTS

In the perspective of time-geography (see Chapter 1)
physical and environmental constraints achieve dominance in their effects on activities. However, in this
study, it is assumed that such immediate constraints
on activity patterns are themselves the product of
societal structure and are, thus, of less underlying
importance than are the gender-role and socio-
economic constraints discussed in Chapter 2. In
particular, physical constraints are not viewed here
as causal elements (able to be incorporated into
regression or causal path analysis) but as relational
factors. Thus, their relationship with activity
patterns has been demonstrated by many research
studies and will be tested in this study.
    The physical constraints discussed in this
Chapter will be those of distance and mobility and
the provision of opportunity. In each case, the
nature of the constraint will first be considered,
followed by the influence of the constraint on
activity patterns. Wherever sufficient information
is available from previous studies, distinctions
between types of activity will be drawn.

Distance and Mobility

1.   The nature of the constraint

a)   Distance

    In geographical studies distance has always been
viewed as a primary constraint on interaction and
activities (Hillman, 1970,266). An extensive
literature exists on the importance of distance, for
example, in work location, social interaction
patterns and patterns of leisure and recreational
activities; some of this literature will be reviewed

later. The actual measurement of distance has varied
between studies: thus, straight line distance has in
some cases been replaced by other measures such as
monetary or time cost, in the interests of obtaining
a higher degree of explanation.
'Nevertheless, it has been suggested that
accessibility, rather than proximity, is becoming the
key determinant of urban form...The implication of
this argument is that improved communications and the
extension of physical mobility afforded by the car,
negate the "frictional" effect of distance' (Hillman,
1970,268). The significant point to be brought out
here is that the negation of the distance constraint
acts differentially as between different groups in
society. Hillman notes (1970,268-269) that the
widely held views on improved accessibility and the
consequent lessening of the distance constraint,'...
only take account of the requirements of adults with
cars, and ignore the needs of large sections of the
community which have to be very dependent on local
activities, and for whom accessibility and proximity
are synonomous' (my emphasis).

b)   Mobility

The notions of 'accessibility' and 'mobility'
are widely used, both in the academic literature and
more generally and encompass many different ideas.
It is,therefore,essential that a strict definition be
applied and adhered to in this study. The idea of
'accessibility' is related to the provision of
facilities to which access is sought and this
concept will,therefore,be mainly dealt with in a
later section of this chapter, which considers the
constraint of provision of opportunity. The idea of
'mobility' is more directly related to the question
of distance and will be dealt with here. Following
Hillman et al., (1976,51), 'mobility' can be defined
in terms of, firstly, the ability to use different
forms of travel and, secondly, the availability of
methods of travel. Although these two aspects of
personal mobility interact to a considerable extent,
in some cases only one constraint may be operative.
For example, in Hillman et al's., (1976) study of
mobility among young mothers, it was found that 29
per cent of women with driving licences in car owning
households (and therefore able to travel by car) did
not have the optional use of a car (in other words,
that form of transport was not available to them).
On the other hand, this same survey found that, even
where buses were available as a means of transport,

they were used very little because of the difficulties involved in that travel mode, especially when
the women were accompanied by their children. As
Mann (1965,162) states, 'Transporting the infant on
buses becomes a major tactical operation.'
    As has been noted in Chapter 1, the concept of
mobility has been stressed very heavily in the time-
geographic approach to the study of activity
patterns. It is the level of mobility which determines the width of the daily 'prism' within which
activities can take place because of the importance
of time constraints. For the woman with a young
child, 'Mobility is limited by the needs of feeding
times and the distance that can be covered when
pushing a pram' (Mann, 1965,162). In such a case,
the 'daily life environment' is very small in extent.
'It is clear that an individual must derive services,
information, and connections from the social complex
formed by the people and institutions within the
daily-life environment open to him' (sic)(Peet, 1975,
568).

c)   Differential individual mobility

    Hillman was the first writer to publicise widely
the fairly obvious, but neglected, point that
individual mobility is not the same thing as
household mobility, since '...the family operates as
a unit on a relatively small number of the total
journeys made by the individuals within it...'
(Hillman, 1970,51 - see also, Bannister, 1977,3). In
particular, there is a great difference between the
levels of access to a car by women and men (see
Passwell, 1976,5). The myth of a future age in which
car availability will be universal (at least in the
Western world) is fairly deeply entrenched. It
underlies the ideas of Webber on 'non-place'
communities (Webber, 1964b) and on a lesser scale
influences many American writers. Thus, Gans (1961a,
138), for example, writes that '...the increase in
two-car families and women's greater willingness to
drive are gradually reducing the traditional immobility of the housewife.' One fundamental point is
overlooked by Gans and many other writers; this is,
that the more a society relies on cars as a means of
transport, the more constrained in mobility is the
person without a car (Palm and Pred, 1974,23). Thus,
in the suburban sprawl of American cities where '...
the automobile is essential as a means of carrying
out the most mundane of activities' (Palm and Pred,
1974,29), those without the normal use of a car

suffer the greatest mobility problems.

Hayford (1974,16-17) relates these problems of individual differences in mobility to the structure of power in society: she suggests that,'The dominance of men in the public sphere means that the paths of movement that are available in an area reflect the needs of men as they move from one type of space to another...Relative expenditures on expressways and public transportation can in part be understood by looking at which sex drives most of the cars on the former and which rides the buses of the latter...Women do not have the same freedom to move in space or to organise space that men have.' Again, writing of the situation in American cities, Koutsopoulos and Schmidt (1976,32) note that car-less groups in the population are often ignored as a minority in overall urban transportation planning and therefore public transport development is unco- ordinated (see Jones et al., 1983, for an attempt at incorporating a real understanding of travel behav- iour into the transportation planning process).

d)   Re-emphasis of the distance constraint

In America, cities have sprawled to such an extent that a local solution to accessibility problems appears to be impossible. There is, there- fore,an emphasis in geographical literature on public transport provision as a means of overcoming the mobility constraints of the car-less. In Britain, urban development has been much more severely contained (see Hall et al., 1973) but even here, 'The catchment areas of urban facilities are contin- uously growing larger because of the wider range of services that they provide' (Hillman, 1970,54 - see also, Mitchell and Town, 1977,1). In addition, there has been the growth of specifically car-oriented patterns of activity - for example, the development of hypermarkets. In these ways, society has become more dependent on cars as a means of transport and hence more 'inequitable' in terms of access possibil- ities. Hillman et al., (1973,72) stress that,'In all areas, the importance of proximity of local facili- ties...cannot be over-emphasised'. Because car- availability can never be universal, there must be a return to the consideration of distance as a signif- icant constraint on activity patterns. Public transport can never operate as a really optional alternative to car transport because of the many problems inherent in its operation - problems of reliability, frequency, convenience, the effort

involved in its use and perceived and actual cost.
  The weight of research evidence therefore, seems
to go against the approval of an increasing car-
orientation in society on the grounds of universal
car accessibility and in favour of an emphasis on
distance-minimisation as the means of increasing
equity as between all groups in society. Lee (1968,
264) states that '...planning should be directed
towards heterogeneous physical and social layouts,
deliberately emphasising the local (and therefore
most effortless) satisfaction of needs.' In
particular, it is felt that,'The comparative
immobility of the young mother and small child
demands a local solution...' (Pritchard, 1967,29).
It is this planning philosophy which, as Hillman et
al., (1976,xviii) recognise, lies behind the planning
of local facilities in New Towns. Even in a car-
oriented new city such as Milton Keynes, 'activity
centres' have been designed in such a way that every
resident lives within 500 metres of basic services
and facilities (Milton Keynes Development Corporation, 1970,36). It is,therefore,recognised, at
least by some, that distance remains a constraint on
activity patterns because the ability to overcome the
constraint is not available to all, due to low levels
of personal mobility.

2.   The influence of the constraint on activity
      patterns

a)   The extent of activity space

  'Mothers of young children have the greatest
problems of mobility, and many have to restrict their
journeys to those that can be made on foot; as a
result, their activities are very influenced by
physical proximity' (Hillman, 1970,26). The extent
of activity space for such women is very limited, at
least during weekdays. The existence of public
transport does not seem to expand their activity
space very noticeably since women with young children
do not tend to use such transport very much (see
Paaswell, 1976,6). For example, Hillman's survey
'...shows that women's use of buses is surprisingly
low, even for those in households without a car. It
indicates that the women prefer instead to use nearby
facilities - even if they are smaller; to adjust or
delay activities in order to be able to travel by car
(if there is one in the household); or to make fewer
trips and sometimes to engage in fewer activities'
(Hillman et al., 1976,104).

b)   Local orientation of activities

    If there is a boundary which marks the edge of
the individual's 'activity space', this may correspond to a time constraint, as could be described in
terms of Hagerstrand's 'prism'-width, or it may
represent something far more subjective than this.
There have been a number of studies (for examples,
Lee, 1968; Eyles, 1968) on people's perceptions of
their 'neighbourhood' and these have shown how strong
is the sense of identification with local areas. For
example, Lee (1968,263) remarks that,'Neighbourhood,
it seems, remains a highly salient phenomenon of
urban living.' People who are very restricted in
their mobility are most likely to form a close association with their immediate area and this association having been formed, they are unlikely to pursue
activities far beyond its boundary. Thus, the local-
isation process is circular in causation.
    Many attempts have been made to show that local
services and facilities are of little importance to
residents but generally without success. As long
ago as 1947, Foley (1950) surveyed households in St.
Louis in order to establish the decline in importance
of local facilities but he found that the opposite
was true. The majority of activities took place in
the immediate residential area and for women the use
of local facilities was absolutely dominant. A
recent study by Everitt (1976), attempting to test
Webber's idea of 'non-place' urban realms, found
instead a significant physical tie to the local area,
particularly among women.
    To take, firstly, the case of outside employ-
ment, Hillman et al., (1976,97,98), note the dominant
importance of the location of potential workplaces
in relation to home in determining the ability of
women with young families to work at all. For these
women, walking was the most common journey mode to
work (in constrast to their husbands' use of cars).
    The use of local shopping facilities has already
been stressed. Hillman's survey (1976,77) showed
that of all day-to-day shopping trips, 68 per cent
were made on foot. Women are not generally in a
position of optional car use for shopping trips and a
survey in Watford (Daws and McCulloch, 1974,19)
provides evidence to support this point; it found
that on weekdays only 23 per cent of Watford housewives had a car available for shopping purposes,
whereas 64 per cent of households owned cars. The
results of a survey in Milton Keynes also '...under-
line the importance of car-ownership and car-

availability as crucial determinants in explaining
shopping patterns' (Milton Keynes Development
Corporation, 1974,50).
    Local orientation also occurs in the case of
recreation patterns. Hillman et al., (1976,91)
found that a ten minute walk appeared to represent
the distance which would be travelled by young
mothers in order to visit a park. This finding is
confirmed by other studies, notably the Greater
London recreation survey (1968,6) and Balmer's study
in Liverpool (1974,116). There are some activities,
however,which do not seem to be so affected by the
distance constraint. One example is attendance in
adult education centres; Lee (1966) found no
relationship between enrolment in classes and
distance from home. However, in the case of women
with young children, the effect of the distance
constraint may be masked by an even more important
constraint - the need to attend a centre which has
child care facilities.

c)   Home visiting activity

    Of all types of activity, perhaps the most
studied with respect to the importance of distance is
home visiting and friendship patterns (see Athanasiou
and Yoshioka, 1973, and Forrest, 1974 for reviews of
previous studies). However, much early work related
to friendship patterns in completely homogeneous
communities; for example, Festinger et al's., (1950)
study of a student housing area. Gans hypothesised
that, in a less homogeneous area, friendship patterns
would be dependent on homogeneity of background
rather than propinquity and supported this hypothesis with evidence from his (1967) study of
Levittown, New Jersey. But Athanasiou and Yoshioka
(1973,61) found that distance operated as an important variable even in a heterogeneous social environment: 'Apparently propinquity plays a part in the
formation and maintenance of friendships among women
who may have little in common besides life-cycle
stage. In order for friendships to be maintained
over moderate or large distances, however, additional
similarities in social class must be present.' (Both
life cycle stage, as a common attribute in visiting
patterns and social class exclusivity in social
activity, have been discussed already in Chapter 2).
    Since personal mobility is very restricted for
the woman with young children, she is inevitably
constrained to participate in home visiting at a very
local level. Gans (1961a,183) admits that '...young

mothers must usually be able to find compatible
people...within a relatively small radius. Should
they fail to do so, they may become the unhappy
isolated suburban housewives about whom so much has
been written.' A similar point is made by Carey and
Mapes (1972,11-12), speaking of English housing
estates: '...the housewife, particularly if she is
also a mother of young children, may be largely
confined to the estate. If she is unable to make
social contacts elsewhere the socialization process
in the immediate locality is likely to be more urgent
and exacting for her.'
    A considerable volume of literature has examined
the different levels of personal mobility between
different social classes but as previously shown,
household mobility is not necessarily the same thing
as individual mobility. In particular, much has been
made of the ability of middle class people to travel
widely in their home visiting activity and maintain
social relationships over great distances. Muller
(1976,15) for example, referring to the work of
Webber on non-propinquitous communities, states that,
'The widely dispersed life spaces of middle-class
suburbanites, who increasingly participate in social
networks which function with little regard for
distance or territoriality, typify the unhitching of
communities from geographically-fixed localities.'
Bracey (1964,97), however, points out the great
difference between America and Britain in mobility
levels. In particular, American women are more
likely to have access to a car during the daytime,
although even in a car-dependent city such as Los
Angeles, it has been shown that a large percentage of
women are without the use of a car on weekdays.
Obviously, higher class people tend to be the two-car
owners and it is middle class wives who are more
easily able to overcome distance in visiting friends,
whereas working class wives must be content to
socialise close to home (Gans, 1961a,138). However,
an English study by Carey and Mapes (1972) shows that
the availability of a second car to the wife is not
correlated with home visiting activity away from the
immediate environment and that (at least in this
study) distance does represent an important
constraint on visiting patterns for all housewives.
    It is generally agreed that distance does not
operate in quite the same way as a constraint on
visiting activity with relatives as with friends. A
great deal of sociological enquiry has been directed
at the nature and importance of kinship networks.
Firth et al., (1969,3) stress the social (as opposed

to the biological) determination of kinship. They
found their (middle class) informants to be highly
selective in their choice of social contacts from
among their (biological) kinship group, however close
the potential contacts might live. They stress the
fact that, 'In urban conditions geographical proximity
in itself does not imply that contact between kin
should be frequent or intense.' In general, they
found that contact was maintained with members of the
natal family, wherever they lived but other kin
relationships were more related to geographical
distance. In summary, it might be said that distance
becomes an important constraint on visiting activity
with kin after the operation of the selection process
and the social determination of the kinship network.
       This is, surely, equally true of working class
kinship networks. The 'traditional' working class
community (such as that described by Dennis et al.,
1956) was based on strong extended family linkages
and close geographical proximity; the perceived
kinship network was large. The removal of younger
members of such communities to peripheral estates did
not initially alter this perception. The social
definition of kinship remained as before, with its
established pattern of interdependence and visiting
obligations (see Field and Neill, 1957). In seeking
to maintain this pattern, distance became an extremely important constraint to overcome. Young and
Willmott (1957,III) particularly note the importance
of fare costs as a constraint on the maintenance of
kinship visiting patterns between residents of
'Greenleigh' and Bethnal Green. They also stress the
poverty of social relationships on the estates,
especially for women at home; this could be interpreted, in the light of the foregoing discussion, as
the result of geographically wide, socially defined
kinship networks, in which interaction is inhibited
by the constraint of distance. A quite different
situation has more recently been described by Gavron
(1966) who found her working class respondents in
London to have very limited, effective kinship networks, despite the close proximity of kin members.
       Visiting patterns with relatives and those with
friends do differ from each other. Although it is
not entirely true that one chooses one's friends
while relatives are pre-determined - it has been
shown that kinship is also a socially defined phenomenon - it is nevertheless obvious that relatives are
known even where they live at a distance, while the
average person will not have equivalent information
about potential friends not living in the immediate

vicinity. Distance, as a consequence, appears to be less important in the choice of kinship-based social interaction, but because of this, it acts as a more important constraint on actual visiting activity. Thus, the young mother, having chosen the relatives with whom she wishes to maintain social contact, with little regard for proximity, finds herself constrained by distance (both in time and cost terms) in establishing her actual visiting patterns. By contrast, proximity appears to be a crucial variable in the choice of friends for the woman with a young child (due to the constraint imposed by lack of personal mobility) and, in consequence, actual visiting patterns are less constrained by problems of distance.

Provision of Opportunity

1. The nature of the constraint

a) Spatial inequality

This constraint concerns the question of accessibility in a spatial sense, in contrast to the distance and mobility constraint, discussed above, which determines physical accessibility and the income constraint (see Chapter 2) which determines social accessibility. We are concerned here with the actual provision of services and facilities and, in general, of spatial opportunity to undertake desired activities.

Inequalities in society have long been recognised and studied but 'Only recently has attention been directed to the geographical or spatial dimensions of inequality' (Pahl, 1968,16). Simmie (1974, 85) views society as a conflict between groups competing for scarce resources and, therefore, for the improvement of their situation in the social structure. He stresses that this social structure is the key to the spatial structure and that it is necessary first to understand the differential possession of scarce resources by different groups before one can understand patterns of spatial differentiation (Simmie, 1974,86). In other words, he considers that spatial inequality is merely a by-product of social inequality.

The same view is held by many writers, notably those critical of the workings of capitalism such as Peet (1975,569): 'Just as the capitalist system of production must lead to a hierarchical social class structure, so it must provide differentiated social resource environments in which each class reproduces itself.' American literature dealing with spatial inequality also tends to support this view, that the spatial structure is the result of the social structure, in that race relations problems are seen as the determinants of spatial problems such as ghetto formation (see Glazer, 1967,89; Kennedy, 1967,114; Meltzer and Whitley, 1967,134). The Chicago school of human ecology represents yet another group of writers who have viewed spatial patterns in the city as 'natural' results of social inequality and conflict between societal groups. The same point has recently been made by Ward and Dubos (1974,136) who stress the causal connection between the dominance of socially segregated rural in-migrants and the existence of pockets of dilapidated housing, poor services and generally impoverished environment.

Pahl, (1968,14) supports the general view that the social system is an important determinant of spatial structure but he also goes further than this and suggests the importance of location, in itself, as a source of inequality: 'At present it is known that territorial inequality is substantial and that men (sic) with the same occupation, income and family characteristics have substantially different life chances in different localities' (Pahl, 1971b,135-136). Recently, there has been a strong interest in the use of 'social indicators' to give an accurate spatial picture of variations in the 'quality of life' or 'social well-being' between regions, cities or intra-urban areas (Knox, 1975; Smith, 1973). The basis of this movement is the belief that accurate and useful policies can only be built on a sound foundation of factual evidence. More generally, Chisholm and Manners (1971,3) note the increasing contrasts between central city and suburban areas in terms of housing standards, educational facilities and social provisions (see also Ambrose,1974,203). This is, of course, no new pattern of inequality, as can be seen, for example, in Engels' description of conditions in English cities in 1844. A modern case study, of St. Ann's in Nottingham, is presented by Coates and Silburn (1970).

It is obviously impossible for everyone to live in an equally advantageous position in relation to all urban resources and facilities (Pahl, 1975,297). The problem is not that spatial disparities exist, but that they reinforce social inequalities. 'Those provisions which are administered by local or national government are critical determinants of life chances' (Pahl, 1971b,132) and, if allocated according to need, could lead to a redistribution of real income within society. Harvey also states that, 'The real income of an individual can be changed by changing the resources available to him' (Harvey, 1975, 68). But the situation remains that the poorest members of society are condemned to live, not only in the worst inner city housing but with a low level of access to urban resources in general. An example here could be the provision of public open space, the lack of which is highly correlated with low social status and inner city location (Tivers, 1976). As Hardy (1973,83-84) states, 'Deficiency in recreation space is one facet of multiple deprivation. Understandably, it does not attract the same degree of attention as housing or income levels, but it represents one more component in the total complex of poverty: in leisure as at work access to urban resources is restricted.'

However, inner city, low status areas may not be the only ones which suffer from objective deprivation in terms of access to resources. Many fringe suburban areas in Britain are severely lacking in services and facilities of one kind or another. Particularly poorly provided for are the numerous housing estate areas which have sprung up around the fringes of the old, non-metropolitan towns of south-east England, during the last ten or fifteen years. A major problem here is of course inherent in the lower residential densities than those which prevail in central city areas - namely, the problem of providing services efficiently without thereby condemning a large part of the population to low standards of accessibility (U.K. Central Housing Committee, 1967, 30).

b)   The provision of child care facilities

i)   Inadequacy of services

One particular aspect of the provision of opportunity constraint which is of great importance to women with young children concerns the provision of child care facilities. There is substantial inequality in the spatial distribution of such facilities (as is also the case with respect to other services and facilities as shown above) but in addition there is near-universal agreement in the literature that existing day care services for young children in Britain are totally inadequate overall and that they should be expanded to meet the demand for such

services. These research conclusions, of course, fly
directly in the face of current government policy
(1979 onwards) to restrict nursery expansion and to
strengthen the ideological emphasis on women's role
in the care of pre-school children. It is only
possible to understand the present situation in the
provision of child care by considering the historical
trends in the light of such changing ideological
emphases, which are themselves clearly related to
economic and national needs for employed labour.

ii) Historical trends in provision

     Over the last forty years there have been many
changes in economic conditions in this country,
which have led to differential demands for the
employment of women workers. At the same time,
changes in social conditions have slowly altered the
position of women (although, in reality, probably to
a lesser extent than is widely believed). The
provision of child care facilities outside the home
has occurred as a response to these sets of changes.
However, if one simply charts the changes in numbers
of day care places over the years in relation to
stated government policy at the time, one overlooks
the complex economic and social interrelationships
which lie behind such changes in provision. These
interrelationships can best be understood by tracing
the historical development of child care provision
alongside changes in economic and social conditions.
For the purposes of this study reference will only be
made to the comparatively recent past, although a
clearer understanding of such interrelationships
would require the consideration of data over a much
longer time-span.
     The beginning of the second world war marks a
convenient starting point for the study of changes
in day care provision. In 1938 there were 104 day
nurseries in England and Wales. By 1941 this number
had risen to 194, and in 1944, 1,559 day nurseries
provided full-time places for over 68,000 pre-school
children and a further 109 part-time nurseries
catered for 3,625 children. This provision was in
addition to the 35,000 places for children in
nursery schools and classes and the 103,000 places
in the reception classes of elementary schools
(Tizard et al., 1976,70-72). The causes of this
enormous expansion in child-care provision are not
difficult to identify. Particularly from 1941
onwards, women were increasingly needed to occupy
men's jobs and to sustain the 'war effort'. It was

63

recognised that any great expansion of the labour force in this direction would require a parallel expansion of child care facilities. Thus wartime nurseries were set up, most remaining open for very long hours each day. The pre-war Hadow Report (Consultative Committee on Infant and Nursery Schools, 1933) had supported the traditional view that the best place for a child under five was with his/her mother at home. Within the space of a decade ideological emphasis had shifted completely. Because women were needed in the labour force, it became necessary to emphasise the social value of day nursery provision for pre-school children, alongside the national need for 'service to the state' in the form of employment.

It did not take long for official views to change again. The immediate post-war era saw the replacement of women workers by men and the concomitant re-emphasis of women's child care role. The provision of child care by the state being no longer in the national interest, it was rapidly re-asserted that the right place for a young child was with his/her mother. Child care provision was to be restricted either to purely educational ends (thus many wartime nurseries were handed over to local education authorities for conversion to nursery schools) or to remedial purposes (for those '...children whose mothers are constrained by individual circumstances to go out to work or whose home conditions are in themselves unsatisfactory from the health point of view, or whose mothers are incapable for some good reason of undertaking the full care of their children.' (Ministry of Health circular 221/45, quoted in Tizard et al., 1976,73)). Day care was firmly divided between the Ministries of Education and of Health and has remained largely unco-ordinated in its provision up to the present time.

It had proved necessary to justify the expansion of wartime provision in terms of the value of outside child care. It now became necessary to justify the cut-back in provision by reference to the young child's need of his/her own mother. Extremely influential, both at this time and throughout the succeeding post-war period, was the research work of John Bowlby, the British psychologist. Working for the World Health Organisation he produced in 1951 his seminal report, Maternal Care and Mental Health which, by raising the issue of 'maternal deprivation', was to have a lasting impact on the ideology of childcare provision. In this and succeeding works, his thesis was developed that '...a child is deprived if for any reason he is removed from his mother's care' (Bowlby, 1953,14). Despite the fact that his research was based on studies undertaken in resident- ial institutions, such as children's homes, its results were generalised to apply to all day care situations. These results provided a convenient 'scientific' basis for reducing the number of day nursery places in line with the reduced demand for women in employment and were seized upon eagerly by the government of the time. The ideological emphasis on women's child care role was revitalised and has remained clearly in evidence up to the present day.

Throughout the 1950's, day nurseries steadily closed down while the hoped-for expansion in nursery education failed to take place (officially, because of 'teacher shortages'). The same situation continued into the early 1960's when, however, the private sector intervened for the first time on a large scale with the beginning of the Playgroup Movement. This movement, with its avowedly 'educat- ional' aims, was responsible for the setting up of some 15,000 playgroups in England by 1972 (Tizard et al., 1976,78). But part-time child care of the sort supplied by such private, fee-paying institutions was of little or no value to working mothers, the number of whom was steadily beginning to rise again in this period of economic expansion. Such women turned increasingly to childminders for the provision of full-day care. Required under legislation dating from 1948 to register with local authorities if minding children for profit, childminders increased in numbers during this period both legally and illegally but particularly the latter. As Tizard et al., (1976,79) say, 'The law is...a dead letter, and it is known that most minders are not in fact regis- tered. Consequently, the official numbers...are mis- leading rather than informative.' Known child- minding, however, extended to 32,000 places by 1966.

Despite the surge of interest in pre-school facilities from the private sector, fewer than 9 per cent of all children under five had access to any 'official' form of child care provision by 1966. In particular, there had been no expansion in educational facilities, despite the post-war switch of ideological emphasis from day care to the educat- ional needs of young children. The Plowden Report of the following year stated unequivocally: 'The under fives are the only age group for whom no extra educa- tional provision of any kind has been made since 1944...Nursery education on a large scale remains an

unfulfilled promise' (Central Advisory Council for
Education (England), 1967,116). Influenced by the
work of different 'experts' with conflicting ideas
(including, of course, Bowlby), the Report itself
appeared contradictory in its approach to the need
for pre-school provision. On the one hand, it sought
to establish that '...nursery provision on a substantial scale is desirable, not only on educational
grounds, but also for social, health and welfare
considerations' (page 117) and came out in support of
the argument that young children with mothers out at
work are not worse-off than their contemporaries
providing that alternative care is made available
(page 120). On the other hand, the Report argued
that the expansion of nursery education should take
place in part-time schooling, 'because young children
should not be separated for long from their mothers'
(Page 121) and stated that only a minority (15 per
cent of three and four year olds) would need full-
time nursery education because their parents were
unable to care for them. Working mothers who chose
to work full-time were certainly not to be supported
by the state: 'We do not believe that full-time
nursery places should be provided even for children
who might tolerate separation without harm, except
for exceptionally good reasons' (my emphasis) (page
127). Finally, the Report calculated (on the basis
of little real evidence concerning parental wishes)
that only one-half of three year olds and 90 per cent
of four year olds would actually attend nursery
schools (page 126). Its recommendations concerning
the number of places needed to be provided, therefore, were conservative, even given the restricted
scope of the provision in general.
  The expansion of part-time education provides an
interesting example of the ideological justification
of a situation originally caused by economic conditions. In 1960 there were only about 3,400 children
receiving part-time nursery education and in that
year the Ministry of Education issued a circular (no.
8/60) commending the principle of part-time schooling
on the grounds that funds were not available for any
expansion of nursery schools; by this means, more
children could be offered places without increasing
the overall cost (Tizard et al., 1976,76). Only
seven years later, the Plowden Report came out
strongly in favour of part-time nursery education,
not explicitly on the grounds of cost but influenced
by theories on 'maternal deprivation'. The 1972
White Paper on education (Department of Education and
Science, 1972) accepted the conclusions of the

Plowden Report and, as Tizard et al., (1976,76)
note, '...by the 1970's...the numbers of part-time
pupils had increased dramatically, and part-time
education for the under fives had become not just a
regrettable practical necessity but a policy justified on educational grounds and a principle for
future expansion'.

Whatever the relationship between supply and
demand in nursery education, it remained obvious that
daycare was still desperately needed by many families. Nursery school hours (even full-time) were
simply not long enough to provide satisfactory care
for the children of full-time workers, while the
problem of school holidays was of great significance.
However, the 'official' view was set firmly against
any encouragement of women to go out to work, except
in cases of 'exceptional' need: 'It is the stated
government view that two or so hours away from mother
is as much as most children can take, and this is all
most of them are going to get' (Tizard et al., 1976,
102). For some, however, a different policy was to
apply. As far back as 1945, there had existed
certain criteria of 'need' which were designed to
apply to special cases - notably those where housing
conditions were very poor or where the mother concerned was incapable of caring for her children. In
1968, the Seebohm report was published (Committee on
Local Authority and Allied Personal Social Services,
1968). Amongst other matters, this report was
concerned with the provision of day nursery facilities and recommended that these should be increased
once again to match the 'need' for such services.
The criteria of 'need' were little different from
those employed in 1945, although lone parents and low
income families were specifically included in the
list of those 'needing' day care. In 1969 the
decline in the number of day nurseries finally ended
and nursery places began to increase again, although
much of the new provision was to be 'on the cheap' -
using existing premises and voluntary staff and
providing only part-time care (Tizard et al., 1976,
87).

As a result of increases in part-time education
and day care, by 1973 about 23 per cent of children
under five in England and Wales (excluding those with
unregistered childminders) were receiving some form
of pre-school care, compared to only 9 per cent in
1966. This clearly fell far short of even the
conservative estimates of 'demand' and 'need' discussed in government reports. But, in addition,
there had been no official recognition of the child

care needs of families where both parents worked
outside the home (except in the case of the very low
income families), despite the fact that,'The rate of
increase in employment for the mothers of under fives
has been faster than for all married women under
sixty' (Mackie and Pattullo, 1977,114). The state
did not intend to help women workers in defiance of
its own child care ideology. At the same time, since
most new employment for women with children was part-
time, there was not the same obligation placed on
employers for the provision of creche facilities as
had been traditional in industries employing full-
time women workers (for example the Lancashire cotton
industry). Thus, child care provision remained woe-
fully inadequate and increasing numbers of children
came to be looked after by unregistered childminders,
and unpaid relatives and friends, in conditions which
were often far from satisfactory.

The 1970's have seen the passage to law of the
Equal Pay and Sex Discrimination Acts, intended to
end discrimination against women in the world of
work. There has also been a concomitant rise in the
expectations of women, based at least partly on the
'raising of consciousness' achieved by the Women's
Movement. The question of paid employment is closely
tied up with the supply of child care facilities, not
only for the very young but also for school-age
children during holiday and after-school periods.
Recently, two reports have emerged which stress the
need to consider the difficulties of working mothers
(Bone, 1977; Central Policy Review Staff, 1978).

The 'official' view overall, however, remains
unchanged. An inability to meet the financial costs
involved in providing adequate pre-school facilities
is justified by resort to the old 'maternal deprivation' theories (Smith, 1979). The general economic
situation is also of great relevance here. The
expansion of employment for women in the ten years
between 1971 and 1981 was mainly in the part-time
service sector and there was thus no effective
demand by employers for the state to provide parallel
child care facilities. In the present era of economic cuts and rising unemployment, combined with far-
reaching technological developments, there would
appear to be even less reason for the government to
implement a policy of expanding pre-school provision,
since it is very likely that a large percentage of
part-time, unskilled jobs will simply disappear in
the near future. The present re-emphasis on the
'natural' role of women in child care must be seen in
the light of both these economic elements: cost

limitations on the provision and maintenance of
facilities and a potential lessening of demand from
employers for women workers (especially those with
'other commitments'), 'In times of reduced demand for
female labour the ideological messages enshrined in
child care theories tend to move away from the
emphasis on early social contacts for the pre-school
child and the dangers of maternal smothering and towards the ghastly consequences of maternal deprivation' (Holland, 1981,36).

iii) The supply of child care

As previously mentioned, the management of child
care facilities falls under the control of two
different government departments (although there have
been some recent attempts to co-ordinate services at
local level - see Bradley, 1982). Nursery schools
and classes in primary schools are the responsibility
of the Department of Education and Science, while day
nurseries, playgroups and childminders are the
concern of the Department of Health and Social
Security. Nursery schools and classes provide their
services free-of-charge to parents but they rarely
admit children under the age of three and the majority of places are for part-time education (either
morning or afternoon sessions, on every weekday).
Nationally, the majority of places for children under
five are in non-nursery classes in primary schools.
Most of the children occupying these places are
'rising fives' - that is, four year olds who are
admitted to school at the beginning of the term in
which they reach the age of five or one term before
that. The figure of 30 per cent of children under
five in some form of day care (Central Policy Review
Staff, 1978) should, therefore, be considered in the
light of the fact that one in six of those are
receiving precisely one term of pre-school education
as their allocation of child care.

Of the facilities controlled by the Department
of Health and Social Security, only day nurseries are
provided by local authorities and even these charge
fees to parents according to means. The percentage
of children cared for in such nurseries is today very
small and strict criteria of 'need' are assumed in
judging applicants. Most places are reserved for
children of lone parents who are out at work full-
time. Day nurseries normally accept young children
of any age up to five years, as do many private
nurseries, although the latter charge a widely varying range of fees for attendance and are also highly

dissimilar in their hours and conditions. Some
private day nurseries are run by voluntary groups and
some are directly government-funded, while others are
run as private, profit-making concerns. By far the
largest proportion of children receiving day care,
outside of primary and nursery schools, attend playgroups. The origin of the Playgroup Movement has
already been discussed in the preceding section.
Like private nurseries, playgroups vary considerably
in their opening hours and method of organisation,
although most provide either morning or afternoon
sessions on fewer than five days per week and charge
a fairly small fee for attendance. Some expect
mothers to help on a rota basis while others have
trained staff to run them.

Childminders, although theoretically under state
control, provide a rather different service for
parents and their contribution to child care will
here be considered in rather more detail. As has
already been noted, childminders are required by law
to register with local Social Services Departments
but this registration has been seen by many '...more
as a form of control than of support' (Urben, 1977,
46) and large numbers remain unregistered. (For
details concerning legislation, see London Council of
Social Service, 1977, Chapter II.) Figures exist
only for the percentage of children under five cared
for by registered childminders and no really accurate
estimate is available of the numbers of children
with childminders in total. Unregistered childminders are estimated by different researchers to
care for between 100,000 and 500,000 children (Ellis,
1978,116). Childminders are particularly important
for the care they provide for very young children
(under three years of age) for whom very little
alternative provision is made.

Recently, there has been considerable government
interest in an expansion of childminding; '... the
government sees it as the easiest way of meeting
demand for pre-school care. It is cheap, and is
thought likely to remain so even when its most un-
acceptable aspects have been remedied' (Hannon, 1978,
304). But such arguments ignore the point that '...
childminding is a cheap option mainly because it
depends on childminders being exploited' (Moss, 1978,
693). Indeed, 'Childminding may itself be seen as
evidence of the need for day care facilities for
families with pre-school children' (Hannon, 1978,
304), since so many childminders are themselves the
mothers of young children, for whom this type of
home-working offers the only possible form of paid

employment. 'The pay minders receive and the
conditions in which they work puts limits on the kind
of care they can be expected to provide' (Hannon,
1978,304). Smith, summarising the results of work by
child psychologists in the era since Bowlby says
that '...child-minding could...be a good stable
means of substitute care for a working mother with
young children. But this depends on the quality of
minding. And what little we know about childminding
in Britain suggests the quality is often poor with
an unstimulating environment for the children'
(Smith, 1979,506).

If standards are low, then it is essential that
ways be found to raise them since, as Whicheloe
(1977,49) justly remarks, '...poor quality day care
quite unjustly perpetuates the belief that day care
adversely affects the child'. But standards cannot
be raised 'on the cheap'. While self-help schemes
amongst childminders and the formation of a National
Childminding Association in 1977 have begun to raise
the status of registered minders in certain areas,
at no cost to the state, the Department of the Environment - funded, Groveway scheme for salaried childminders in Lambeth illustrates well the problems of
attempting a new approach with insufficient state
financial resources (see Healy, 1977). Under this
scheme, childminders were trained at a local day
nursery and paid directly by the project. Salaries
were very low and recruiting was a major problem.
Hannon concludes that,'The Groveway Scheme was
effectively subsidised by the minders themselves...
Just as there is no such thing as a free lunch in
real world economics, there is no such thing as cheap
pre-school provision. Somebody has to bear the
capital costs (or debt charges) of whatever building
and facilities are used, plus the running costs,
which include labour. Childminding only appears to
be cheap because most of the capital costs are borne
by minders who can also be induced to work for less
than the normal costs of comparable labour' (Hannon,
1978,305). Any future scheme of this type will of
necessity involve a higher level of expenditure and
thus be less competitive economically compared to
the more traditional forms of day care.'

iv) The demand for child care services

'Despite the recent progress and the plans for
expansion there are still no places of any kind for
the great majority of children' (Gittus, 1976,202).
On the other hand, 'Surveys carried out in recent

years show that a majority of parents now want some
day care for their under fives' (Hannon, 1978,304).
As pointed out earlier, the 'need' for day care is
officially defined according to very strict criteria
but it is obvious that a considerable gap exists
between what is provided and what is 'needed' even
assuming this conservative estimate of 'need'. If
the 'need' criteria are relaxed slightly the short-
fall in provision becomes even more apparent. Bone
(1977), for example, included amongst those 'needing'
day care all children with working mothers and also
children with a 'lack of opportunity for play'
(children in the latter category would include those
living in high-rise flats, such as those from families studied by Gittus (1976) and Jephcott (1971).
On this basis she estimated that,'Provision was
wanted for twice as many children as were receiving
it' (Bone, 1977,13) amongst her national sample of
2,500 children under five. In particular, she found
that,'Unmet demand was greatest for two and, particularly, for three year olds' and that the '...desire
for day provision differed little between the social
classes' (Bone, 1977,14). A big preference for
educational provision was revealed by the study and
a general lack of demand for childminding.

Bone was hampered in her estimates of demand for
child care services by the government-imposed
directive to consider 'need' criteria, even though
the latter were interpreted in a more liberal manner
than in earlier official reports (for example, the
1968 Seebohm Report). If, instead of some arbitra-
rily defined 'need', one considers the actual demand
for pre-school provision, the extent of under-supply
becomes all too readily apparent. Research undertaken by the Thomas Coram Research Unit (Moss and
Plewis, 1976) in three areas of London has indicated
that the demand for child care approaches a peak of
90 per cent for three year olds and increases by
only a little more for four year olds. However,
unsatisfied demand is, in fact, proportionately greater
for children under three, reflecting the lack of
provision for this age-group in particular; almost
threequarters of the mothers of two year olds would
like their children to attend some form of pre-school
facility and nearly one-half of the mothers of one
year olds. Like Bone, Moss and Plewis also found
little variation in demand between different social
and cultural groups.

Results such as those quoted above seriously
conflict with the conclusions of the Plowden Report
and the 1972 White Paper on education, that

72

pre-school provision should be confined to children of three or over and that only 50 per cent of three year olds would, in fact, use nursery schools. The additional recommendation that nursery education should be part-time also conflicts with the results of demand studies. Bone found that '...the most common complaint about the facility used related to availability - that is, that sessions were too infrequent, too brief...' (Bone, 1977,17). Moss and Plewis (1976) found that for all age groups the main demand is for child care provision lasting a full school day or longer and this finding is echoed by the Benwell Community Development Project group in their work on day care availability in the Newcastle area (Nursery Action Group/Benwell C.D.P., 1977,19). The latter study found in particular that 72 per cent of their respondents would have worked if adequate child care facilities were available and that five in six part-time workers would work full-time (see also, Leigh, 1980).

Clearly, the real demand for pre-school services far exceeds the available supply. In particular, there is a demand for full-time care, which would enable mothers to work and for greatly increased provision for children under three. What is equally clear, however, is that such a demand is very unlikely to be met in the present economic and political climate. Rather, '...the implied reasoning (of government)...is that, if services are not provided, then mothers will be obliged to stay at home and enjoy their proper role as mother and wife. The main result is, however, that many working mothers have to make child-care arrangements that are not satisfactory for them or their children; they feel guilty and their children may suffer, fulfilling too often the expectation that it is a bad thing for mothers of young children to go to work' (Tizard, Moss and Perry, 1976,145).

2. The influence of the constraint on activity patterns

a) Differences between areas

'The more resources which a group has at its command the more options and alternatives it has with respect to the quality of its social and physical environment and the better able it is to control or determine what that environment will be' (Meltzer and Whitley, 1967,145).

As the above quotation suggests, those groups

which possess power and money can largely determine
the nature of their physical environment and thus
effectively limit their activity constraints. However, women with young children must surely be one
of the best examples of a group with very little
power in society. As a result we would not expect to
find a perfect match between the spatial opportunity
needs of women and the provision of relevant services
and facilities. Because of the prevailing spatial
patterns of variation in such provision (which have
been discussed earlier) women in different areas
will be subject to differing degrees of constraint on
their spatial behaviour.

In order to understand the influence of the
constraint of lack of provision of opportunity, it
is necessary to consider women's activities in two
categories: those undertaken <u>with</u> children and
those undertaken <u>without</u> children.

b)   <u>Activities with children - local orientation</u>

'The level of provision and the spatial arrangement of urban facilities might be viewed as placing
constraints on the ease with which activities can be
carried out' (Daws and McCulloch, 1974,11). As we
have seen, the mobility problems of women with young
children are most equitably dealt with by providing
shops and services locally. In this context, it is
interesting to look at the results of two surveys
which have attempted to establish <u>which</u> facilities
are most needed close to home. A government research
study in Reading (Ministry of Housing and Local
Government, 1966,12) found that the greatest demand
for proximity occurred in the case of shops and bus
stops. Families with children obviously valued
closeness to schools and playgrounds, while proximity
to parks was important for most people. A later
survey by the Building Research Establishment (Daws
and McCulloch, 1974) in Watford found that people
most valued proximity to shops, medical care, bus
stops and open space, while those with children again
mentioned schools and closeness to a library was
also considered important. The results of the two
surveys are remarkably similar, although the respondents to the Watford survey appeared to emphasise
medical care (doctors' surgeries, dentists and child
health clinics) as being a local need, whereas the
Reading respondents did not put this so high on their
lists of local needs. There is, therefore, a coherent
group of services and facilities which is considered
essential to be provided locally.

The problems of planning for local provision of services to satisfy the needs of residents have been faced in particular by the New Town development corporations. Pritchard (1967,34) points out that the main need is to provide a service with convenient access, at the right focal point for those the facility is to serve and at the right time. But this is not normally a simple planning operation and the results may not be as equitable as they were intended to be. Thus, even in planned New Towns, the lack of provision of some important services at the local level imposes a constraint on activity patterns. In unplanned suburbia or on new peripheral estates, the situation may be far worse (see, CES Ltd., 1984). Burtenshaw (1973,688) notes the plight of wives of relocated (decentralised) workers: '... the housebound wife is more cut off from the facilities she had access to in the London suburbs. The convenient shops are no longer those with the best selection, quality or lowest prices, but those within pram-pushing distance.' There is often also a shortage of social, leisure and community facilities (Bracey, 1964,73; Rapoport and Rapoport, 1975, 344). Young and Willmott (1957,116), speaking of the residents of 'Greenleigh', contend that,'One reason people have so little to do with neighbours is the absence of places to meet them.' Although Gans (1972,372), for one, considers that for most people community facilities are relatively unimportant, Hillman (1970,54) stresses that '...the urban environment may play a dominant role in encouraging or discouraging individuals from engaging in leisure interests outside the home and it is thus an important influence on the extent of their participation in urban activities.'

c)   Activities without children - child care needs

Some leisure activities obviously involve children - one example would be the use of local playgrounds and parks - and these are most restricted by lack of local provision. However, other leisure activities (and other activities generally), which women may wish to participate in, are more constrained by a lack of provision of child care facilities (Rapoport and Rapoport, 1975,196). One example here is attendance at adult education centres. Pahl (1962,17) notes the dominance of housewives among the adult student population but points out that young women are not able to attend classes except at the few centres where child care facilities are

75

available, The same point is made in the Southwark recreation survey (London Borough of Southwark, 1970, 37).

Perhaps the greatest demand, however, is for child care facilities which will enable young mothers to be economically-active. For most women, the existence of such facilities is a necessary pre-condition for working but, even in the planned New Towns, there is no comprehensive provision of child care services (Milton Keynes Development Corporation, 1974,61), even where this has been an important planning goal (Milton Keynes Development Corporation, 1970,57). The problem of lack of child care facilities is exacerbated by the lack of suitable part-time employment opportunities in many areas. Consequently, many women are not able to work when they would otherwise wish to do so. The Milton Keynes household survey (1974,56), for example, found that 39 per cent of housewives without jobs would like to work if suitable opportunities existed, combined with child care facilities. As in the case of services provision, it is also true that work opportunities of a suitable nature are most readily available in the inner areas of cities, while outer suburban estates have little to offer in the way of employment (Thorns, 1972,118; CES Ltd., 1984). The separation of home from work due to suburban growth is discussed also by McDowell (1983) in the context of women's employment opportunities. Jobs with associated nursery facilities are exceedingly rare and the 'coupling' constraint which operates on women, having to take children to a nursery in one place and then travel to another place to work, may make that pattern of activity impossible to under-take. (The work by Lenntorp (1977) in Sweden on this problem, using a computer simulation model, is of particular interest.)

d)   The subjective opportunity constraint

Throughout this section the objective constraint of lack of provision of opportunities has been considered but there is also a significant subjective constraint which may operate to restrict activity patterns. Lack of information concerning opportunities may act as a spatial constraint in the same way as it also controls social access to resources, (see Chapter 2). If people are ignorant of the location of facilities, whether they actually exist or not is largely irrelevant in terms of their activity patterns. Although every person carries a

'mental map' of the environment, it would seem
likely that more newly-settled residents in an area
would have less complete information about spatial
opportunities than older residents. Since actual
activity patterns depend on the use of these opportunities, lack of knowledge concerning them will
obviously serve as a constraint on activities.
Similarly, incorrect information may also restrict
activities, whether this be concerning the value of
adult education classes or the quality of particular
shops. How people perceive spatial opportunities
determine to a large extent how they will use them.

Variables for the Empirical Study

There are far fewer problems involved in the choice
of suitable variables for studying physical
constraints on activity patterns than in the case of
societal constraints (see Chapter 2). Mobility
levels can be determined quite well from the data
relating to car availability and the use of public
transport. Distance information must be obtained in
a rather arbitrary way; generally straight line
distances can be reasonably applied, although these
may, of course, represent biased estimates of actual
distances travelled to activities. In many cases the
use of time as a surrogate for distance can be usefully considered, as is the case in parts of this
survey.
    The provision of services and facilities within
the study area including the provision of child care
services can be ascertained from maps and other
background information. Spatial differences in the
supply of employment opportunities are, however,
virtually impossible to discover at the local level
(without extensive field survey work.) This study,
therefore, includes the collection of objective data
concerning the provision of services but does not
include access to employment, except on the broad
scale or in terms of the measurement of actual
journeys to work.

Chapter 4

BACKGROUND TO THE EMPIRICAL STUDY

The preceding two chapters have discussed literature concerning the nature of societal and physical constraints and the influence of these constraints on activity patterns of individuals. The concluding section of Chapter 1 has outlined the conceptual approach of this study. The purpose of this chapter is to develop the research model related to the empirical study and to discuss the methodology of the study. In order to collect relevant data, a questionnaire survey was undertaken. This was supplemented by information from the 1971 Census (enumeration district data) and by details concerning the actual provision of services and facilities in the area concerned. This chapter will discuss briefly the formulation of the questionnaire used, the choice of the study area and the sampling and data collection procedure employed in the empirical study. The principal methods of data analysis will also be introduced.

Hypotheses to be Tested and the Derivation of the Questionnaire

1.   The hypotheses

      The research model (Fig. 2) indicates the influences (numbered arrows) related to the structure of actual activity patterns. Societal constraints are taken to be the underlying influences on the activity patterns of women with young children. They are directly a reflection of the structure of society at a point in time and form the framework within which other (physical or smaller scale) constraints operate. They also influence attitudes which are themselves important influences on activity preferences. The influences (numbered 1) can be described

78

and exemplified from a qualitative, historical viewpoint (see Chapter 3) but it would be beyond the
scope of this thesis to attempt to <u>quantify</u> the
nature and importance of such influences or to test
statistically any specific hypotheses related to
them. Similarly, Influence numbered 6 (which
suggests that activity patterns may encourage
attitude change and subsequent modification of
activities) is not testable using cross-sectional
data of the type collected for this research project.
    Thus, the hypotheses which this study seeks to
examine, by means of data analytic techniques, are as
follows:

1)   Societal constraints, in their objective or
practical manifestation, directly influence
activity choices and hence actual activity patterns
of women with young children (Influence numbered
 2).
2.   Physical constraints also influence the activities of women with young children, through the modification of activity preferences (Influence numbered
 3).
3.   Constraints, operating through modified activity
choices, serve to restrict both the pattern of
'normal' activities in the long term and the number,
variety and specific content of activities on a
particular day (Influence numbered 4).
4.   Attitudes held by women with young children are
a major influence on their activity preferences and
choices and consequently on their actual activity
patterns (Influence numbered 5).
5.   The quality of life, experienced by women with
young children, is closely inter-related with
attitudes held by them (Influence numbered 7). It
is also strongly influenced by actual activity
patterns (Influence numbered 8).

2.   Operationalisation of the hypotheses

    In order to examine the hypotheses listed above,
it was necessary to define variables which could be
said to measure (to some degree at least) the
different elements contained within the hypotheses.

a)   Societal constraints

1.   Gender-role. Measures of variation in the
impact of the gender-role constraint are potentially
very wide-ranging and only a small number of these
measures were selected for actual inclusion in the

**Figure 2: The Research Model: Cross-sectional view of
the nature and influence of constraints on the
activity patterns of women with young children**

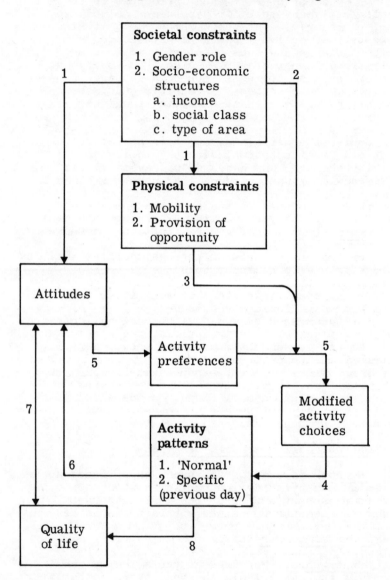

questionnaire. The choice of variables was dictated
by the focus on child care in the study; those selected were the measures considered most important in
differentiating between women in their experience of
child care and included personal characteristics
thought to influence the interpretation of the gender-
role constraint. Variables included the number and
ages of children, the present age of the woman and
her age at the birth of her first child, the length
of time each day during which the woman was solely
responsible for children, the husband's age, his
attitudes and degree of helpfulness, the proximity,
and availability as a source of help of family and
friends and the woman's own childhood experience of
having a mother out at work.

2.   Income. It was very difficult to define a reliable variable to investigate this constraint.
Household income before tax (as perceived by the
woman) was selected as the most appropriate measure.

3.   Social class. This was measured by reference to
the socio-economic status of the woman's husband, of
her own family when she was a child and in relation
to her own work status in her last full-time job and
in her present job (if working). Education levels
(of the woman and her husband) and type of dwelling
tenure were also considered relevant to the consideration of social class.

4.   Type of area. Neighbourhood characteristics
measured included the social class, tenure type and
age-group character and degree of homogeneity or
heterogeneity of the enumeration district within
which the woman lived and her own family's correspondence (or lack of correspondence) to the majority
characteristics.

b)   Physical Constraints

1.   Mobility. Mobility was related to household car
ownership, the weekday availability of a car to the
woman and her ability to drive, the frequency of
using buses and trains and problems related to their
use, the frequency of travelling outside the local
area, problems involved in walking, health considerations, the time spent in travelling to activity
centres and the actual locations of facilities used.

2.   Provision of opportunity. The provision of
opportunity was assessed in terms of the relative

location and accessibility of, for example, shops,
parks, homes of family and friends, nursery schools,
library and adult education facilities and employment opportunities. Knowledge concerning provision
was assumed to be represented by length of residence
in the local area and also whether or not the respondent had known the area as a child.

c)   Attitudes

Variables related to the attitudes of women with
young children consisted, firstly, of individual
attitude variables which combined to form two attitude dimensions - one related to the general position
of women in society and the other specifically
related to paid employment. Other attitude variables
included the reasons for working/not working, working
part-time, a measure of home/work orientation and
the degree of commitment to further training;
reasons for shopping in particular localities, the
perception of similarity with friends, reasons for
not taking part in desired social activities and
perception of the convenience and friendliness of
the local area. Attitudes towards the responsibility
of children were considered in relation to the use of
nursery schools, reasons for not leaving children
with anyone else and the enjoyment (or otherwise) of
motherhood and its responsibilities.

d)   Activity preferences

Variables included the existence (or non-
existence) of a desire to work, either now or in the
future, an expressed desire to participate in certain
social activities and the intention to use nursery
schools.

e)   Quality of life

The variable developed in relation to overall
life satisfaction consisted of a set of scales, defined in terms of bipolar descriptive adjectives.
Time-budget out-of-home activities and the location
of services and facilities formed the variables relating to objective quality of life.

f)   Activity patterns

Finally, modified activity choices and their
geographical expression as activity patterns were
described by variables relating, firstly, to 'normal'

activities and, secondly, to the specific activities
undertaken on the previous day. 'Normal' activities
included work status, hours of work, work location
and mode of travel to work; frequency of shopping
trips, the timing of main shopping journeys and
locations of shopping centres used; frequency of
park visiting, location of parks used and activities
undertaken in parks; frequency and location of home
visiting, attendance at regular social activities,
frequency of public transport use and the actual use
of nursery schools and child-minders. Specific
activity patterns of the previous day were described
by variables indicating the type, number and variety
of activities undertaken, the timing of these
activities and the total time spent out of home, the
location of activities and journey time and mode for
reaching them and the presence (or absence) of young
children at the activity locations.

3.   Derivation of the questionnaire

Having established which variables would be used
to examine the research hypotheses, the next step was
to formulate a questionnaire (and associated data
collection procedures) in order to assemble data relating to these variables. Altogether, five drafts
were constructed during the design procedure and, at
each stage, both individual questions and the complete schedule were piloted on a small sample of respondents. Minor modifications and major changes were
then incorporated in the succeeding version of the
questionnaire.

In particular, the problem of whether to use
open or closed questions was investigated. In its
final form the questionnaire contained predominantly
closed questions with pre-coded answers because of
the logistical problem of dealing with such a large
number of variables. In any event, most social researchers (see, for example, Oppenheim, 1968,41;
Moser and Kalton, 1971,341-347) believe that open-
ended questions offer as many problems as do closed
questions; in particular, there is the problem of
ensuring accurate and unbiased recording of information by interviewers. Information is bound to be lost
at some stage of the research procedure, even if only
at the final computing stage, so the argument for not
closing questions, on the basis of loss of information, is a poor one, especially in cases where a very
large quantity of data is to be collected. Of
course, not all questions can be pre-coded and it is
in any case sensible to keep some open-ended

questions in order to maintain or stimulate the
interest of the respondent.

The actual wording of questions is subject to
problems of reliability and validity. The problem of
reliability relates to the accuracy of questions - to
their stability, dependability and predictability
(Kerlinger, 1969,430). Reliability can be improved
by unambiguous wording of questions, together with
clear and standard instructions to interviewers. The
problem of validity concerns the actual content of
questions; in effect, are we measuring what we think
we are measuring? (Kerlinger, 1969,444). These
problems, of reliability and validity, are of greatest significance in relation to attitude measurement
but are of importance with respect to all survey
questions. The best method of avoiding the problems
is to use forms of questions previously developed by
other researchers and, therefore, already tested for
reliability and validity (Kerlinger, 1969,491).

Thus, a large number of relevant questions were
taken from previous questionnaires in the formulation
of the interview schedule for this study. Questions
on mobility came from the 'Housewives Mobility Study'
(1973) questionnaire, developed by Hillman and
Whalley at Political and Economic Planning (now the
Policy Studies Institute). Questions on employment
status, the helpfulness and attitudes of husbands
and, in particular, the attitudes of women towards
their position in society and towards paid employment
for women, were taken from the 'Protective Legislation Survey' (1976) pilot questionnaire, developed
by the Social Survey Division of the Office of Population Censuses and Surveys. Questions concerning
the convenience of the local area and the local
public transport service, the desire by women to work
and their reasons for working, possible health
problems and attitudes to motherhood, came from the
'American Quality of Life Survey' questionnaire
(Campbell et al., 1976, Appendix B). Questions on
desired social activities and education level and
the semantic differential scale relating to satisfaction with life were taken from the 'British Quality
of Life Survey' (1975) questionnaire, developed by
Hall and his associates at the Social Science
Research Council Survey Unit.

It is worthwhile reiterating the fact that
problems of reliability and validity are of greatest
importance in relation to attitude questions. The
present study required the testing of attitudes using
a Likert scale (a five-point scale comprising a set
of attitude statements) which, though developed using

a less laborious procedure than a Thurstone scale, would still require a great deal of time to set up properly (Oppenheim, 1968,133). Since a relevant scale had already been developed (by Marsh at the Office of Population Censuses and Surveys), it was a great saving in time and also preferable in terms of accuracy to use this existing scale. Similarly, in the case of the semantic differential used in the questionnaire, the actual scales were taken directly from the Social Science Research Council Survey Unit's 'Quality of Life' survey. The semantic differential is a technique for measuring different kinds of meaning (or semantic dimensions) which are used in conceptualising an object or idea (Elms, 1976,27). It consists of a number of bipolar adjectival scales, which are in themselves a type of Likert scale and, therefore, subject to the same restrictive and perfectionist approach to formulation as the attitude scales previously mentioned.

Having determined the specific content of the questionnaire, it was then necessary to assemble the questions in some sort of logical sequence. Basically, the final schedule dealt with different types of activity in turn since this was considered a format which could be more easily followed by respondents than a sequence based on particular constraints. The final form of the questionnaire is shown in Appendix A.

Choice of Study Area and Overview of its General Characteristics

1. Choice of study area

From within the designated general population of women with children under school age, it was necessary to select a study population in a particular area. It was decided to choose a south London borough as the study area, both because of ease of access for interviewing and because the focus of the study was to be on urban activity patterns. One borough was to be selected rather than several, in order to control for Council policy in the provision of services and facilities.

The choice of the borough to be used in the survey was based on a number of specific requirements. These were as follows:

1) Most importantly, the chosen borough should be as heterogeneous as possible.

2)   Related to the above requirement, the borough should probably be located in the inner suburban zone of London - that is, spanning the border between 'inner' and 'outer' city characteristics (for example, in terms of car ownership, residential density, housing age and type, and service provision), in order to aid the description of variations in activity patterns within the borough.

3)   Taking the average values for different variables relating to social class, housing and mobility across the chosen borough, they should correspond as closely as possible to the average values for Greater London as a whole.

4)   The borough should, preferably, have only a small number of new Commonwealth immigrants among its total population, since it would be attempted to exclude these from the final sample of respondents (on the grounds that activity patterns would vary greatly between different ethnic groups (Deakin, 1970; Hiro, 1971) and that it was hoped to control for this factor).

5)   The borough should be generally well-supplied with public transport facilities of a variety of types, in order that variations in activity patterns could be related to the proximity of transport routes. A borough served by both underground and British Rail train services, as well as buses, would be chosen.

6)   The chosen borough should not be dominated by one major retail centre since the existence of such a centre could be expected to distort the patterns of local retail provision and the use of local facilities.

7)   The borough should be compact in shape, in order to eliminate the need to take account of distance to the centre of London.

Having determined the above list of requirements, maps from the 'Social Atlas of London' (Shepherd et al., 1974) were consulted in order to select the borough to be used for the survey. Visual impressions were checked by reference to 1971 Census data. After consideration, the London borough of Merton was selected as the survey area, since it met the above list of conditions better than any other borough.

BACKGROUND TO THE EMPIRICAL STUDY

2. General characteristics of the borough of Merton

Merton is located in a middle-distance position
in relation to the urban core. The average road
distance to central London is approximately nine
miles. The borough comprises two parliamentary
constituencies (in the north, Merton and Wimbledon
and in the south-east, Merton, Morden and Mitcham)
(see Map 1) with very different socio-economic
characteristics (Table 1). In fact, differences in
social group representation at the constituency level
would be even greater if Morden ward were excluded
from consideration in its constituency and Wimbledon
East ward in its constituency. Higher socio-economic
groups are more particularly concentrated in the
Merton and Wimbledon constituency and skilled manual
workers in the Merton, Morden and Mitcham constituency.

The borough is divided into 14 wards and 375
Census enumeration districts. Map 1 indicates the
location of ward boundaries and Table 1 shows the
ward percentages of economically active males in each
of the four major social groups in 1971 (the census
year preceding the present survey). In general, the
northern and western wards of the borough contain
more professional and managerial and fewer manual,
workers, by comparison with wards in the eastern part
of the borough. The population sizes and social
composition of enumeration districts is considered
below, in relation to sampling procedure for the
survey.

Historically, the present London borough of
Merton comprised two boroughs (Wimbledon, Mitcham)
and one urban district (Merton and Morden) within
the County of Surrey. These merged only in 1965,
with the establishment of the Greater London Council.
It is to be expected, therefore, that physical
conditions should vary considerably within the
present borough, partly as a result of previous
planning decisions. In addition, the predominant age
of the housing stock varies between the north and
south of the borough, the northern area having been
almost completely developed before 1914 and the
southern half being mainly the product of inter-war
development.

The overall patterns of provision of services
and facilities (for example, shops, parks and adult
education centres) within the borough are described
in relation to specific activities in the following
chapters.

Map 1   Merton: Parliamentary Constituencies and Wards

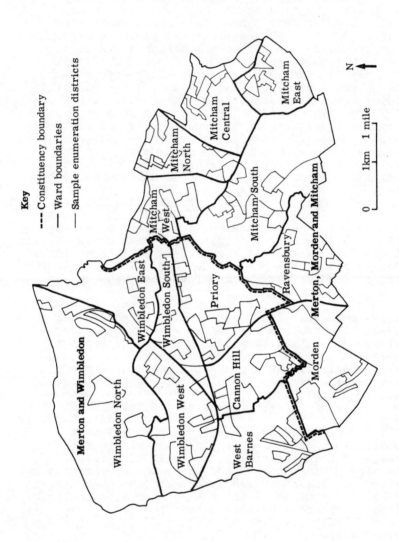

Table 1 Socio-Economic Characteristics of Merton Wards and Constituencies, 1971 (percentage of economically active males in different social groups)[1]

	Professional and Managerial	Other non-manual	Skilled Manual	Semi-skilled and un-skilled manual
Wards				
Mitcham Central	16.4	29.9	37.6	16.1
Mitcham East	14.0	26.3	39.0	20.8
Mitcham North	13.4	24.3	45.1	17.2
Mitcham South	15.3	18.8	44.2	21.8
Mitcham West	14.8	18.4	37.9	28.8
Morden	25.2	27.3	36.5	10.9
Ravensbury	11.6	22.7	42.6	23.1
Constituency				
Merton, Morden and Mitcham	15.8	23.8	40.7	19.6
Wards				
Cannon Hill	21.7	24.6	33.1	20.6
Priory	22.8	27.5	32.4	17.4
West Barnes	31.3	34.6	22.9	11.2
Wimbledon East	13.1	26.8	38.7	21.3
Wimbledon North	41.4	29.6	17.0	12.0
Wimbledon South	20.5	25.3	34.1	20.2
Wimbledon West	40.7	31.6	14.3	13.4
Constituency				
Merton and Wimbledon	27.5	28.5	27.3	16.6

Note: 1. Source of data: G.L.C. Intelligence Unit (1974)

Sampling Procedure and Data Collection and Analysis

1. Sampling procedure

Having determined the location of the study area, it was then necessary to establish a sampling procedure for the selection of actual respondents to

be interviewed. Most work on activity patterns so
far undertaken has used the household as the primary
unit of study. One suspects that the relative ease
of acquisition of empirical data and of sampling at
the household level might be influential in encouraging this existing emphasis on household studies.
Households can be fairly easily sampled, either
randomly or in some other way, from electoral registers. By contrast, activity studies of population
sub-groups are both less common and more difficult to
undertake since the specific location of sub-group
members may be unknown, while basic demographic and
other data concerning the group as a whole may not be
available. The procedure for obtaining the required
sample of 400 respondents is described in some detail
in Appendix B. Briefly, a sample of 100 enumeration
districts (e.d.s) within the borough of Merton was
established. Within each of these sample e.d.s four
respondents were to be found.

2. Data collection

    The interviewing period was set as 13th-30th
September, 1977. The restricted length of this
period was determined by the need to control for the
season of the year in analysing activity data.
September was chosen as a suitable month because the
weather could be expected to be favourable and,
therefore, time-budget data collected would reflect
a maximum level of out-of-home activity participation. The survey could not be undertaken before the
beginning of the school term because the focus of the
study was to be the weekday activity patterns of
women, alone with their children under five. The
interviewing period was, therefore, timed to begin in
the first full week of the school term. This timing
could be criticised on the grounds that activity
patterns might not be regularised so early in the new
term but weather factors dictated that the interviewing period should not extend too far into the autumn.
    All interviews were carried out during the day-
time hours on weekdays. In fact, only Tuesday to
Friday of each of the three weeks were used for
interviewing since the questionnaire included the
collection of time-budget information relating to the
previous day's activities and it was considered that
respondents would not accurately remember their
activities of the previous Friday on the following
Monday. This meant, of course, that no activity
patterns were recorded for Fridays but this was not
felt to be too much of a disadvantage since Friday is

possibly an exceptional weekday in terms of activities; for example, the Household Interview Survey
conducted by the London borough of Enfield (1975)
found that Friday was the most popular shopping day
for convenience goods.

Since respondents had not been pre-selected in
the sampling procedure, it was impossible to avoid
some bias in the selection of the sample. The
sample was obviously weighted towards women who spent
more time at home and, in particular, against those
who were out at work full-time. As can be seen from
Table 2, the sample overrepresented the proportion
working shorter hours by comparison with figures
from the 1971 Census. However, this was not considered a weakness in the survey since the study was
intended to be oriented towards the problems of
housebound mothers, rather than towards those of
full-time working women. One-third of the employed
women in the sample worked at home; therefore, the
overwhelming majority of respondents (80 per cent)
could be classed as 'housebound'.

The normal research procedure carried out after
the selection of respondents is to compare the
characteristics of the sample with those of the
population from which the sample is drawn. However,
in the case of women with young children most
characteristics of the population are not known. As
illustrated in Table 2, employment status is recorded
in the Census tabulations but the only other characteristic of this group which is known (for 1971) is
the proportion of women with children under five,
living in households without a husband present. The
1971 Census for the borough of Merton gave this
figure as 5.4 per cent of the total. In this survey,
nineteen respondents (or 4.7 per cent of the total)
were living in households without a husband present.

The acceptance of interviewers was almost certainly facilitated by the fact that all interviewers
were women, mainly themselves with young children
and they were, therefore, able to relate to their
respondents very well (see McDowell and Bowlby, 1983,
102). Acceptance of the purpose of the survey among
respondents was also encouraged by the publication of
a feature article in the local newspaper which was
read by most families.

Data from the questionnaire survey for each
respondent were supplemented by information from two
sources. In the first place, 1971 e.d. Census data
were used to define variables indicating the type of
area in which each respondent lived; in particular,
attention was paid to social class composition,

Table 2   Employment status and hours of work

Women with dependent children aged 0 - 4

	England & Wales (1971)*		L.B. of Merton (1971)**		Sample (1977)	
	No.	%	No.	%	No.	%
Total women	283,304	100	865	100	400	100
In employment	53,463	18.9	216	25.0	114	28.5
Hours worked						
<8	6,168	2.2	21	2.4	31	7.7
8–12	5,504	1.9	21	2.4	32	8.0
12–18	7,238	2.6	24	2.8	14	3.5
18–21	8,479	3.0	40	4.6	13	3.3
21–24	2,275	0.8	5	0.6	3	0.7
24–30	4,913	1.7	22	2.5	6	1.5
30+	15,894	5.6	72	8.3	12	3.0
not stated	2,992	1.1	11	1.3	3	0.8

*   Figures from Table 53 of Census 1971, England and Wales, Household
     Composition Tables Part III (10% sample)

**   Figures from Tables HCA 1-6 of 1971 Census: Special Tables (10% sample)

predominant mode of dwelling tenure, age-structure and car ownership level in the e.d.s concerned. Secondly, the actual provision of services and facilities, in relation to each selected e.d., was quantified and the resulting variables added to the data for the relevant respondents.

3. Data analysis

The principal methods of analysis performed on the survey data involved cross-tabulation and correlation techniques. As is common in social science research, the .05 level of significance was selected as the appropriate level at which to determine the significance, or otherwise, of relationships tested using chi-square or the correlation coefficient (r). Very few of the variables in the data set were measured at an interval level so it was inevitable that cross-tabulation would form the predominant mode of analysis.

For relationships involving nominal level variables, the relevant chi-square statistic was computed together with its level of significance. For relationships involving two ordinal level variables (or one ordinal level variable and one dichotomous variable), the statistic, gamma, was computed. Gamma can be interpreted as the percentage improvement (on random chance prediction) in the prediction of the order on the dependent variable afforded by knowing the order on the independent variable. The conventions for describing gamma scores are well-established (see Pine, 1977,136); a score of 0 indicates no association between two variables and a score between -.09 and +.09 indicates a negligible association, whilst a score greater than -.09 or +.09 is indicative of a definite relationship between variables. The discussion of gamma scores in the following chapters will use the conventional descriptive phrases indicative of the strength of associations discovered.

Interval-level data were inter-related using the Pearson product moment correlation coefficient together with its level of significance. Where it was considered useful to inter-relate categorical and interval-level variables, either the interval-level variables were put into categories (for example, age-group rather than specific age) or the categorical variables were collapsed into dichotomies for inclusion in correlation analysis. The latter procedure is commonly employed in the analysis of questionnaire data so much of which is always

measured at the nominal level only. As Anderson and
Zelditch (1975,168) point out '...any dichotomy can
be interpreted as involving measurement at any of
the three levels...we may assume that any interval
between (the two values) represents "equal intervals"
since there is just one interval.' Therefore, there
is no reason why a dichotomous variable should not be
included in correlation analysis: such a variable
approximates to an interval-level variable and
assumptions regarding level of measurement are not
violated (Anderson and Zelditch, 1975,169 - see also,
Pine, 1977,116).

    Additional forms of analysis performed on the
data will be discussed in relation to their results
in the following chapters.

Chapter 5

PAID EMPLOYMENT

In 1978 there were about 900,000 children under five
in Great Britain whose mothers were in paid employment, compared to 700,000 in 1971 (Central Policy
Review Staff, 1978). Census tabulations for 1971
show that nearly 19 per cent of all women with dependent children aged 0-4 in England and Wales were at
work, the majority part-time (see Table 2). Within
the study area (the London Borough of Merton) the
percentage was even higher; here, one-quarter of
women with young children were in employment. As
mentioned in Chapter 4, the sampling procedure for
the survey tended to under-represent full-time
workers but in total it recorded 28.5 per cent of
respondents as being in paid employment.
        In this research, employment status and attend-
ant attitudes and aspirations are seen as key
variables in differentiating sub-groups of the
population under study. In the first place, these
variables can be viewed as statistically dependent
and attempts can be made to relate employment to the
influences and constraints on activity introduced in
Chapters 2 and 3; in particular, employment status
and attitudes can be seen as the most important outcomes of gender-role ideology. In the second place,
employment status itself may be viewed as an
independent variable, influencing all other weekday
activities of women with young children and being a
major determinant of satisfaction levels and attitudes in general. In this chapter, the factors influencing participation in paid employment will be
considered; in the following chapter, employment
status will be discussed as one factor influencing
other types of activity.
        The part of the questionnaire relating to paid
employment was longer and more complex than any other
section on women's activities, reflecting a

subjective judgement on the personal importance of
work status and attendant attitudes and aspirations
to the lives of individual women. The role of attitudes recurs as a constant theme in this chapter
is, therefore, considered in general at the outset.

    In the analytic section of the chapter respond-
ents are firstly categorised as being either in paid
employment or not in paid employment in order to look
at the question of who works and why. For the purpose of this simple categorisation, no account is
taken of the number of hours worked or whether the
work is home-based or located outside the home. As
indicated in Fig. 3, present employment status is
hypothesised as being influenced by a number of
social, physical and cultural constraints, which are
themselves modified and/or reinforced by the personal
attitudes of individual women. It is important to
determine the extent to which attitudes, particularly
those relating to women's employment, interrelate
closely with actual work status, independent of the
effect of other constraints and influences and
similarly, the extent to which other, more tangible,
constraints directly influence employment status.

    In the second part of the data analysis,
attention is focused only on those respondents who
are in paid employment of some type. The purpose of
this section is to look at the actual conditions of
work experienced by mothers of young children. Here,
consideration is given to the location of the work
place, to the hours of working and to the 'status'
of the work undertaken. A major theme running
through this section is the dominance of gender-role
ideology in determining the situation of working
mothers.

    The third part of the analysis focuses specif-
ically on those women who are 'tied to home' as full-
time housewives and discusses their preferences for
present employment status. It suggests that a desire
to 'take an outside job right now' is closely related
to personal attitudes on the one hand and also to
other social and physical factors on the other.

    Finally, the fourth section of the analysis
considers, more generally, the employment preferences
and expectations of all respondents, both in terms of
present and of future employment. Attention is paid
particularly to the relationship between work status
and generally preferred work status, in order to
attempt to define the constraints which influence
some women to work, or not to work, in opposition to
their own preferences.

Figure 3: Relationships to be tested concerning employment

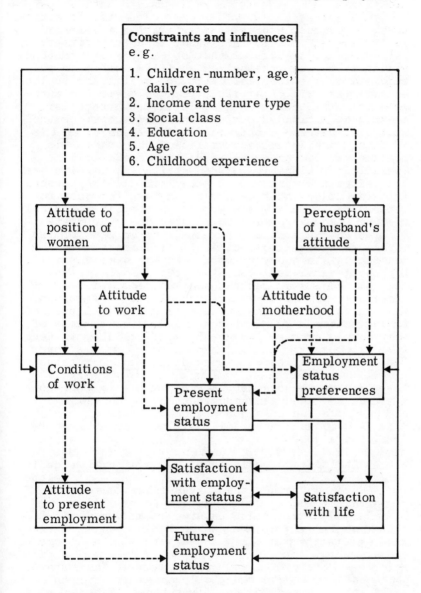

The Role of Attitudes and the Use of Attitude Questions

In the previous Chapter, the derivation and use of attitude questions in this study is briefly described. Fig. 3 suggests that objective constraints on activities are themselves modified and/or reinforced by the personal attitudes of individual women. The role of attitudes can be basically envisaged in a 'filtering' sense, in that, while it is clear that attitudes perform a major function in mediating between constraints and influences on the one hand and actual activities on the other, the precise way in which this mediation occurs and the specific relationship between attitudes and behaviour is difficult to predict in detail (Elms, 1976,41ff).
The major attitude questions used in the survey comprise a Likert-type scale of six statements (derived from a scale developed by the Office of Population Censuses and Surveys), which were chosen to represent two distinct attitude dimensions - one concerning attitudes to work and the other concerning the general position of women in society. To each of these statements the respondent was asked to agree or disagree on a five-point scale. The actual statements used in the questionnaire, listed not as in the schedule but in terms of the dimensions which they were chosen to represent, were as follows:

Attitude to work dimension

1. 'Having her own job is the best way a woman can become a complete and independent person.'
2. 'A woman needs a job of her own'.
3. 'A woman and her family will all benefit if she does a job.'

Attitude to position of women dimension

4. 'Husbands rather than wives should have the final voice in family matters.'
5. 'A job is all right but for a woman real fulfulment lies in a home and children.'
6. 'A woman's place is in the home.'

It is clear from a consideration of the above statements that a thoroughly 'progressive' viewpoint would entail assent to the first three statements and dissent to the remaining three, while a 'traditional' viewpoint would entail the reverse situation. However, as stated previously, these two groups of

statements do, in fact, represent two clearly defined
dimensions of attitude, rather than a unidimensional
approach to the nature of women's lives. This fact
was established by consulting the results of the
O.P.C.S. survey referred to and was further confirmed by analysis of data from the Merton survey.

Factor analysis of some type is commonly used
by psychologists to assess the validity of attitude
dimensions (Kerlinger, 1969,680), despite purist
statistical objections to the use of attitude scales
as interval level data. A principal components
analysis (using varimax rotation) was, therefore, performed on the data derived from the six attitude
statements listed above. This analysis resulted in
the production of two components with eigen values
greater than 1, together accounting for 58 per cent
of the total variance. The component loadings are
indicated below (the variables being described in
terms of the statement numbers used in the above
list).

	Component 1	Component 2
Work 1	.03	.78
Work 2	.09	.81
Work 3	-.05	.68
Women's position 4	.72	-.05
Women's position 5	.76	-.02
Women's position 6	.81	.15

Component 2 can be described very easily as representing 'attitudes to work' and Component 1 obviously
refers to general 'attitudes to the position of
women', the correlation between them being r=.07.

The results of this analysis confirm the lack
of unidimensionality in the attitude data and consequently justify the use of the two attitude dimensions
separately in subsequent discussion of the inter-
relationship between attitudes, constraints and
activities. In general, it is most useful to
consider the dimensions as two separate scales; for
this purpose, a respondent's scores on each of the
three variables comprising a scale are added and
then divided by three (after reversing the scores on
'negative' variables so that high scores in every
case represent 'progressive' attitudes). This
combined score is used in subsequent analyses against
other variables. This procedure is justified by the
lack of association between the variables making up
the two dimensions, which renders the alternative
procedure - the use of component scores - unnecessary
(the 'summed and divided' scale scores being far more

readily comprehensible in subsequent use than the latter would be). In some cases, however, it would appear useful to employ attitudes to one particular statement, rather than combined scale scores, in the analysis of activity data, particularly where non-parametric statistical techniques are being used and this procedure is followed on occasions both in this and in subsequent chapters.

The whole question of the use of attitude data in parametric statistics can not be explored in detail here. It is perhaps sufficient to note the widely divergent opinions of psychologists and statisticians concerning the 'level' of data obtained from attitude scales. Obviously, if such scales are considered as providing only ordinal-level data (that is, as 'techniques for placing people on a continuum in relation to one another, in relative and not in absolute, terms' (Oppenheim, 1966,121), then they can neither produce summated scores, nor can they be factor analysed. It is generally accepted, however, that '...most psychological...scales approximate interval equality fairly well' (Kerlinger, 1969,427) and, therefore, with care can be used in parametric statistical analysis.

In addition to the Likert-type scale of attitude statements discussed in detail above, a number of other individual questions designed to elicit respondents' attitudes were included in the questionnaire for the Merton survey and some of these are of specific importance in dealing with the question of paid employment. The influence of a gender-role constraint on employment status is considered both in relation to the woman's attitude to the responsibilities of motherhood, to her reasons for working, not working or working part-time and also to her perception of her husband's attitude to the question of her own employment status (see Fig. 3). With regard to the latter, it is evident from many studies that '...the woman's perception of her spouse's commitment to the idea of women having careers is an important determinant of her own pattern of work/career orientation' (Fogarty, Rapoport and Rapoport, 1971,319). The true attitudes of husbands can be very influential (for example, Ginsberg (1977,80), in her recent study of housebound women with pre-school children, found that nearly two-thirds of the husbands in her study objected to their wives working outside the home) but probably more important as a behavioural guide is the wife's perception of her husband's attitude.

Findings from the Survey

1.   Who Works and Why

A simple division between those in paid employment and those not in paid employment provides us
with a first categorisation of sample respondents.
As previously mentioned, just under 30 per cent of
the sample were engaged in some type of paid work at
the time of the questionnaire survey.

a)   Attitude relationships

As shown in Fig. 3, present employment status
is expected to be directly related to various attitude dimensions and this anticipated connection
provides us with a useful starting point to the
analysis. Taking firstly the 'attitude to work'
dimension (whose derivation is described in the
previous section), the degree of association between
this variable and the dichotomised variable, employment status, was found to be $r=.22$ which, although
not representing a high degree of accordance, is
significant at the .001 level of significance.
The next step in the analysis is to ascertain
the extent to which 'attitudes to work' are related
both to other attitudes and to the constraints which
are hypothesised to influence work status (see Fig.
3). Those variables which could not be measured on
an interval scale were, therefore, dichotomised and
correlated with the 'attitude to work' dimension. The
results of the correlation analysis are shown in
Table 3 (specifications of variables used in this and
later tables are listed in Appendix C). Using the
.05 level of significance, it can be seen that six
associations of variables give significant outcomes.
A positive ('progressive') attitude to women working
is related to a lower terminal age of education, to
having a husband working in a manual occupation and
to non-owner occupier housing tenure status. Since
the latter three variables are all inter-related at
the .001 level of significance, it is clear that they
can be considered, for most purposes, as representing
one socio-economic 'dimension' in the data. In
addition, 'attitude to work' is significantly related
to the experience of having had a mother out at work
when the respondent was a young child and it is
negatively related to the age of the respondent's
husband (surprisingly, not to the age of the woman
herself), neither of which associations is unexpected. The presence or absence of a husband appears to

Table 3 Correlation of 'attitude to work' with other variables

	No. of children under 5	Age of youngest child	S.e.g. of husband	Terminal education age	Age of husband	Age of respondent
'Attitude to work'	r=-.04 (p=.22)	r=.05 (p=.15)	r=-.16* (p=.001)	r=-.15* (p=.001)	r=-.09* (p=.04)	r=-.06 (p=.13)

	Childhood experience	Tenure of Household	Presence/ absence of husband	Husband's attitude	Attitude to motherhood
'Attitude to work'	r=.08* (p=.05)	r=-.17* (p=.001)	r=-.04 (p=.20)	r=.03 (p=.29)	r=-.13* (p=.004)

* Relationship significant at the .05 level of significance

be unimportant in determining 'attitude to work' as
does the woman's perception of her husband's attitude
to her work status but there is a negative (and
significant) relationship between 'work' and 'motherhood' attitudes; those who assert that they 'often'
or 'sometimes' experience a desire to be free from
motherhood responsibilities are more likely to hold
'progressive' attitudes to work. This relationship
is, again, not unexpected.

        Since so many variables are closely related
to the possession of certain attitudes to work, it is
possible that the relationship between attitudes and
actual employment status can be explained simply by
the effect of these other variables. A partial correlation analysis was, therefore, carried out. The
results indicate that the influence of attitudes
stands independent of the effect of other variables,
despite the fact that these are individually related
to the 'attitude to work' dimension. In no case does
the effect of controlling for another variable serve
to alter the correlation coefficient between work
attitudes and employment status by more than .01 and
the latter relationship remains significant at the
.001 level of significance in all cases.

        Having established the importance of the
'attitude to work' dimension as a correlate of
present employment status, it is now useful to disaggregate the scores on this attitude dimension and
consider in more detail individual responses to particular statements. Approximately half of all respondents were shown to be in agreement with the three
statements concerned (55 per cent with the first
statement, 53 per cent with the second and 49 per
cent with the third). Fewest respondents (30 per
cent) disagree with the statement that 'a woman needs
a job of her own'. As would be expected from the
previous discussion, women who are in paid work at
the present time hold the most positive attitudes to
the question of the need for women's employment but
the trend is by no means universal. Indeed, just
under one-fifth of employed women disagree with the
idea that 'a woman needs a job of her own'. Similarly, it is interesting to note that 66 per cent of
those respondents who agree with the statement concerned are, in fact, full-time housewives, indicating a
possible measure of dissatisfaction with their present lives (see Appendix D, Table D1).

        If one looks only at those full-time housewives
who say that they 'agree very much', both with the
statement that 'a woman needs a job of her own' and
with the statement that 'having her own job is the

best way a woman can become a complete and independent person' (a total of 27 respondents), one definitely finds a lower level of general satisfaction with life than in the sample as a whole. In particular, one-third of all respondents who state that their lives are 'extremely boring' come from this small group of 27 women, while no member of the group feels their life to be 'free' rather than 'tied down' and all of them intend to return to work when the children are at school full-time. A simple analysis of data relating to these women reveals that they are younger than the sample as a whole and are more likely to have babies under two years of age, they tend to be the wives of skilled manual workers and, in particular, they have a much lower terminal age of education than the sample as a whole. It was amongst such women that very real signs of depression and apathy were visible to interviewers. Depressive illness is far more widespread amongst mothers of young children, particularly amongst working class women, than is commonly believed (see Chapter 2).

Having considered attitudes to work as important determinants of present employment status, we can now go on to consider the influence of other attitudes on paid employment for women with young children. Taking firstly the question relating to 'motherhood responsibilities',it is interesting to note that, despite the existence of a significant relationship between this variable and the 'attitude to work' dimension (see Table 3), there is virtually no relationship between a 'desire to be free from motherhood responsibilities' and actual paid employment (the correlation of these two variables gives a result, $r=.04$ ($p=.23$)). Nor does this 'attitude to motherhood responsibility' variable appear to be related closely to other characteristics of respondents, for example, age, education or age of the youngest child. The only significant relationship, in fact, occurs between this attitude question and the variable describing the presence or absence of a husband in the household; those living in households with no husband present are more likely than others to have experienced a 'desire to be free from motherhood responsibilities', at least occasionally ($r=.09$ ($p=.04$)).

Overall, nearly half of the sample (48.5 per cent) admitted that they had experienced such a desire on some occasions, including some 47 per cent of all full-time housewives. This latter fact, however, appears to conflict with the main reasons given by housewives for not taking part in paid employment

at the present time. While 33 per cent (of full-time
housewives) refer to a sense of 'duty' in relation to
the care of their children, more than twice as many
(76 per cent) give, as a major reason for not working, their 'desire' to be with their children while
they are young. If one abstracts this single answer
('desire to be with children') from the various
reasons for not working and, using it as a dichotomous variable, correlates it with various other
characteristics of the respondents, it is interesting
to note that only one significant relationship
results; that with the age of the youngest child
($r=-.11$ ($p=.04$)). Social class, the education level
of the woman concerned and her age are all of no
importance and, similarly, there is no significant
relationship with the woman's childhood experience of
having a mother at work. All these variables might
have been hypothesised to influence 'desire to be
with children' as a reason for not being in paid employment. The fact that the presence of a very young
child (under two years) is significantly related to a
'desire to be with children' is to be expected and
this relationship may help to account for the
apparent contradiction of attitudes amongst full-time
housewives which has been referred to earlier.
Although finding motherhood responsibilities irksome
on occasions, the majority of housewives with babies
would certainly feel that a 'desire to be with their
children while they were young' was a valid and
important reason for not being in paid employment,
while this feeling might well become less pervasive
as the youngest child grew towards school age.
     The final attitude question to be considered in
this section is the woman's perception of her
husband's attitude regarding her own employment
status (see Appendix D, Table D2). The vast majority
of respondents with husbands present in the household
consider that their husbands display an entirely
liberal attitude to the question of their work status
(a finding which appears to conflict with Ginsberg's
(1977) result). Few women acknowledge the existence
of any discouragement from their husbands (only 7
full-time housewives definitely state elsewhere that
their husbands would not allow them to work),
although even fewer point to an active encouragement
from them to go out to work and most of those who
are subject to discouragement are in fact full-time
housewives. Overall, there is a low positive relationship between the respondent's perception of her
husband's attitude and her actual employment status,
although this attitude variable can hardly be

considered as a major determining factor in relation to paid employment.

b)   The direct influence of constraints

Fig. 3 hypothesises not only a set of influences exerted by socio-economic, demographic and other characteristics of respondents mediated through various attitudes but also the independent influence of constraints - both societal and physical - on present employment status.

It has been strongly suggested in Chapter 2 that the presence of young children acts as an ideological constraint on women's employment; indeed, this is one manifestation of the overall gender-role constraint with which this research is primarily concerned. However, the data from the survey do not confirm a significant relationship between the number of young children (under five years) which a woman has and her employment status (r=-.04 (p=.24)). Much more important as an influence on employment status is the age of the youngest child in the family (see Appendix D, Table D3 for corroboration of this finding, see Jephcott, 1962,97). There is, as would be expected, a fairly consistent fall in the percentage of women who are full-time housewives, as the age of the youngest child increases. Commensurate with this decline is an increase in the percentage of women in paid work (from 17 per cent of those whose youngest child is under one year old to 38 per cent of those whose youngest child is four).

Related to the effect on employment status of the age of the youngest child is the question of whether or not any of the children has a sleep during the daytime. A child who needs to go to bed during the day is not so easily left with some other person and there is, of course, a strong relationship between the need for a sleep and a younger age. Overall, two-thirds of respondents reported that at least one of their children normally had a sleep at some time during the day.

The ability to leave a young child in the care of some other person is, of course, fundamental to the ability to take part in paid employment outside the home. There are a few occupations which enable children to accompany their mothers to work (for example, house cleaning) but in the vast majority of cases substitute child care is necessary. The provision and use of nursery facilities is more thoroughly dealt with in Chapter 8. Here it suffices to point out that women who are out at work are more

likely to have their children at some type of nursery
school than are those who are full-time housewives
and that the former are more likely to have their
children in half-time schooling (in a State nursery
class/school), while the latter are more likely to be
using private playgroups where the children attend
for fewer hours each week. However, as many as 38
per cent of women who go out to work do not have any
child at nursery school, possibly in many cases because of the short, inflexible hours of child care
which are provided and which often do not fit the
requirements of working women. It is notable that
only half of those respondents who work in Central
London send their children to nursery schools and
this tends to be full-time, indicating the lack of
coincidence between nursery school and working hours
and between nursery and work locations. By comparison, 72 per cent of women working in the local area
(within ordinary walking distance of home) have
children at nursery school (mainly part-time). As is
also true in France, 'Co-ordinating work hours and
commuting time to correspond with hours of child-care
facilities is a daily harassment for many mothers'
(Fodor, 1978,473).

Gender-role ideology and specifically in this
instance the belief that a woman should be at home
to care for her own children, although 'passed on' to
the child through a variety of social institutions,
is certainly reinforced by the conditioning received
by the child in the family home. It is interesting,
therefore, to look at the direct relationship between
the respondent's childhood experience of whether her
own mother worked and her present employment status.
It will be recalled that childhood experience has
already been shown to be positively related to the
'attitude to work' dimension. However, this is one
instance in which no direct relationship is evident
in the data; although the two variables are
positively associated the correlation coefficient is
low ($r=.05$) and is not significant at the .05 level
of significance ($p=.14$). In fact, as many as 69 per
cent of women whose own mothers were at work when
they were children are themselves now full-time
housewives.

In addition to gender-role considerations, one
cannot overlook the potential importance of social
class as a determinant of employment status. As
already indicated, social class (as measured by the
socio-economic group of the husband), terminal age of
education and mode of housing tenure are closely
inter-related variables, each of these variables

being also significantly related to the 'attitude to work' dimension. Table 4 indicates the actual degree of association between these and other 'social' variables and also relates them individually to employment status. It is interesting to note that none of the relationships involving employment status proves to be significant at the .05 level of significance, while all of the inter-relationships between the 'social' variables are significant (most of them at the .001 level). Social class itself, hypothesised as an important determining factor as regards employment status, proves to be not significantly related to the latter variable even in partial correlation analysis, although the direction of relationship is as anticipated - namely, that the wives of men in manual occupations are more likely to be in paid employment than those with husbands in non-manual occupations.

If a husband's employment group is not significantly related, as a variable, to the woman's own employment status, one might still expect the actual activities of her husband to influence whether or not a woman is engaged in paid work. In particular, it would be difficult for a woman with young children to work at all without some domestic help. Although it is true that some richer families might employ outside help, in general respondents in this sample would rely primarily on their husbands for housework and child care assistance. However, while a large minority of respondents consider their husbands to provide insufficient help around the home, particularly with housework (26 per cent) but also with child care (16 per cent), there is little or no difference between employment status groups in this respect.

The hours during which a husband is away from home on each working day is definitely related to employment status, however. Women appear to be increasingly less likely to go out to work and more likely to be full-time housewives as their husbands' hours out of home increase. In addition, the wives of shift-workers are more likely to be in outside employment than the sample as a whole, probably because their husbands are available to care for the children during some part of the day. This pattern is, however, reversed for wives of men on rolling three-shift systems presumably because a constant change in shift provides no 'regularity' for a wife to base her own employment on.

Related to the questions of both child care provided by the husband and also family income is

Table 4   Inter-correlation of employment status and 'social' variables

	S.e.g. of husband	Terminal education age	Tenure of household	Family income	Presence/ absence husband	Age of respondent
Employment status	r=-.06 (p=.11)	r=-.07 (p=.08)	r=.05 (p=.15)	r=.07 (p=.08)	r=-.07 (p=.09)	r=.08 (p=.06)
S.e.g. of husband		r=.47* (p=.001)	r=.28* (p=.001)	r=.25* (p=.001)	– –	r=.17* (p=.001)
Terminal education age			r=.19* (p=.001)	r=.19* (p=.001)	r=.10* (p=.02)	r=-.16* (p=.001)
Tenure of household				r=.34* (p=.001)	r=.17* (p=.001)	r=.28* (p=.001)
Family income					r=.34* (p=.001)	r=.11* (p=.03)
Presence/ Absence husband						r=.20* (p=.001)

* Relationship significant at the .05 level of significance

the situation concerning the employment status of
women without husbands. On the basis of the previous
discussion, it would be expected that women who are
lone parents would find it more difficult to go out
to work than those who have husbands to share their
child care responsibilities, if only in a minor way.
But, at the same time, the lack of a husband's
income coming into the family must encourage lone
parents to take paid employment (Table 4 indicates a
close relationship between the absence of a husband
from the household and low family income). Thus,
there are contradictory forces influencing these
women and the survey found no significant difference
between those with and those without husbands in
terms of employment status (see Table 4). There is
a tendency, however, for lone parents to be more
likely to go out to work and less likely to be full-
time housewives; in fact, 8 out of 19 women in the
sample living in households without a husband present
undertake paid employment, compared to 28.5 per cent
of the total sample.

The relationship between the family's need for
extra income and the employment status of the wife is
complicated by the fact that the wife's income is
included in household income in this survey. However, it is clear, as would be expected, that a
smaller percentage of families where the wife is in
employment fall into the lowest income group (up to
£3,000 per annum). It is also clear that the
majority of families with working mothers enjoy only
'average' household incomes; were it not for the
employment of the respondents concerned, these
families would fall into the 'low' income group. The
encouragement of extra financial resources is clearly
an important determinant of the decision to take paid
employment for many women. In answer to the
question: 'What is your main reason for working?',
36 per cent of employed respondents say that money is
the overriding reason, while less than half this
number (16 per cent) state that 'other' reasons are
more important than money and none of these are lone
parents.

Using the socio-economic group of the husband as
a surrogate for income, it is interesting to note
that the wives of manual workers are much more likely
to be working primarily because they need to earn
extra money, while 'other' reasons are equally or
more important to the wives of non-manual workers;
the correlation coefficient between social class and
reasons for working is r=-.19 (p=.02). Overall, 64
per cent of the respondents in paid employment

mention 'other' reasons for working. Of these, over
half consider the break from home and the provision
of an outside interest to be an important reason for
working. Other reasons given include the opportunity
to use previous training and the enjoyment of contact
with other people. Such 'other' reasons are most
commonly cited by women who are more highly educated,
as can be seen from Table 5, which shows a moderate
relationship between education level and reasons for
working. The group with the lowest terminal education age is dominated by the need to consider money
first as a reason for taking up paid employment.
This fact,in turn,is probably related to the type of
job which is open to women with few or no qualifications although, in fact, as will be shown in the next
section, few women with young children are in the
position of being able to obtain jobs of a high
quality.
     The lack of child care facilities has already
been mentioned as a major physical constraint on
employment activity and the whole question of pre-
school child care will be discussed in Chapter 8.
Other physical constraints include a lack of provision of job opportunities and a lack of personal
mobility. As far as the provision of opportunity is
concerned, no data are available at district level to
show variations in job supply across the borough of
Merton. It is instructive, however, to consider that
of 286 non-employed respondents in this survey, only
17 mention the lack of suitable jobs (either in terms
of the type of work or in terms of the hours of
work) as a reason for not being in employment. As
far as can be ascertained, the level of personal
mobility also does not seem to be very important in
determining employment status; 41 per cent of women
in paid employment have regular weekday access to a
car and, on the other hand, 29 per cent of full-time
housewives do so. In fact, far more respondents walk
or go by bus than use cars for travelling to work,
mainly because of the short distances involved.
     In summary, the analysis of data relating to
present employment status highlights the importance
of 'attitude to work' as an independent determinant
of employment status. While the possession of certain attitudes is itself closely related to various
'social' characteristics of respondents, these
characteristics do not appear to operate as direct
constraints on employment status. The most important
direct determinant of work status appears to be the
age of the youngest child in the family; in particular relatively few women with babies under two years

Table 5   Cross-tabulation of reason for working, with terminal education age

(Percentages in brackets)

	-15	16	17-18	19+	Total
'Money is by far the most important reason I work'	22(51.2)	14(42.4)	3(13.6)	1(6.7)	40(35.4)
'Money is important but other reasons are equally important'	17(39.5)	16(48.5)	12(54.5)	10(66.7)	55(48.7)
'Other reasons are more important than money'	4(9.3)	3(9.1)	7(31.8)	4(26.7)	18(15.9)
Total	43(100.0)	33(100.0)	22(100.0)	15(100.0)	113(100.0)

gamma = .47   (287 missing cases)

of age are engaged in paid employment. The absence
of a husband from the household and low family
income have also been suggested as encouraging
women to take paid work. Financial reasons are most
commonly cited by employees as determining their own
employment status, while reasons connected with the
care of children dominate the answers of full-time
housewives to the question of their non-engagement
in paid employment.

2. Conditions of paid employment

This section of the data analysis focuses
entirely on those respondents who are in paid employment and deals with the actual conditions of work
experienced by such women, in order to present a
fuller picture of the life style of working mothers
with young children.

a) Work location

Reference to Fig. 1 will show the ideological
framework within which women's employment takes
place. One of the results of societal emphasis on a
domestic, child-centred role for women is a local or
home-based orientation of employment (see White,
1977,41). Of 114 respondents in paid employment in
the Merton survey, nearly one-third (37) worked
entirely at home. For many women with young
children, working in their own home provides the
only possible outlet to paid employment, due to the
inadequacies (and cost) of child care provision,
combined with a general belief that women should be
at home to care for their own children. The existence of home-working in turn serves to reinforce the
home-based and child-centred status of these women,
making them subject to a double constraint on activities, since they must care for their children themselves as well as finding time for their work duties.
In contrast, those who are able to go out to work
have freed themselves, at least for some hours a day
(or week), from their domestic roles.
It is interesting to look at the characteristics
of home-workers as opposed to those who work outside
the home. A significant relationship exists between
home-working and a more 'traditional' 'attitude to
work' ($r=.24$ ($p=.005$)) but surprisingly not between
working at home and a 'traditional''attitude to the
position of women' ($r=-.04$($p=.34$)). Home-workers
tend to be more highly educated ($r=-.16$ ($p=.05$)) and
come from families with higher joint incomes ($r=-.15$

(p=.05)) than those who go out to work. They are
also much more likely than outside workers to think
of themselves firstly as housewives rather than as
'working women' (r=.30 (p=.001)). But, perhaps most
importantly from the point of view of work
conditions, home-workers are more likely than those
working outside the home to occupy lower 'status'
jobs than before the birth of their children (r=.17
(p=.04)): the question of job 'status' is raised
again later.

The majority of employed respondents work outside the home, as we have seen, but most outside
workers are still very locally-oriented in their
employment; 37 per cent have a journey of only five
minutes or less to get to work and 70 per cent
travel for no longer than ten minutes. This local
orientation of work is the main spatial result of the
gender-role constraint on employment. Out of 77 respondents who go out to work, only six work in Central
London, while 40 per cent of women who were employed
before the birth of their children did so and 36 per
cent of respondents' husbands do so at present. In
addition, only 19 of 292 respondents who intend to go
out to work when their children are all at school
full-time expect to work in Central London, while
220 (75 per cent) intend to work locally and a
further 27 will probably work at home. This last
point serves to illustrate the deeply ingrained
effect of gender-role restrictions on employment.
Locally-based work provides the opportunity for
mothers to accompany their children to and from
school and also avoids extensive and time-consuming
journeys to work, but it is fairly unlikely to offer
the same degree of interest or opportunity for
advancement as employment 'up in town'. It seems
clear from selected case-studies and more generally
from Census information that, while employment in
general has decentralised greatly from Central London
to suburban locations in the last twenty years,
clerical employment and, especially higher-grade
clerical work, has tended to remain in the central
area, while less skilled work has been more subject
to decentralisation; in particular, work in retailing is more readily available in the suburbs (Tivers,
1979). It is notable that most respondents now working as supermarket cashiers and shop-workers were
formerly employed in clerical jobs before the birth
of their children.

b)   Working hours

Another very important result of gender-role

114

restrictions on employment is the prevalence of part-
time working amongst women with young children. As
Table 2 shows, an overwhelming majority of working
respondents are employed for less than 30 hours each
week. This contrasts markedly with a figure of 92
per cent of all respondents in the survey, working
full-time before the birth of their children. Home-
workers most notably work short hours, 73 per cent
being employed for less than 12 hours per week. The
length of a woman's work hours out of home can be
taken in some measure as an indication of her commitment to employment; certainly there is a correlation
between work hours out of home and a 'progressive'
'attitude to work'(r=.22 (p=.001)).

Nearly half of all respondents in paid employment work only in the evenings or at weekends and
the percentage is even higher taking only outside
workers into account (see Appendix D, Table D4). The
accepted principle is that working hours must fit in
with other family arrangements (see also, Speakman,
1983). If one divides the 'working' sample into
'regular' and 'casual' workers (by calling all those
who work at home and all those outside workers who
are in paid employment only in the evenings, at weekends or on less than two weekdays each week,
'casual' workers), very different attitudes and group
characteristics might be expected from the two groups
which result. In particular, while there has been
shown to be a close relationship between 'attitude to
work' and actual work status (in the preceding
section), there is no definite reason to suppose that
such attitudes should be related to 'regular' or
'casual' working (although home-workers have already
been shown to hold more 'traditional' attitudes than
those who work outside the home). On the other hand,
one might certainly expect to find a close relationship between 'attitude to the position of women' and
the 'casual' work variable, since, 'casual' workers
are so obviously subject to gender-role differentiation, the ideology of which is enshrined in the
'attitude to the position of women' dimension. Table
6 illustrates the actual relationships which exist
between 'regular' or 'casual' working and these two
attitude dimensions. In addition, other variables
which are significantly related to the 'casual/
regular' work variable are included in the table.

As can be clearly seen, the importance of the
two attitude dimensions is reversed from what might
have been expected; as in the case of outside versus
home-workers, there is, in fact, a relationship between
'regular' working and 'progressive' attitudes to

Table 6   Correlation of 'regular/casual' working,
with attitude dimensions and other
(significantly related) variables

	'Attitude to work'	'Attitude to position of women'	Family income	Tenure of household
'regular/casual' working	r=.23* (p=.007)	r=.05 (p=.31)	r=-.19* (p=.02)	r=-.19* (p=.02)

	Age of husband	Presence/absence of husband	No.of children under 5	Attitude to present employment
'regular/casual' working	r=-.29* (p=.001)	r=-.25* (p=.004)	r=-.20* (p=.02)	r=.38* (p=.001)

* Relationship significant at the .05 level of significance

work, while there is no significant relationship with
the more general 'attitude to the position of women'
dimension. The latter result is perhaps more surprising than the former and it was felt worthwhile to
expand the analysis by looking again at the relationship between 'regular' or 'casual' working and the
more general attitude dimension, controlling for the
possible influence of other variables (including
those indicated in Table 6). The partial correlation
coefficients produced were in every case little different from the zero-order coefficient and it was
concluded,therefore,that this attitude variable was
of no use in discriminating between 'regular' and
'casual' workers.

The characteristics of 'casual', as opposed to
'regular' workers can be listed from Table 6;
'casual' workers come from families with higher joint
incomes, they are more likely to be owner-occupiers,
they are more likely to live in households with a
husband present and, if this is so, then they tend
also to have older husbands than 'regular' workers.
They also have more young children (under five
years). Surprisingly 'casual' working is not significantly related to education, social class, the age

of the woman herself or the age of her youngest
child. Nor is it related to 'reasons for working',
although one might have expected 'casual' employees
to show less concern for money as a reason for
working and be more interested in 'other' reasons,
than 'regular' workers. In fact, if one looks only
at evening/weekend workers (as one sub-group of
'casual' workers), it can be clearly seen that these
women are much more likely to stress 'other' reasons
for working and to consider paid employment as an
'escape from home' during a time which is most convenient for the rest of the family. Most striking of
all, perhaps,from Table 6 is the definite relationship evident between 'casual' working and a belief
in being a 'housewife with a job' (and vice versa,
that between 'regular' working and self-judgement as
a 'working woman who also runs a home'). This latter
variable, which can be considered as representing an
'attitude to present employment', will be further
considered later.

Indicative of a continuing child care constraint
on employment for women is the fact that, while 80
per cent of respondents state that they intend to
undertake paid employment when their children are all
at school, only 19 per cent of future potential
workers expect to be employed full-time. The influence of gender-role ideology is here very apparent:
most women simply do not expect ever to be principal,
or even equal, breadwinners for their families. In
addition, even when all children are at school full-
time, there remains the problem of arranging child
care for after-school hours and holidays. But
certainly many women also feel a personal desire to
spend as much time as possible with their children,
both at present and in the future; of 99 respondents
at present working part-time, 72 give as a reason for
not working full-time their 'desire to be with their
children', while 39 express feelings of 'duty' towards them. Other reasons are of much less importance to this presently-employed group. Respondents
stating a 'desire to be with their children' as a
reason for working part-time at present are more
likely to have husbands in non-manual occupations
$(r=.15 \ (p=.05))$ and to have a youngest child aged
under two years $(r=-.15(p=.05))$, but there is no
relationship between the dichotomous 'desire to be
with children' variable and either terminal education age or present age of the respondent. Nor is
there any relationship at all with the 'attitude to
work' dimension $(r=-.01 \ (p=.47))$, whilst that with
the 'attitude to the position of women' combined

117

variable is in the opposite direction from what might
have been expected $(r=.24$ $(p=.005))$; it appears
that part-time workers with more 'progressive'
attitudes to women's general position are also more
likely to state a 'desire to be with their children'
as a reason for not working full-time.

When those who intend to work only part-time in
the future are considered, a much larger group (21
per cent) cite the lack of provision of child care
for out-of-school hours as a reason for not working
full-time. A further 22 per cent stress their 'duty
to be with their children' as a reason. The respondents giving these answers cannot, however, be identified separately in terms of social or attitudinal
characteristics; no variables appear to be significantly related to the possession of these views.
Despite the greater importance of these constraint-
oriented reasons among those who intend to work only
part-time in the future, still a large majority state
that their 'desire to be with their children' is a
major factor determining their future working hours.
The need to fit in time for housework is also cited
as an important reason when considering future work.

c)   The 'status' of jobs

Together with a decrease in the number of hours
worked and the distance travelled to work, women at
present in paid employment have also tended to suffer
a fall in the 'status' (or 'quality') of jobs undertaken (see also, Elias and Main, 1982). This tendency is difficult to illustrate objectively, due to the
coarse classification of socio-economic status employed in Census publications and also for comparative
purposes in this study. However, it is clear that,
for example, many former secretaries now undertake
home typing duties or work as Saturday shop assistan-
ts and that very many women from all types of employment background now work as cleaners and childminders, jobs which imply a reinforcement of the domestic role. A new variable was,therefore,created to
identify present job 'status' in relation to previous
'status', which was based on subjective criteria in
the absence of more quantifiable data.

It appears that present home-workers are much
more likely to have experienced a drop in 'status'
than are those who are out at work, even though the
latter are more likely to have changed jobs since
their children were born (see Appendix D, Table D5).
Over half of all home-workers have had to accept work
of a lower'status'; this situation reflects the

number of such women who are employed as childminders or piece-workers. The 'status' of jobs is
also closely related to working hours. Amongst
weekend and evening workers, for example, 52 per cent
are in lower 'status' jobs than previously, while 17
per cent perform the same type of job as before they
had children. This is contrasted by the situation
for full-time weekday workers: only 2 out of 11
respondents working for 30 hours or more each week
are in lower 'status' jobs, while 5 are in the same
type of work as previously.

There is also a spatial variation in job
'status' decline. Those working in Central London
are least likely to be in lower 'status' jobs, while
those who work locally are most likely to be so.
This situation is obviously related to the fact that
most women at present working in Central London are
in the same actual jobs as before. Those with jobs
of a lower 'status' than their former full-time jobs
are the most likely to state that money is by far the
most important reason for them being in employment;
those who are in the same jobs as previously are the
most likely to cite 'other' reasons as being more
important. Similarly, those with lower 'status' jobs
are more likely than any other group to think of
themselves as 'housewives with a job', rather than as
'working women who also run a home'.

Bringing together all the facts listed above, it
would seem likely that respondents with lower
'status' jobs now than the ones they previously
occupied would have less positive attitudes towards
the importance of work for women. However, this is
not so (see Appendix D, Table D6). There is, in fact,
very little difference between those who have kept
the same jobs and those who have taken lower 'status'
jobs, in terms of their belief in the fulfilment
offered by employment. It is those who have taken
different jobs but with a similar 'status' who are
least convinced about the value of work as an agent
of independence and satisfaction. There is thus once
again strong evidence for a clash of attitudes and a
difference between attitudes and behaviour for the
individual woman. Those who hold a positive attitude
concerning the fulfilling nature of employment, but
who are constrained to work in low 'status' jobs,
mainly for the money they offer, must inevitably
suffer from a personal lack of satisfaction. (This
point is taken up again in Chapter 9.) Significantly, more women with lower 'status' jobs do not intend
to work at all in the future (20 per cent) than the
respondents in any other group, possibly because of

their present work experience. But even more notable
is the fact that almost all of the remainder are
concerned to get back to jobs of a higher 'status'
again.

d)   'Attitude to present employment'

    The typical working conditions of women with
young children, in terms of location, hours and
'status', combine to support an ideological belief
in the 'peripheral' nature of women's employment.
Thus, in answer to the question: 'Do you think of
yourself primarily as a housewife who has a job or as
a working woman who also runs a home?', only 18
employed respondents state that they consider themselves to be primarily 'working women'. It is
interesting to consider some of the characteristics
of this work-oriented small group of respondents.
Not surprisingly, a much higher percentage of respondents living in households without a husband
present think of themselves primarily as 'working
women' (50 per cent) than do married respondents (13
per cent); these two variables are related by a
correlation coefficient of r=-.26 (p=.003). Also
related to household structure is the fact that all
employed women with three or more dependent children
in total consider themselves to be mainly 'housewives' while in contrast, half of those with only one
child think of themselves as 'workers'. The situation is even more clearly defined taking only children under five into account; in fact, all 18
respondents who consider themselves to be primarily
'working women' have only one child under five. The
age of this one child tends to be rather older than
the age of the youngest child in families where
women think of themselves firstly as 'housewives'.
    The majority of women who consider themselves
mainly 'workers' are concentrated in partly-skilled
and unskilled manual occupations (half of them having
left school before the age of 16 and more than half
having come from working-class families themselves),
although most of those who are married have husbands
in white-collar occupations. In addition, as would
be expected, most of these women work longer hours
than do those who consider themselves to be 'housewives' but it is important to note that even of
those respondents working full-time (30 hours or more
each week), over half think of themselves firstly as
housewives. Work-oriented women tend to be employed
further away from home and, in particular, only one
of them works actually at home, compared to 38 (42

120

per cent) of those who consider themselves as
'housewives'.

A consideration of attitude data suggests that
those who think of themselves firstly as 'working
women' have the most positive attitudes towards the
need for women's employment of any sub-group within
the total sample; the relationship with the
'attitude to work' dimension is of the order, r=.43
(p=.001). In particular, in response to the statement: 'A woman and her family will all benefit if
she does a job', all 18 respondents are in agreement,
compared to only half of the total sample. Similarly, work-oriented women are more likely to experience a desire to be free from motherhood responsibilities at least occasionally but they are not more
likely themselves to have had mothers out at work
when they were young.

Finally, it is instructive to note that none of
the respondents who think of themselves primarily as
'workers' perceive their husbands' attitude to their
working to be one of discouragement but, on the other
hand, just as many of them as in the sample as a
whole complain of a lack of domestic help from their
husbands. In the end, despite certain attitudes on
the part of both women and their husbands to the
contrary, 'The addition of paid work to the housewife's activities does not mean she is no longer a
housewife' (Oakley, 1974,38). The position of
economic dependence and the status of being a 'non-
worker' remain even when the housewife also works
outside the home; such is the primacy of the housewife role in the value system of society.

In summary, the conditions of work experienced
by women with young children are influenced strongly
by ideological emphasis on a home-oriented and
gender-differentiated role for women. The data from
the Merton survey emphasise a:) the home-based or
locally-oriented nature of employment for such women,
b) the prevalence of part-time and 'casual' working,
c) the low 'status' of jobs undertaken and the drop
in 'status' from previous occupations for many women,
and d) the primacy of the 'housewife' role in the
minds of working women.

3. Housewives' preferences with respect to employment

The previous section has considered the disadvantaged position of women with young children in the
field of employment. This section, in contrast,
looks at women who are 'tied to home' as full-time

housewives and at their present aspirations concerning outside employment. In answer to the question: 'If you could have someone to take care of things here at home, would you like to take an outside job right now, or are you happy enough to be at home?', 69 per cent state that they are 'happy at home' (or are unsure), while 31 per cent say that they would prefer to go out to work.

a)   The role of attitudes

We have noted earlier that the 'attitude to work' dimension is a key variable in determining present employment status and in relation to working conditions. If a close relationship between attitudes and actual behaviour can be observed in the data, as in these cases, then it is even more likely that close relationships will be found between attitudes and preferences. Thus, it is not unexpected to find significant relationships existing between the employment status preferences of full-time housewives and major attitudinal variables (see Table 7). It is particularly interesting to note the connection between a desire to go out to work at the present time and 'progressive' attitudes to the general position of women, since this latter attitude variable has not proved a significant differentiating variable up to this point in the analysis. Housewives who would prefer to be out at work are more likely than others to experience, at least occasionally, a desire for freedom from motherhood responsibilities, which result is entirely to be expected.

Table 7	Correlation of employment status preference with attitude variables (full-time housewives)			
	'Attitude to work'	'Attitude to position of women'	Attitude to motherhood	Husband's attitude
Employment status preference	r=.32* (p=.001)	r=.10* (p=.05)	r=-.27* (p=.001)	r=-.08 (p=.09)

*Relationship significant at the .05 level of significance

The perceived attitude of husbands does not, however, seem to be important as a determinant of employment status preference for these women.

Related to the question of attitudes are the reasons for not being at work at the present time. Many respondents wishing to work outside the home cite a 'desire to be with their children' as a main reason for not working, despite the fact that they have previously stated a desire to take an outside job if they 'could have someone to take care of things here at home'. This suggests an ambivalence in attitudes, although it is possible that some women unconsciously exclude the care of children from their consideration of the domestic role. In general, however, there is a negative relationship between wanting to go out to work now and citing a 'desire to be with children' as a reason for not working ($r = -.18 (p = .001)$), a relationship which remains unchanged even when the effects of other attitudes are taken into account in partial correlation analyses. Of some interest is the relatively large number of women (preferring to go out to work now) who state that they are unable to work because of a lack of suitable child care facilities. (This point is taken up again later in Chapter 8.)

The vast majority of respondents, who would like to go out to work now, intend to do so when their children are all at school full-time (86 per cent), while the percentage intending to take an outside job among those who are at present 'happy at home' is considerably smaller (64 per cent). The former are more likely to intend to work full-time in the future, although most of them, as in the sample as a whole, expect to work only part-time.

b)   Characteristics of housewives with contrasting preferences

Full-time housewives who would really prefer to go out to work at the present time may be different-iated from those who are 'happy at home', not only in terms of attitudinal differences but also in terms of the social and physical characteristics which determine particular styles of life. Significant relationships between employment status preference and other variables are illustrated in Table 8. Those who would like to take an outside job tend not to be the mothers of young babies or toddlers (under two years). In contrast, the actual number of young children seems to be an unimportant factor ($r = .03 (p = .34)$), as does the mother's own age ($r = -.02 (p = .39)$).

Table 8   Correlation of employment status preference
with other variables

(full-time housewives)

	Age of youngest child	Presence/ absence of husband	S.e.g. of husband
Employment status preference	r=.11* (p=.03)	r=-.10* (p=.04)	r=-.19* (p=.001)

	Car Avail- ability	Tenure of household	Flat dwelling
Employment status preference	r=-.18* (p=.001)	r=-.13* (p=.02)	r=.10* (p=.04)

*Relationship significant at the .05 level of
significance

It is interesting to note, however, that one-quarter
of those who would prefer to go out to work now had
their first child before the age of 20, compared to
only one in nine of those who say they are 'happy at
home'.
     A present preference for paid employment might
be expected to relate closely to previous work
experience; thus one might expect women who previously worked in higher level occupations, often
requiring high qualifications, to have a greater
orientation to working at the present time than those
whose work experience was limited to low-grade manual
jobs. In fact, the opposite is more likely to be the
case. Although the relationship between employment
status preference and previous occupation (in terms
of non-manual and manual employment categories) is
not significant (r=-.06 (p=.15)), it is interesting
that only 3 out of 16 (19 per cent) respondents who
previously worked in managerial and professional
occupations would prefer to go out to work now,
whereas 12 out of 20 (38 per cent) respondents who
used to hold partly-skilled and unskilled manual jobs
would prefer to do so.
     This finding might relate to the differing

predisposition of respondents to take part in other (social) activities, partly since previous job 'status' is clearly related to terminal age of full-time education. It is certainly traditional in sociological literature to consider educated, middle class housewives as the 'joiners' of clubs and the initiators of home visiting patterns, rather than their working class counterparts (see also Chapter 6). A new variable was, therefore, computed from counts made on seven existing variables relating to frequencies of home visiting, park use and travel outside the local area and to club and adult education attendance. The new variable purported to differentiate between respondents on the basis of a quantitative measure of social activities. Results show clearly that respondents who would prefer to go out to work take part in fewer social activities than those who say they are 'happy at home'.

However, the ability to take part in many outside activities depends crucially on a level of personal mobility which is simply not available to very many respondents. Table 8 shows a significant negative relationship between a preference for present employment and having a car available on a daily basis (that is, having a car at home and being able to drive it). Car availability is, of course, closely related to higher social class and higher family income but even when the effect of these two variables is taken into account in partial correlation analyses, car availability remains significantly related to employment preference. Presumably, those who have effective access to the 'outside world' are not so likely to prefer to go back to work immediately, regardless of their social class or family income.

Social class (measured by husband's socio-economic group) is, however, also very closely related to employment status preference (see Table 8); those with husbands in manual jobs are more likely to prefer to go out to work now than respondents with husbands in white-collar occupations. Interestingly, family income does not appear as an independent influence on preferences ($r=-.01$ ($p=.42$)), although the actual presence or absence of a husband in the household is an important factor and this is clearly related to 'family' income in the case of women who are full-time housewives. A desire to work, in terms of thereby acquiring extra money, can also be related to type of present housing tenure (see Table 8). It is clear that respondents living in council housing and in private rented

accommodation are far more likely to prefer to go out
to work than those who live in owner-occupied
housing. Respondents living in flats are also more
likely to want to go out to work than are those who
live in houses, perhaps reflecting a desire to obtain
a house for their growing families. However, too
much attention should not be focused uncritically on
these latter results; if one takes into account the
effect of social class, the relationships between
employment status preference and both tenure type and
flat dwelling effectively disappear (with tenure of
household, the partial correlation coefficient drops
to $r=-.07(p=.12)$ and with flat dwelling it decreases
to $r=.06$ $(p=.17))$.

In summary, this section has attempted to assess
the situation of full-time housewives in relation to
their present employment status preferences. A
desire to 'take an outside job right now', has been
shown to be closely related to personal attitudes,
both to work, to the general position of women and
to motherhood responsibilities. Social class and car
availability, together with the age of the youngest
child in the family, stand as the most important
other variables relating to employment status preference.

4.   General employment preferences of respondents

Another perspective on employment status is
provided by considering general preferences in the
area of work. Many women who are at present 'housebound' may be content to remain at home while they
have young children but this does not mean that in
general they would not prefer to go out to work.
Similarly, there may be other women who are forced by
economic or other circumstances to go out to work,
while their general preference may be to remain at
home. All respondents were, therefore, asked the
question: 'Leaving your family circumstances aside,
on the whole, would you prefer to stay at home or go
out to work?'; 270 (67.5 per cent) replied that they
would prefer to work and 115 (28.5 per cent) that
they would rather stay at home, while 15 were undec-
ided.

Table 9 shows that there is virtually no relationship between present employment status and
generally preferred status. Present home-workers are
most likely, of the three groups, to prefer in
general to stay at home but present outside workers
are only marginally more likely to prefer to go out
to work (in general) than are those who are full-

PAID EMPLOYMENT

Table 9 Cross tabulation of generally preferred
employment status, with actual employment
status at the present time

(percentages in brackets)

	Out at work	Work at home	Not in employment	Total
Prefer to stay at home	18(23.4)	13(35.1)	84(29.4)	115(28.5)
Prefer to go out to work	54(70.1)	23(62.2)	193(67.5)	270(67.5)
Don't know	5(6.5)	1(2.7)	9(3.1)	15(3.7)
Total	77(100.0)	37(100.0)	286(100.0)	400(100.0)

chi-square = 3.50 (p=.48)

time housewives. Leaving aside those respondents who
work at home (and adding 'don't know' replies to the
'prefer to stay at home' category), an interesting,
secondary piece of analysis is suggested by the
results shown in Table 9. By combining the two
variables (present employment status, and generally
preferred employment status) a new variable can be
created which has four categories: 1) those who are
out at work and who prefer to work in general, 2)
those who are out at work but would prefer to stay at
home, 3) those who are not in employment and who
would prefer to stay at home in any case and
finally, 4) those who are full-time housewives at
present but in general would prefer to go out to
work. In looking closely at inter-relationships with
this new variable (which we can call 'satisfaction
with employment status'), we may perhaps achieve a
better understanding of the relative importance of
choice and constraint factors in determining employment status; categories 1 and 3 of this variable can
be seen as examples of 'choice' situations, while
categories 2 and 4 clearly represent situations of
'constraint'.

a)   Attitude relationships

      As in previous sections, it is useful initially
to consider the relationships between the dependent
variable (in this case, 'satisfaction with employment
status') and the different attitudinal variables
defined at the beginning of the chapter. For the
purposes of use in cross-tabulation analysis, the
attitude dimensions representing 'attitude to work'
and 'attitude to the position of women' were firstly
recoded into categorised form and the variables were
then inter-related with the 'satisfaction with
employment status' variable (see Appendix D, Tables
D7 and D8). The relationship in both cases is
clearly significant; as would be expected, work-
oriented preference situations are positively
related to 'progressive' attitudes, while home-
oriented preferences are related to 'traditional'
attitudes. What is perhaps more interesting, however, is the lack of co-ordination of attitudes,
preferences and actual behaviour in some individual
cases. For example, five respondents who are at
present in employment and who would, in general,
prefer to work, have negative ('traditional') attitudes to the importance of employment for women.
Also nine respondents who hold 'progressive' attitudes to work and who are actually at work would, in
general, prefer to stay at home. Similarly, seven-
teen housewives who prefer to stay at home hold
'progressive' attitudes to the importance of work for
women, while as many as 57 full-time housewives who
would really prefer to go out to work, in fact hold
negative attitudes to women's employment! A similar
variation in responses, indicating discrepancies
which may exist, for individual reasons, between
attitudes, preferences and behaviour, occurs in
relation to the 'attitude to the position of women'
variable. The reasons for such discrepancies could
only be sought in the personal circumstances of the
respondents concerned, in a survey of much greater
depth than the present one. Here it suffices simply
to point out the apparent lack of co-ordination in
the various aspects of some women's lives.
      Taking now the other major attitude variables,
the data show firstly that the respondent's perception of her husband's attitude is of no importance in
influencing her own 'satisfaction with employment
status'. The relationship with the 'attitude to
motherhood responsibilities' variable is of some
interest (see Appendix D, Table D9). Full-time
housewives who prefer being at home are much more

likely to state that they have 'never experienced a
desire to be free from motherhood responsibilities'
than women in any other category. Conversely,
working women who prefer going out to work are most
likely to feel that they have experienced such a
desire, at least occasionally. Respondents in the
other two 'constraint' categories are, however, very
similar in their reactions to this attitude question;
in both cases, a slight majority of respondents admit
to having experienced some desire to be free from
motherhood responsibilities.

b)   Characteristics of respondents in 'choice' and
     'constraint' situations

     Throughout this chapter, reference has constan-
tly been made to 'social' variables which are seen to
have some influence on the attitudes and behaviour of
respondents. In this final section we will attempt
to relate these 'social' characteristics to women in
different categories of 'choice' and 'constraint'
situations. The most obvious constraint on activities to be considered when dealing with women with
young children as a group, is the very presence of
young children. In particular, it could reasonably
be expected that full-time housewives who would
prefer to go out to work would have more and/or
younger children than those actually out at work and
satisfied with that situation. This hypothesis is
borne out by the results of cross-tabulation analysis
(see Appendix D, Table D10). As we have already noted
earlier in the chapter, full-time housewives are much
more likely to have young babies in their care than
are those who go out to work. In fact there is
virtually no difference between people in 'choice'
and 'constraint' situations in terms of the age of
their youngest child; housewives, both preferring to
work and preferring to stay at home, have younger
children than those out at work, whether the latter
actually prefer to be working or not. The number of
young children which a woman has seems to be virtually unrelated to her 'satisfaction with employment
status'(see Appendix D, Table D11).
     Another likely constraint on employment status,
leading either to a 'satisfied' or a 'dissatisfied'
situation, is that of family income. In particular,
it might be expected that lone mothers (who are in
any case over-represented amongst employed respondents) would tend to be those who, although out at
work, would really prefer to stay at home. This
supposition is not, however, supported by the data;

women without husbands present in the household are
no more likely to be 'unwilling' workers than are
married women. The financial situation of the family
must, however, influence many women to work when they
would really prefer not to. Obtaining extra money is
obviously a more important reason for working amongst
those who would prefer to stay at home than amongst
those who would rather go out to work (see Appendix
D, Table D12). Most notable is the fact that not one
respondent in the 'prefer to stay at home' category
is working primarily for reasons other than monetary
ones. However, it is an interesting fact that women
who would prefer not to be out at work and who
clearly work largely for financial reasons, in fact,
tend to live in households with higher incomes than
those who are satisfied to be out at work (see
Appendix D, Table D13). Looking now at the full-time
housewives, a clearer picture of income constraints
on preferences is visible; those who would really
prefer to go out to work do, in fact, as one would
expect, live in households with lower incomes than
those who would prefer to stay at home.

Social class (measured in terms of the husband's
socio-economic group) has already been mentioned
several times in this chapter as an important differentiating factor in relation to employment variables. Here it might reasonably be hypothesised that
'choice' and 'constraint' situations with regard to
employment status could be related, respectively, to
middle class and working class families since it is
a commonplace finding that choice is very class-
based (Harper and Richards, 1979,164). However, the
analysis does not support this hypothesis (see
Appendix D, Table D14). Housewives who would prefer
to stay at home are, indeed, more likely to have
husbands in managerial or professional occupations
but outside workers who prefer to go out to work
tend, on the other hand, to have husbands in skilled
manual occupations. The situation is equally
confused with regard to respondents in 'constraint'
oriented situations. It appears that the major
influence is that of social class directly on actual
employment status, rather than as an influence on
'constraint' versus 'choice' situations. The same
type of result is also obtained from a comparison
of terminal education age and the 'satisfaction
with employment status' variable. For example,
those who go out to work but who would prefer to
stay at home are over-represented amongst
respondents with a lower terminal age of full-time
education but those who are in the reverse

situation, being housewives with a desire to go out
to work, are the most likely of all groups to have
received a full-time education beyond the age of 18
years.

For women who are out at work at present, the
difference between 'constraint' and 'choice' situations could well relate to actual conditions of work.
As might be expected, a higher percentage of those
who generally prefer to go out to work (31.5 per
cent) are employed in the same jobs as those they
held before the birth of their children, than of
those who would rather stay at home (21.7 per cent).
On the other hand, judged purely subjectively, it
would appear that more of those who prefer to work
are at present occupied in lower 'status' jobs than
before they had children (42.6 per cent), than is
true of respondents preferring to stay at home (30.4
per cent). There is definitely a close relationship
with working hours however; 40 per cent of 'constrained' employees work for 24 hours or more each
week, compared to only 7 per cent of workers who
prefer to go out to work. In contrast, very few
respondents who work really short hours fall into
this 'constrained' group. An interesting additional
result comes from a consideration of work times; 70
per cent of those who would really prefer to stay at
home are evening or weekend workers only (compared
to 50 per cent of those who prefer to work). But
also, a greater percentage of 'unwilling' workers go
out to work regularly on Monday to Friday each
week, than of 'satisfied' workers (hence, the over-
representation of the former group amongst employees
working 24 hours or more each week).

Whatever constraints are important for individual women in preventing them from occupying 'choice'
situations regarding employment status at the present
time, it is clear from Table 10 that many women hope
to overcome these constraints in the future. Thus, a
very high percentage of present full-time housewives
who would prefer to go out to work, actually expect
to do so when their children are all at school full-
time (80 per cent). Conversely, a fairly large
number of present 'constrained' workers do not intend
to continue working in the future (30 per cent). But
there are still very many respondents who obviously
do not anticipate the lessening of the constraints
which determine their present situations; in particular, 61 per cent of workers who would prefer to
stay at home still expect to be out at work when
their children are all at school. It is also notable
that as many as 57 per cent of present housewives who

Table 10   Cross-tabulation of 'satisfaction with
            employment status', with expected future
            employment status

(percentages in brackets)

	Out at work	Work at home	Not in employment	Total
1) 'Satisfied worker'	48 (88.9)	1 (1.9)	5 (9.3)	54 (100.0)
2) 'Dissatisfied worker'	14 (60.9)	2 (8.7)	7 (30.4)	23 (100.0)
3) 'Satisfied housewife'	53 (57.0)	6 (6.5)	34 (36.6)	93 (100.0)
4) 'Dissatisfied housewife'	155 (80.3)	9 (4.7)	29 (15.0)	193 (100.0)
Total	270 (74.4)	18 (5.0)	75 (20.7)	363 (100.0)

chi-square = 27.74   (p=.001)   (37 missing cases)

are quite happy to stay at home anticipate being in
employment in the future, indicating the possible
existence of other constraints from which those in
'choice' situations at the present time may tempor-
arily be shielded.
    As a concluding comment, it is useful to check
the hypothesised model of 'choice' versus
'constraint' situations against the data indicating
the general level of 'satisfaction with life'
experienced by respondents in different categories.
For this purpose, the four categories of the 'satisfaction with employment status' variable were collapsed into two cases by combining categories
representing 'choice' situations (1 and 3) and those
representing 'constraint' situations (2 and 4) respectively. The dichotomous variable so produced was
correlated with the total score on the semantic differential scale which was used to measure overall
'satisfaction with life'. (The derivation of this
scale is described in Chapter 4 and results relating

to it are discussed more fully in Chapter 9.) The
resulting correlation coefficient of r=.16 is
significant at the .001 level of significance and
indicates a relationship between low general
'satisfaction with life' and occupying a 'constraint'
situation in relation to employment status (and vice
versa).

In summary, by combining general preferences
relating to employment status with actual work
status it has been possible to consider respondents
in terms of 'choice' and 'constraint' situations.
Discrepancies in individual cases occur within an
overall picture of relationship between preferences
and attitudes. Although situations of 'choice' and
'constraint' clearly do exist and have validity in
determining general 'satisfaction with life' at the
present time and also future employment status, the
'social' variables tested against preferences seem
to act as a greater influence directly on actual
employment status than on 'choice' versus
'constraint' situations.

5.   General summary of survey findings

The findings related to the analysis of employment data point to the importance of attitudes
(particularly attitudes connected with work) in
determining both preferences and actual employment
status (at present and in the future). The most
important other variables influencing employment
status and preferences are the age of the youngest
child in the family and the inter-linked 'social'
variables (income, social class and car availability). Those who work at present, or who would
prefer to do so, tend to be women with older children and those in lower 'social groups'.

The nature of employment for women with young
children has also been emphasised. Most working
respondents are in employment at home or in the
local area, they occupy part-time jobs and very
often take work which is lower in 'status' than
their previous employment before the birth of their
children. The vast majority of respondents expect
to work in the future, whether or not they would
actually prefer to do so.

The employment data have indicated very clearly
the importance of the gender-role constraint (and
the allied physical constraint of lack of child
care provision) in influencing both the ability to
work and the conditions of work for women with
young children. However, paid employment is not the

general preference of all respondents, particularly those in higher 'social groups' and it is also evident that the constraint of low income is influential in encouraging employment at the present time for many women. Clearly, while all respondents are subject to gender-role restrictions on employment, it is the higher income, higher social class women who are more easily able to overcome this constraint in part, in that they choose to take employment, or who are more satisfied in accepting a non-employed role, if they are full-time housewives.

Chapter 6

NON-EMPLOYMENT ACTIVITIES

The previous chapter has attempted to analyse and
interpret data from the questionnaire survey which
relate to paid employment. Because employment status
may be of fundamental importance in determining the
structure of daily activity patterns (whether or not
paid work is undertaken actually during the daytime)
and also because employment offers its own system of
social, as well as economic, benefits and costs, it
seemed right to devote a whole chapter to this
subject. In contrast, it is possible (and in the
context of this study also desirable) to consider
other daytime activities in a more summary fashion.
The questionnaire used in the study contained questions relating to a wide range of daily activities
but these questions as a whole were intentionally
more limited in scope than those dealing with paid
employment.
    Fig. 4 indicates the range of activities
studied. Activities other than paid employment can
be divided into two types: those which constitute
types of 'unpaid work' and those which could be
described as 'leisure' activities. There is some
practical justification for such a division of
activities, although the two categories should not in
any sense be seen as mutually exclusive, nor should
the division itself be taken to parallel the methodological distinction between 'obligatory' and 'discretionary' activities employed, for example, by
Chapin and Logan (1969,310). It is,of course,true
that for many women shopping (even for food) is certainly a leisure activity and that they find a major
source of adult companionship through taking their
children to and from school each day. Equally, many
so-called 'leisure' activities are undertaken almost
entirely as aspects of the child care function and,
therefore,should probably be better considered as

135

Figure 4: The range of daily activities considered

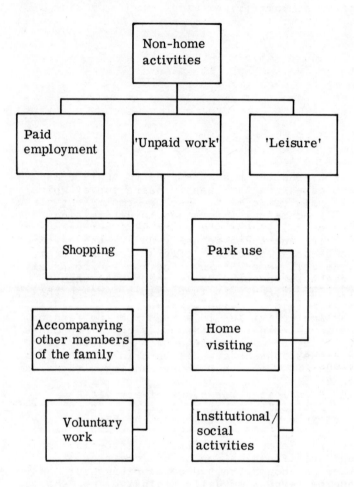

'unpaid work'. The categorisation suggested here is intended simply to promote order and structure in the data to be analysed, rather than to provide a definitive framework of analysis.

Data relating to non-employment activities originate from three sources in the questionnaire; in the first place, from direct questioning of respondents regarding activities <u>normally</u> undertaken, frequencies of participation, distances travelled and other relevant issues and in the second place from the detailed time-budget accounts of the previous day's actual out-of-home activities. The third source of data consists of objective measures of the spatial supply of facilities (shops, schools, parks and so on) in relation to the location of respondents. This chapter attempts to bring together these three data sources in an integrated manner, in order to present a complete picture of non-employment activities. In addition, the data analysis deals with the inter-relationships between activities and the 'social' and ideological influences identified in the previous chapter. Much of the data presented in this chapter is categorical in nature and (unlike the situation in Chapter 5) little benefit is here obtained from collapsing variables into dichotomised forms in order to employ correlation techniques; in most cases, the loss of information thereby occurring would be too great to justify this course of action. Analysis of the data in this chapter is, therefore, limited almost entirely to the use of cross-tabulations.

Unpaid Work

Whether or not they are in paid employment, it is undoubtedly true that women with young children spend much of their waking life 'working'. As has been indicated in Chapter 2, time-budget studies illustrate clearly that women in general and women with children in particular spend long hours performing domestic tasks and also enjoy fewer hours of real leisure a day than their husbands, who are often considered to be the ones 'at work'. Much of this unpaid labour (which is not thought of as 'work' by society at large or even by most women) takes place entirely in the home and as such is not the concern of this research, except in so far as the physical 'burden' of housework and child care may serve to restrict activities outside the home, while the ideological 'burden' of gender-role differentiation may make participation in certain outside activities impossible. The unpaid work which takes place outside the home is concerned with 'servicing' the family (or the community).

1. Shopping

The section in the questionnaire dealing with shopping specifically relates to the purchase of food and general goods, since it is the servicing function of shopping that is the focus of attention here rather than a leisure function (made explicit in fashion clothes shopping for example).

a) Weekday shopping

In answer to the question: 'How often, on weekdays during the daytime, do you go out to buy food or general items?', 35.5 per cent of respondents state that they go every day and a further 46 per cent that they shop two or three times a week. This might seem to represent an extremely and, perhaps an unreliably, high degree of shopping participation, but the time-budget survey which relates to the previous day's actual activities shows that 60 per cent of respondents did, in fact, go shopping (or go out to use services) on the day before the interview and that shopping ranks second only to accompanying children to school as the most predominant out-of-home activity.

Although, in fact, most respondents shop very frequently, there are some notable differences between different groups of respondents. As anticipated from previous findings reported in Chapter 2, it does appear that the wives of professional and managerial workers tend to shop less frequently than other women (see Appendix D, Table D15). The wives of skilled manual workers tend to be the most frequent shoppers. 20 respondents reportedly do not shop on weekdays at all, these being predominantly the wives of non-manual workers. However, there does appear to be an important intervening variable in the relationship under consideration. Women of higher social class also tend to have cars available for use on weekdays; those with husbands in professional and managerial occupations make up 23 per cent of respondents without cars available for use but 47 per cent of those with a car available. In fact, when car availability is taken into account in a three-way cross-tabulation analysis, the relationship between social class and frequency of shopping diminishes considerably. The existence of

Table 11   Cross-tabulation of frequency of weekday
            shopping, with car availability

(percentages in brackets)

	Car not available	Car available	Total
Every day	112(43.6)	30(24.4)	142(37.4)
2 or 3 times per week	118(45.9)	65(52.8)	183(48.2)
Once a week or less often	27(10.5)	28(22.8)	55(14.5)
Total	257(100.0)	123(100.0)	380(100.0)

gamma = .38   (20 missing cases)

private transport would seem likely to encourage
fewer, more major shopping trips, since more goods
can be carried at any one time; indeed 23 per cent
of respondents with a car available shop once a week
or less often on weekdays, while only 11 per cent of
those without a car go shopping this infrequently
(see Table 11). Although walking is clearly the most
important mode of travel to shops, as many as 22 per
cent of shopping trips, described in the time-budget
study as occurring on the previous day, were made by
car.
     The percentage of respondents shopping on a
daily basis decreases with increasing family income,
although there is only a low positive association
between the two variables (see Appendix D, Table
D16). Also of interest is the fact that it is women
in the above-average income group (£5-7000 per annum)
who are most likely to shop only once a week or less
often, rather than those in the highest income
category. Perhaps this is because the latter,
although personally mobile, are free of the financial
necessity of making major trips to supermarkets
(which is what shopping once a week would suggest).
     As indicated in Chapter 5, paid employment can
be viewed not only as a dependent variable but also
as an independent influence affecting other weekday
activities. It is, therefore, interesting to consider
the relationship between employment status (and hours

of work) and shopping frequency. In fact, there is
no significant relationship with employment status
overall (see Appendix D, Table D17) but the hypothesis that shopping could be combined with travel
from work would seem to be supported by the fact
that those who work on every weekday are most likely
to shop every day, while those who work on fewer
than five weekdays are much more likely to go shopping on two or three days a week. Similarly, those
who work longer hours each week are more likely to
shop every day than those working shorter hours. Unfortunately, the hypothesis does not seem to be
supported by the time-budget data, which indicates
that only three respondents experienced a work/
shopping activity combination during the day before
interview. However, it is probable that those who
work all day shop mainly at lunch times and, therefore, that the occurrence of shopping could be under-
recorded in the time-budget survey.

Besides paid employment, other activities might
be presumed to influence shopping frequency. In
particular, it could be hypothesised that women who
take part in very few, or infrequent, social activities would be likely to go shopping more often, if
only to maintain a contact with the 'outside world'.
The computed variable which sought to represent
degree of social participation (already referred to
in the previous chapter) was, therefore, compared with
shopping frequency. The resulting association is
negligible but, if anything, there is a tendency for
those who take part in fewer social activities to
shop less frequently than the others. Similarly,
looking at just the particular social activity of
home visiting, it appears that people tend to do
'everything or nothing' - that is, the frequency of
home visiting (with both relatives and friends) is
positively related to shopping frequency.

It is the existence of gender-role differentiation which makes women the chief family shoppers as
well as the child minders but, on the other hand, it
would seem likely that the age and number of young
children that a woman has will have some influence
on her frequency of shopping trips, due to the
problems of keeping control of children at the same
time as making purchases. (The time-budget survey
of the previous day's activities indicates that
children accompanied their mothers on 87 per cent of
shopping trips made on the day before interview.)
The questionnaire results indicate that women with
two or more young children are slightly less likely
to shop every day than those with only one child

under five. They are also more likely to go shopping only once a week or less often (see Appendix D, Table D18).

The age of the youngest child in the family would also be expected to influence shopping frequency, since older children are much easier to keep under control than are young toddlers, while very few shops have facilities to enable women with prams to enter. However, in fact, there appears to be very little difference in the propensity to shop on a daily basis as between women with babies or toddlers, and others, although those with a child under two are slightly more likely to go shopping only once a week or less often. Since children are an obvious handicap to efficient shopping it would seem likely that those with a child at nursery school would be more likely to shop frequently than those whose children are at home all day. The reverse, however, is the case; 45 per cent of women with no child at nursery school or playgroup go shopping every day, while only 30 per cent of those with children in such daytime care shop on a daily basis. Perhaps, in this case, shopping is seen as a way of simply taking children out and as 'something to do', rather than as a purely servicing task (see also, Gittus, 1976,63).

Having considered some potential personal influences on shopping behaviour, such as class and income, car availability and child care responsibilities, it is of great importance to take into account also the question of supply - of the provision of opportunity in terms of shopping centres; their size, location and accessibility to respondents. Map 2 shows the distribution of shops in the borough of Merton. Shopping centres are graded into size categories according to the number of shops which they contain, although there is an additional category, Grade 5 centres, which are classified as District shopping centres (Hillier, Parker May & Rowden, 1974,5). This report describes District centres as 'shopping centres which satisfy the main weekly shopping needs of the population for food and also routine durable goods'.) As a first stage in considering respondents' use of different centres, the frequency of weekday shopping can be compared with the grade of shopping centre normally used for such shopping.

Table 12 indicates the existence of two other centre categories; Grade 6 centres have been categorised as minor shopping centres outside the borough of Merton and Grade 7 centres are major centres outside the borough (for example, Croydon, Kingston,

141

Map 2 Merton: Distribution and grades of shopping centres

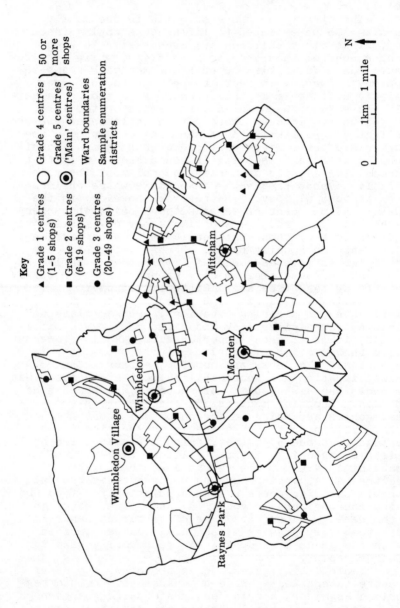

Key

▲ Grade 1 centres (1–5 shops)

■ Grade 2 centres (6–19 shops)

● Grade 3 centres (20–49 shops)

○ Grade 4 centres ⎫ 50 or
⦿ Grade 5 centres ⎬ more
('Main' centres) ⎭ shops

— Ward boundaries

— Sample enumeration districts

Wimbledon Village

Wimbledon

Raynes Park

Morden

Mitcham

N

0   1km 1 mile

Tooting, Wandsworth (Arndale Centre) and Central London). The overall grading of centres should not be viewed as representing a simple ordinal scale. The relationship between frequency of shopping and grade of shopping centre, illustrated in Table 12, is clearly significant, there being a decline in the likelihood of daily shopping with an increase in shopping centre size, for centres within the borough (centres graded 1 to 5 inclusive). The frequency of use of Grade 7 centres is, however, surprising high. It is interesting that Grade 6 centres are visited comparatively infrequently and this is almost cert- ainly related to their structural characteristics. Many of these minor centres just outside the borough (for example, North Cheam) contain large super- markets, which are the type of shops tending to be visited less frequently than small shops. Overall, it is important to note that half of all respondents (51 per cent) normally shop at District centres within the borough (Grade 5 centres); the next largest category comprises those using Grade 2 (local) shopping centres (17 per cent). Only 16 per cent of respondents normally use centres outside the borough for weekday shopping, despite their relative proximity to Merton and the lack of a 'Major Strategic Shopping Centre' (as defined by the 1968 Greater London Development Plan (Hillier Parker May & Rowden, 1974,3))within the borough.

Social class seems to be of some importance in determining the grade of centre used for weekday shopping, higher class people being more likely to use main borough centres than lower class respond- ents; for example, 63 per cent of those with husbands in professional and managerial occupations shop in main centres while, in comparison, only 35 per cent of those with husbands who are partly- skilled or unskilled manual workers do so. If car availability is taken into account, an interesting situation emerges. In the case of respondents to whom a car is not available, there is no relation- ship at all between social class and the grade of shopping centre patronised but in the case of car users a strong relationship exists. Related to both social class and car availability is the fact that higher income respondents are also much more likely to shop at main borough centres than are those from lower income families. The lowest income/class respondents are, however, more likely to go shopping outside the borough, probably because these centres contain the major cheap supermarkets. This is des- pite the fact that (without exception) these women

Table 12   Cross-tabulation of frequency of weekday shopping, with grade of shopping centre used for weekday shopping (percentages in brackets)

	1 or 2	3 or 4	5	6	7	Total
Every day	40(54.1)	24(46.2)	59(30.3)	8(24.2)	11(42.3)	142(37.4)
2 or 3 times per week	26(35.1)	22(42.3)	110(56.4)	14(42.4)	11(42.3)	183(48.2)
Once a week or less often	8(10.8)	6(11.5)	26(13.3)	11(33.3)	4(15.4)	55(14.5)
Total	74(100.0) (19.5)	52(100.0) (13.7)	195(100.0) (51.3)	33(100.0) (8.7)	26(100.0) (6.8)	380(100.0) (100.0)

chi-square = 26.36   (p=.001)   (20 missing cases)

do not have cars available to them for use on weekdays.

As might be expected, there is a close relationship between the grade of centre normally used
for weekday shopping and whether or not the shops
actually used are the closest to home (see Appendix
D, Table D19). Practically everyone using centres
of Grades 1 to 4 (small local, to large, borough
centres) is, in fact, using the closest shops to home
and this, in turn, accounts, at least partly, for the
greater frequency of shopping taking place in these
centres which has already been noted. (Results show
that there is, in fact, a close relationship between
shopping frequency and whether or not the centre
used is the closest to home). In contrast, only
just over half of all respondents using District
centres (53 per cent) are using their nearest shops
on weekdays, fewer than 40 per cent using minor
shopping centres outside the borough are doing so
and no one who normally visits a major centre outside the borough is using the nearest shops to home.
In addition, as the grade of the nearest shopping
centre to home gets higher, the actual use of these
nearest shops increases; for example, only 34 per
cent of respondents who live closest to small local
(Grade 1) centres are actually using their nearest
shops for weekday shopping, while 90 per cent of
those whose nearest shops comprise a District (Grade
5) centre normally use this centre. Also of importance is the fact that respondents who normally shop
in centres outside the borough live, almost exclusively, closest to centres of Grades 1 and 2.

In answer to the question: 'Would you describe
the shops you normally use, on weekdays, as local
shops - that is, are they within ordinary walking
distance of your home?'- 88 per cent of respondents
answer in the affirmative. Not unexpectedly, respondents' identification of their centres as local
or non-local is strongly related to their frequency
of shopping (see Appendix D, Table D20); 41 per cent
of those using 'local' shops go shopping every day
compared to only 9 per cent of those using 'non-
local' shops, while the situation is reversed when
considering those who shop only once a week or less
often.

The reasons given by respondents for using
either local or non-local shops are of some interest.
Of those who use local shops, 30 per cent state that
they do not go further afield to bigger centres because of the difficulties and inconvenience involved
in travelling, 21 per cent mention the problem of

taking children with them in particular and another
18 per cent state simply that shopping further away
from home is 'too much trouble'. For 20 per cent of
these respondents, the 'local' shops already comprise a main shopping centre, while a further 16 per
cent assert their lack of need to shop further
afield on weekdays since they do most of their shopping on a 'main' trip each week. The expense of
fares and the lack of time available are given as
other, less important, reasons, while 10 per cent
simply state that they 'prefer to use local shops'.
Of the 46 respondents who normally use non-local
shops, 33 (72 per cent) give as a reason for doing
so the fact that local shops are too expensive
26 (57 per cent) cite the limited range of goods
available in local shops. No other reason is mentioned by any significant number of respondents.

It is hardly surprising that such a large percentage of respondents (88 per cent) use 'local'
shops for weekday shopping, since the vast majority
of people in Merton live very close to shops: 73 per
cent of respondents live within one quarter of a
mile walk of a shopping centre containing at least
six shops (as defined in Hillier Parker May & Rowden,
1974). These women are more likely to shop on a
daily basis than are those who live further away but
the difference is not very great, probably because
most of the latter live within half a mile of such a
centre (70 per cent of respondents report having
travelled for no more than ten minutes to shops on
the previous day).

b)   'Main' shopping trips

Besides weekday shopping, respondents were also
questioned as to whether they go on a main shopping
trip at any time, for example, at the weekends or in
the evening. 74 per cent state that they do go on
such a trip and the percentage is even higher where
the shopping centre used on weekdays is of a low
grade (see Table 13), probably because weekday users
of small local shops are more likely to stock up on
major items on a main shopping trip. If a bigger
shopping centre is used for ordinary weekday trips,
respondents are much less likely to go on a main
shopping trip as well, although even of those normally using major centres outside the borough for
weekday shopping, half also go on a main shopping
trip. Distance from home to a main shopping centre
does not seem to be important at all in determining
whether a main shopping trip will be undertaken,

Table 13   Cross-tabulation of use of main shopping trip, with grade of centre used for weekday shopping

(Percentages in brackets)

	1	2	3	4	5	6	7	Total
Yes	9(90.0)	54(84.4)	37(82.2)	5(71.4)	134(68.7)	27(81.8)	13(50.0)	279(73.4)
No	1(10.0)	10(15.6)	8(17.8)	2(28.6)	61(31.3)	6(18.2)	13(50.0)	101(26.6)
Total	10(100)	64(100)	45(100)	7(100)	195(100)	33(100)	26(100)	380(100)

chi-square = 17.86   (p=.007)   (20 missing cases)

despite the fact that half of all main shopping
trips are to District centres within Merton and a
further quarter are to major centres outside the
borough. It might be thought that the availability
of a car would be the intervening variable here and
indeed, 32 per cent of main shopping trips are undertaken when there is a car available for use but
amongst those who do not use a car for such trips,
about the same percentage live more than 20 minutes
walk (or one mile) from a main centre as amongst
those who do use a car.

While 60 per cent of weekday shopping, overall,
is carried out at the closest available shops to
home, only 13 per cent of respondents go to their
nearest shopping centre for main shopping trips and
three-quarters of these are, in fact, using Grade 5
(District) centres. Since main shopping trips,
therefore, often require additional effort and are
less convenient than weekday shopping, it is not
surprising that 34 per cent of respondents who make
these trips are accompanied on them by their husbands, a further 8 per cent go with relatives or
friends and 22 per cent take the opportunity to
leave their children with someone else so that they
can go alone.

Women who go on a main shopping trip as well as
their weekday shopping are most likely to live in
families with average or above average incomes,
while those from the lowest and highest income
families tend not to go on a main trip, the latter
presumably because economy in shopping is not a
necessity and the lowest income respondents
possibly because of a lack of personal mobility. As
mentioned earlier, both family income and social
class are related to car availability but in this
case social class does not appear to be an important
determinant of activity even when car availability
is taken into account. However, considering only
those respondents who do undertake main shopping
trips, it is clear that higher class people are more
likely to use District centres within the borough
for this purpose, while those with husbands in manual
occupations are relatively more likely to use either
local shopping centres or major centres outside
Merton. The situation with regard to income groups
is much less clear-cut, although there is a tendency
for middle-income people to shop outside the borough,
as compared to other groups.

Those who go out to work might normally be
expected to have little time available for weekday
shopping and, therefore, be expected to go on a main

shopping trip at another time. However, it has already been shown that women who go out to work every weekday are most likely to go shopping on a daily basis, as are those who work longer hours each week. Bearing these results in mind, it is not, therefore, surprising that outside workers are, in fact, slightly less likely to engage in main shopping expeditions than either home-workers or full-time housewives (see Appendix D, Table D21). Women who work at home are the most likely to go on a main shopping trip, presumably because they are the most 'tied to home' of any group during weekdays. Nearly half of all employed respondents work only in the evenings or at weekends and, as might be expected, these women are much less likely than others to go on a main shopping trip outside normal weekday hours. Those who do paid work on every weekday and/or for longer hours each week are also less likely to undertake a main shopping trip than those who work less frequently and/or for shorter hours, possibly because it is convenient for the former to do all their shopping on a daily basis and also because of the lesser need for economy with a bigger salary coming in.

2.   Accompanying other members of the family

Numerically by far the most important activity outside the home, reported by respondents in the time-budget survey of the previous day's activities, involved taking children to school or collecting them from school (337 separate trips were made for this purpose). 69 per cent of respondents with children at primary school actually accompanied their children to and/or from school on the day before interview. This percentage is perhaps surprisingly low, considering that Merton is very much an 'urban' borough with all the attendant problems of traffic danger but, in fact, it probably indicates considerable sharing of this specific child-care task between mothers (and in some cases with husbands or other adults). This hypothesis would seem to be supported by the fact that 27 per cent of women with children at nursery school on the previous day did not accompany them to school personally; it would certainly appear unlikely that such very young children would be permitted to travel alone. Childminders and friends are obviously important in many cases for taking children to and from school; eight respondents, for example, without any children over five themselves or any children under five at

149

nursery school are recorded as having accompanied
children to school on the day before interview.

Nowhere in the borough of Merton is the journey
to school a very long one; 80 per cent of respondents report journey times of ten minutes or less. 79
per cent of trips to and from school on the day before interview took place on foot and a further 18
per cent by car. Although walking is, therefore,
clearly the predominant means of getting to school,
it is interesting that the biggest single number of
car trips on the previous day (35 per cent) were
made for the purpose of taking children to school;
this compares with the next most important activity
involving car use - shopping - which occupied 28 per
cent of all trips by car. Shopping is often combined with taking children to school, as indicated by
the time-budget survey which shows 70 such activity
combinations having occurred on the day before
interview, out of a total of 116 activity combinations involving accompanying children. In contrast,
221 trips were made solely for the latter purpose,
while 166 were made entirely for the purpose of
shopping or obtaining services.

It is interesting to speculate about the
implicit value of taking children to school from the
point of view of the mother. It may, in fact,
provide the only form of real social contact which a
woman has with others of her age and domestic circumstances. It was, therefore, thought useful to calcul-
ate the length of time actually spent taking children to school (when this was not combined with any
other activity), less the time spent in travelling
there and back and to compare this amount of time
with indicators of the number of other activities
undertaken and the social characteristics of the
respondents concerned. Results from this exercise
show that the length of time spent at school is, in
fact, positively related both to the number of activities undertaken during the day and specifically to
the probability of making a home visit to a friend
or relative. It does not, therefore, appear that this
type of 'social contact' acts as a compensatory form
of interaction. The clearest relationships are those
between lengh of time spent at school on the one
hand and both social class and tenure mode on the
other. As length of time increases, so does the
likelihood of having a husband in a manual occupation and of living as a council tenant. People who
live in flats are also observed to spend longer at
school than those who live in houses.

In addition to accompanying children to school,

women are also regularly called upon to accompany
other members of the family (for example, chauffeur-
ing husbands to the station to go to work or to
take their children to out-of-school activities,
such as ballet or music lessons). The time-budget
survey reveals that 22 respondents took part in such
activities on the day before interview. Two-thirds
of the trips involved were made by car and the remainder on foot. Only 7 of the journeys took longer
than ten minutes and all but two involved taking
young children along as well.

3. Voluntary work

The remaining form of unpaid work undertaken by
women which should be considered is 'community servicing', either in the form of direct voluntary work
with various institutions or, on a more informal
basis, the provision of daily services for a neighbour or relative. 18 respondents state that they are
called upon to perform this latter type of service,
of whom eight are caring for parents and a further
four for other relatives; only two respondents claim
to be providing a daily service for a neighbour.
Voluntary work in the community is undertaken
by 29 respondents. These women are relatively more
likely to have received a higher education; in fact,
while women educated beyond the age of 18 make up
only 17 per cent of the total sample, they comprise
38 per cent of the respondents undertaking voluntary
work in the community (see Appendix D, Table D22).
Voluntary workers also tend to be older than the
sample as a whole (62 per cent are aged 30 or over,
compared to 45 per cent of respondents overall),
they are over-represented amongst women with husbands
in non-manual occupations and are more likely to
come from families with above average or high
incomes. The latter point is important because it
might immediately be concluded that women from higher
income families would not be 'forced' to take paid
employment and, therefore, could spend time on voluntary work in the community. This supposition would,
however, be quite false. Respondents who do paid
work are also more likely to undertake voluntary
work as well (see Appendix D, Table D23). This is
especially true of those who work at home who,
although making up only 9 per cent of the total
sample, comprise 28 per cent of the respondents who
do voluntary work. No voluntary workers have more
than two children under five, and they are, in fact,
most likely to have only one young child. The

constraint of constant child care also tends to be
lessened for these women, in that three-quarters of
them have their young children at nursery school
(compared to less than half of those who do not
undertake voluntary work) and the majority of these
are in half-time state nursery schooling rather than
attending playgroups with shorter hours. Nevertheless, only eight respondents undertake voluntary work
at a time when their children do not have to accompany them.

Voluntary work is undertaken mainly on a once-a-
week basis or less frequently; only six respondents
claim to do voluntary work on more than one occasion
each week. Most voluntary workers walk to the location where they perform their 'community service'
and, in fact, only five respondents travel by car,
although twelve have a car available for use on weekdays and are able to drive it. This is presumably
because of the short distances involved and, indeed,
17 women have only a five minute journey and a
further eight respondents travel for no more than
ten minutes.

Only 29 respondents at present undertake voluntary work on weekdays but as many as 49 others would
like to do so if they were not constrained by other
commitments, notably their children's need for care.
These 'potential' voluntary workers almost exactly
complement in personal characteristics those respondents who already do voluntary work in that they are
more likely to have husbands in manual occupations,
to come from families with lower incomes and, in
particular, to have been less well-educated. It is
especially notable that all respondents who left
school before the age of 16 either undertake voluntary work now or else would like to do so. Most
'potential' voluntary workers are at present full-
time housewives although a further nine respondents
who are in outside employment would like to do voluntary work, in addition to the six who already do so.

In summary, 'unpaid work' activities (particularly shopping and taking children to school) have been
shown to dominate the out-of-home weekday activities
of women with young children. The **vast majority of**
respondents shop for food or general goods at least
two or three times a week during weekdays, the actual
frequency of shopping being statistically related to
social class (as measured by the socio-economic
group of the husband) and car availability, working
hours (for those in paid employment) and the grade of
shopping centre actually patronised. Almost all respondents normally use 'local' shops (reflecting to a

large extent the widespread distribution of shopping
centres in the borough of Merton). Nearly three-
quarters of the sample undertake 'main' shopping
trips as well as weekday shopping and this form of
activity is closely related in particular to the
grade of shopping centre used on weekdays.

Accompanying children to and from school is
statistically the most important out-of-home
activity undertaken by respondents. Almost all
journeys-to-school are very short and the vast majority take place on foot. Taking children to school
is often combined with shopping trips.

Voluntary work in the community is undertaken
at present by relatively few respondents on weekdays,
although a larger number would like to be involved
in such 'unpaid work' if other commitments did not
prevent them from doing so.

Leisure activities

As pointed out previously, many 'leisure' activities
may be undertaken primarily as aspects of child care,
rather than to promote the respondents' own leisure
opportunities. However, it is convenient for the
purposes of discussion to consider park use, home
visiting and other educational and social
activities as 'leisure' activities. In no way is it
intended to suggest that such activities are necessarily 'discretionary' in nature, nor that they may
not, in fact,provide absolutely essential contacts
with the 'outside world' for many women with young
children.

1.   Park use

In contrast with the figure of 60 per cent of
respondents who went shopping on the day prior to
interview, only 54 women (or 13 per cent of the
total sample) made trips to parks on the previous
day. This was despite the fact that the survey was
carried out during a period of very fine weather and
also that, in answer to the direct question: 'How
often, on average, do you visit a park or children's
playground with your child(ren), on weekdays during
the daytime?' _ 20 per cent of respondents state that
they visit a park every day or nearly every day and
a further 27 per cent that they make a park visit
two or three times each week. Only 15 per cent (60
respondents) say that they never visit a park on
weekdays.

Park visiting activity has often been

associated in the literature with a middle class way
of life (see, for example, Sessons, 1963). It is
interesting, therefore, to begin the analysis of
recreation data with a consideration of the
relationship between the frequency of park-visiting
and social class (measured in terms of the husband's
socio-economic group). It is clear that a higher
proportion of working-class wives never go to parks
than the wives of non-manual workers, while the lowest visiting frequencies of all are found amongst
women with husbands in partly-skilled and unskilled
manual jobs (see Appendix D, Table D24). The overall relationship between social class and park
visiting frequency is,however, negligible and remains so even when car availability is taken into
account. Indeed, the availability of a car, in itself, appears to be of very little importance in
influencing the frequency of park visiting; 46 per
cent of respondents who have a car available for use
on weekdays (and are able to drive it) state that
they visit a park more than once a week, while 37 per
cent of those without a car available do so. The
general lack of importance of car availability presumably relates to the fact that 87 per cent of respondents normally walk when they visit a park (and,
indeed, three-quarters of women who actually visited
a park on the day prior to interview travelled on
foot).
     Since social class and car availability do not
prove to be major determinants of park visiting
activity, it is interesting to consider other possible measures of 'social status' in their relationship with recreation patterns. Since the inculcation
of 'social values' can be directly related to the
process of education, it would seem reasonable to
expect that the more highly educated respondents
would tend to use public open spaces more than those
whose formal education was more limited. This hypothesis, in general, appears to be correct (see
Appendix D, Table D25); in particular, the most
highly educated respondents seem least likely to
avoid park use altogether. There is very little
relationship between park visiting and family income,
although it is interesting that 26 per cent of respondents in the lowest income category (under £3000
per annum) never visit parks, compared to 15 per cent
of the overall sample.
     Viewing the different findings relating 'social
status' variables to park visiting together for a
moment, it is clear that it is the lower class, less
well-educated and lower income respondents who are

the least likely to visit parks on weekdays at all.
Since Chapter 5 has already demonstrated the close
link between such respondents and a propensity to be
in outside paid employment, it would seem likely
that it is,in fact,employment status which is determining park use (basically considered to be a leisure
activity), rather than any level of 'social status'.
Table 14,however,shows a total lack of relationship
between park visiting frequency and present employment status, although it is true that, of respondents
in paid employment, those' who work shorter hours each
week tend to visit parks more frequently. There is
also no clear relationship between the frequency of
weekday shopping (selected as a major aspect of
'unpaid work') and the frequency of park visiting.
Recreation activity does not,therefore,seem to relate
to other, more dominant, types of out-of-home
activity in any definite way.

Since the question in the schedule referring to
park visiting frequency specifically refers to visits
in the company of children (and, in fact, only four
respondents went to parks on the day before interview
without their children), it is interesting to examine
the extent to which the number and age of young
children affects visiting patterns. The number of
young children (under five years) does not appear to
influence park visiting at all but the age of the
youngest child in the family does seem to be an
important deciding factor. While there is little
difference between respondents with different aged
children in terms of frequent park visiting, the
difference is very marked when only those respondents
who never visit parks are considered (see Appendix D,
Table D26). 65 per cent of this latter group have a
youngest child aged under two years (compared to 49
per cent of the total sample). On the other hand,
women with a youngest child aged four are also over-
represented amongst non-park users. There is obviously much less need to take very young babies to parks
than older children, so it is not surprising that
one-quarter of mothers with a child less than one
year old never go to parks on weekdays. It is rather
more surprising that 19 per cent of respondents with
a youngest child aged four also never visit parks.
Further investigation, however, reveals that these
women are more likely to be out at work and working
for longer hours than the sample as a whole.

The personal characteristics of respondents have
often been assumed to determine recreation activity
but in the case of this study only the respondent's
educational level and the age of her youngest child

NON-EMPLOYMENT ACTIVITIES

Table 14   Cross-tabulation of frequency of park visiting, with employment status (and work location)

(Percentages in brackets)

	Out at work	Work at home	Not in employment	Total
More than once a week	32(41.6)	14(37.8)	114(39.9)	160(40.0)
Once a week or less often	34(44.2)	18(48.6)	128(44.8)	180(45.0)
Never	11(14.3)	5(13.5)	44(15.4)	60(15.0)
Total	77(100.0)	37(100.0)	286(100.0)	400(100.0)

chi-square = 0.33   (p=.99)

have been shown to act as important determinants of park visiting frequency. Another factor often mentioned in the literature is the importance of distance to parks; many writers have demonstrated the significance of one quarter of a mile (or ten minutes, walking time) as the clearly defined limit for daily park visiting activity (see Chapter 3). Map 3 shows the distribution of parks and children's playgrounds in the borough of Merton, illustrating their very widespread occurrence. In fact, 82 per cent of respondents live within one quarter of a mile walk of a small local or local park (defined as Grades 1 and 2 parks by Merton council (London Borough of Merton, Appendix B,1974)). In no case is the distance to a park very great (generally less than ½ mile) and no relationship is evident in the data between frequency of park visiting and whether or not the respondent lives within one quarter of a mile of a park. On the other hand, as many as 72 per cent of respondents live more than one quarter of a mile away from a playground, a fact which can be assumed to be of some importance considering the age of the children involved in this survey. Frequency of park visiting does prove to be closely related to distance from a playground; as the former decreases, it is increasingly likely that respondents will live outside one quarter of a mile from the nearest playground.

From previous studies (e.g. Greater London Council Planning Dept., 1968,6; Balmer, 1974,116; Hillman et al., 1976,91; Garbrecht, 1978,14) we would expect most people with young children to travel for no more than ten minutes to reach a park used on weekdays and, in fact, 80 per cent of respondents using parks in this survey do have journeys of ten minutes or less to get to their chosen parks, regardless of the means of transport employed (for example, 80 per cent of those who walk and 86 per cent of those who go by car, travel for less than ten minutes). Nearly half of all park users, in fact, visit open spaces within five minutes of their homes and these are the respondents who are most likely to go to parks on a daily basis (see Appendix D, Table D27). Those with journey times of more than ten minutes tend to visit parks less frequently. This generalised information on journey times is reinforced by the results of the time-budget survey which show that three-quarters of respondents making trips to parks on the day before interview travelled for no more than ten minutes, while 46 per cent made journeys taking only five minutes or less.

Map 3   Merton: Distribution of parks and children's playgrounds

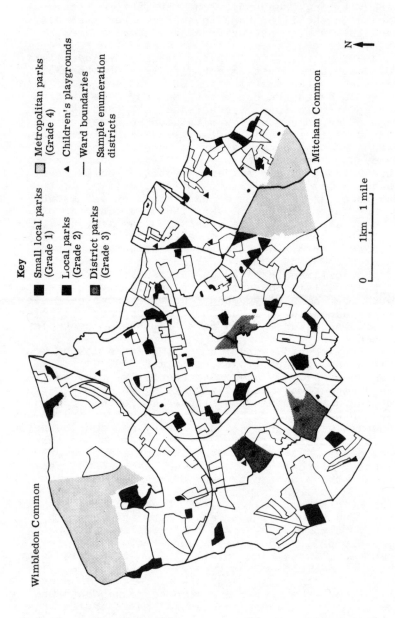

Journey times to parks are short, both because the distribution of parks is relatively uniform throughout Merton and also because the majority of respondents (66 per cent) normally visit the open space which is closest to home. Table 15 demonstrates the substantial positive association between journey times and whether or not the park normally visited is the closest to home. It is interesting to note that 29 respondents visit parks which are not the closest to their homes but which nevertheless lie within five minutes travelling time of home. In some cases this is definitely due to the high density of open space in certain areas of the borough but in other cases short journeys are obviously the result of travelling by car rather than walking, since no less than 71 per cent of trips made by car to parks involve journeys to open space areas which are not the closest to home.

Table 15   Cross-tabulation of whether or not park visited is the closest open space, with journey time to park or playground normally visited

(Percentages in brackets)

	5 mins or less	6-10 mins	More than 10 mins	Total
Yes	132(82.0)	66(62.9)	22(32.4)	220(65.9)
No	29(18.0)	39(37.1)	46(67.6)	114(34.1)
Total	161(100.0)	105(100.0)	68(100.0)	334(100.0)

gamma = .61   (66 missing cases)

The choice of park to be visited clearly relates strongly to proximity but it is nevertheless true that one-third of respondents using parks on weekdays do not visit the closest open space to their homes. This fact raises the issue of the quality of open space available - a factor which is notoriously difficult to define. Certainly, quality can not be simply equated with size, although correlation of the areal extent of the nearest park to the respondent's home, with the variable defining whether or not the park normally visited is the closest to home, gives a coefficient of $r=.11$ ($p=.03$). People do not necessarily visit the closest open space just because it is big but size does appear to act as one determining factor.

The possible importance of a playground in the park which is generally visited has already been alluded to in relation to visiting frequency. For women with young children the existence of a playground could quite reasonably stand as a measure of 'quality' of open space. It is certainly true that nearly 80 per.cent of respondents visit parks with a children's playground in them (compared to 66 per cent who visit the nearest open space of any sort). Women in the sample are clearly quite prepared to travel a little further from home if a park with a playground can thereby be visited. A children's playground may provide not only an interesting play area for the children but also a social focus for the mothers themselves (see Garbrecht, 1978,16). For some women with young children, meeting friends in a park may provide a chance for social interaction not obtainable in any other way. It is interesting that as many as 50 respondents specifically mention 'meeting friends' in describing the way they spend their time while accompanying children to the park. The use of a park with a playground tends to increase as the age of the youngest child rises; thus, only 16 per cent of respondents with a youngest child aged three or four normally visit parks which do not have play facilities, while one-quarter of those with a youngest child under two years of age do so.

Another measure of park 'quality' is provided by the grading system used by Merton council; open space in the borough is graded in terms of both size and perceived importance (which is related to catchment area) (see, London Borough of Merton, Appendix B, 1974). Grade 1 parks are 'small local' parks, Grade 2 are 'local' parks, Grade 3, 'district' parks and Grade 4 are termed 'metropolitan' parks. There is a negligible association overall between the grade of park which is normally visited and visiting frequency (see Appendix D, Table D28) but of great interest is the fact that Grade 4 (metropolitan) parks are the most likely to be visited more than once a week, despite the fact that 68 per cent of users of Grade 4 parks are not using the closest open space to their homes. This suggests that these areas of open space are viewed as being of a higher 'quality' by at least some respondents.

People are prepared to travel for a longer time to visit higher grade parks; for example, while 53 per cent of visitors to Grade 1 parks travel for no

longer than five minutes, only 37 per cent of Grade 4
park users do so. Since there are only two open
space areas in the borough which are accorded Grade 4
(metropolitan) status - namely, Wimbledon and Mitcham
Commons - it is obvious that most respondents would
have to travel some considerable distance to reach
them. It is not, therefore, surprising that while,
overall, 87 per cent of respondents using parks on
weekdays make their journeys on foot, no less than 60
per cent of those who normally visit one of these two
major open space areas travel by car. Car availability is, of course, closely related to social class
and, in fact, 88 per cent of those with a car available
who visit Grade 4 parks have husbands in professional
and managerial occupations, while the remaining 12
per cent are married to other non-manual workers. By
comparison, for those without a car normally available on weekdays there is no apparent relationship
between social class and the grade of park visited.
While 'metropolitan' parks may be distinguished as
higher 'quality' open space areas by some respondents and, therefore, be visited in preference to
closer, more accessible parks, it is nevertheless
true that 82 per cent of respondents normally use
either 'small local' or 'local' parks on weekdays.
There is a definite relationship between the grade of
park visited and the age of the respondent's youngest
child; those with a baby (under the age of 1) most
commonly visit these smaller parks (88 per cent do
so), whilst those with a youngest child aged 4 are
the least likely to do so (73 per cent). This
tendency is even more marked when respondents with
only one child under five are considered separately.
Grade 1 parks, which are often extremely small in
total area, are definitely the least favoured open
space areas. While approximately three-quarters of
respondents living closest to parks of Grades 2, 3 or
4 normally use parks of these grades, respectively,
only 31 per cent of respondents living closest to
Grade 1 parks actually use them in preference to
other parks.
     The above discussion has sought to emphasise
that both proximity and 'quality' (reflected in the
existence of a playground or the grade of park
visited) influence a respondent's choice of open
space to be visited. There remains one further
factor to be taken into account when considering
weekday park visiting - namely, whether or not the
respondent has a garden which can be used for
children's play. A number of writers in the field of
recreation (e.g. Halkett, 1974) have stressed the

importance of gardens as alternative recreation sites
to public open space areas. The results from this
study suggest that a higher percentage of flat
dwellers (22 per cent) than of the sample overall
(17 per cent) go to parks on a daily basis and also
that all respondents living in high blocks of flats
visit parks at least once a week, with half of them
going every day (see also, Gittus, 1976,67). Surprisingly, however, when one takes the sample as a whole
there is no difference at all between those without
a garden and those with a garden in which their
children play in terms of the frequency of park
visiting, although people without a garden seem to be
prepared to travel for a longer time to get to a park
than those with gardens. 32 respondents (9 per cent)
have a garden but say that their children do not play
in it. These are predominantly the mothers of very
young children, who do not 'play' at all in the normal sense of the word (71 per cent of this group have
a youngest child under two years of age). In fact,
over half (57 per cent) of women with only one child,
where this child is less than one year old, fall into the category of having a garden in which children
are said not to play.

The possession of a garden in itself does not
prove to be a very useful differentiating variable in
this study, since 92 per cent of respondents do have
a garden (including half of the flat-dwellers in the
sample). The size and type of garden possessed was
not considered in this survey but these factors are
likely to be of importance in determining the relative use of garden and open space areas, respectively,
for children's play.

2. Home visiting

Visits to the homes of relatives or friends, combined with visits made to respondents' homes by relatives or friends, involved no less than 225 people in
the sample on the day before interview - 56 per cent
of the total. This type of activity, therefore,
clearly represents the most important 'leisure'
activity on weekdays for women with young children.
As suggested in Chapter 2, home visiting may be
emphasised by this group because of their relative
inability to take part in other outside activities.
No distinction is here drawn between visits away from
the respondents' homes and those made to their homes,
since most visiting obviously occurs on a reciprocal
basis.

Visits involving friends seem to be rather more

common than those involving relatives (the former
outnumbering the latter in the ratio 1.5:1 approximately, in the results of the time-budget survey).
70 respondents had a visit with relatives on the
previous day, compared to 131 people who had a visit
with friends, while 24 respondents visited both
friends and relatives. Questioned directly concerning the frequency of visiting (or receiving visits
from) relatives and friends, 108 respondents (29 per
cent) state that they see relatives at least twice a
week, on weekdays during the daytime, while as many
as 231 respondents (62 per cent) claim to see friends
at least twice a week. Clearly, the availability of
friends and family members in the immediate environment influences the possibility of making visits and
it is important to note that while 57 per cent of
respondents have no relatives living in the local
area (defined as that area within ordinary walking
distance of home), only 7 per cent claim to have no
local friends (and nearly half of these have lived in
their local area for less than a year, compared to 8
per cent in the sample as a whole). In fact, visiting
frequencies differ very little when one considers
only those respondents with local relatives and/or
friends; 78 per cent of those with relatives living
nearby visit them at least once a week on weekdays
(51 per cent make visits on at least two weekdays
each week), while 80 per cent of respondents with
local friends see them at least once a week (and 64
per cent, at least twice each week).

Visits exchanged with both relatives and friends
outside the local area are of considerably less numerical significance. 31 per cent of respondents
with non-local relatives and 29 per cent of those
with non-local friends never visit them (or receive
visits from them) on weekdays. Actual visiting
frequencies are, however, slightly higher where relatives are involved rather than friends; in fact, one-
third of all respondents with non-local relatives
visit them at least once a week on weekdays while
only one in five of those with friends living outside
the local area visit them this frequently. While the
extent of visiting activity differs as between local
and non-local friends and relatives, actual patterns
of visiting do not seem to vary substantially when
one considers differences in age, social class,
mmodation and so on. (This is in contrast to the
conclusions of Tallman (1969,66) concerning social
class differences in non-local visiting)). It was,
therefore, considered justifiable, for most purposes,
to combine local and non-local visiting and to

Table 16   Cross-tabulation of frequency of family visiting, with socio-economic group of husband

(percentages in brackets)

	Professional & Managerial	Other non-manual	Skilled Manual	Partly-Skilled & Unskilled	Total
At least twice a week	27(22.0)	19(24.1)	50(36.2)	12(37.5)	108(29.0)
Once a week or less often (includes never)	96(78.0)	60(75.9)	88(63.8)	20(62.5)	264(71.0)
Total	123(100.0)	79(100.0)	138(100.0)	32(100.0)	372(100.0)

gamma = -.25   (28 missing cases)

Table 17 Cross-tabulation of frequency of friend visiting, with socio-economic group of husband

(percentages in brackets)

	Professional & Managerial	Other non-manual	Skilled Manual	Partly-Skilled & Unskilled	Total
At least twice a week	82(66.7)	54(68.4)	81(58.7)	14(43.8)	231(62.1)
Once a week or less often (includes never)	41(33.3)	25(31.6)	57(41.3)	18(56.3)	141(37.9)
Total	123(100.0)	79(100.0)	138(100.0)	32(100.0)	372(100.0)

gamma = .19   (28 missing cases)

consider home visits in only two categories: visits
with relatives and visits with friends, respectively.

Much of the literature previously referred to in
Chapters 2 and 3 of this thesis makes specific reference to social class differences in visiting
patterns and it is interesting, therefore, to
commence this analysis of home visiting activity by
comparing Tables 16 and 17, which indicate the relationships between social class (measured in terms of
the husband's socio-economic group) and frequent
visiting with relatives and friends, respectively.
It is readily apparent that the results here obtained
serve to reinforce those found in other studies;
working class people are the most likely to visit
relatives frequently on weekdays, while middle-class
people are the most likely to visit friends. It is,
however, important to emphasise yet again that
friends tend generally to be visited much more often
than relatives and this is true of people in all
social class groups. Thus, for example, while 38 per
cent of respondents with husbands in partly-skilled
and unskilled manual employment visit relatives at
least twice a week (the highest percentage of any
social class group), 44 per cent of the same group of
respondents visit friends this frequently (which is,
nevertheless, the lowest percentage of any social
class group).

The level of education attained by the respondent is closely related to social class (as already
mentioned in the previous Chapter, the correlation
coefficient between the two variables is r=.46
(p=.001)) and the data dealing with home visiting
underline this fact. The association between education level and family and friend visiting, respectively, is, in fact, stronger than any other relationship concerned with visiting (see Appendix D, Table
D29). The association is particularly close with
respect to visits with relatives, those leaving
school before the age of 16 being more than three
times as likely to make such visits at least twice a
week as those who left full-time education after the
age of 18. Here again, however, it must be borne in
mind that visits with friends are of greater numerical significance for all education groups; thus,
while 40 per cent of those who left school before the
age of 16 frequently visit their relatives on weekdays, 59 per cent of the same group enjoy frequent
visits with their friends. Because of the close
association between education level and social class,
the relationships between education level and

visiting patterns are substantially reduced by taking
social class into account. Since there is a stronger
theoretical reason for considering social class
variations in visiting patterns and since class and
education clearly represent two aspects of the same
'social' dimension, social class, rather than education level, will be used as a major controlling
variable in the remainder of this section.

Alongside the consideration of social class
differences in visiting patterns, the possible importance of different tenure modes and types of local
area should be considered. In particular, studies
have shown the importance of area homogeneity in
encouraging home visiting with friends, while differences as between predominantly owner-occupied and
predominantly council rented areas have also been
suggested. The question of homogeneity was very
difficult to test in this study since the only
available data base comprised the small area statistics of the 1971 Census (at the time of the survey,
already six years out of date and, in the case of
social class at least, providing only 10 per cent sample data). The sampled enumeration districts were, however, assigned to social class and tenure groups on
the basis of predominant characteristics and individual respondents were considered in terms of being
in the same groups as the majority of households in
their areas. However, problems of scale and of
changes in socio-economic structure since 1971, together with the very high level of tenure homogeneity
within Merton enumeration districts, clearly influence the results of studying home visiting patterns
with respect to the 'homogeneity' variables thus
produced and, in fact, there are no relationships
evident between visiting local friends and whether or
not the respondent's social class or tenure mode
coincides with the predominant class or tenure group
of the enumeration district in which she lives.

The predominant tenure mode of an area does,
however, itself relate strongly to local visiting
patterns. While 57 per cent of the sample as a whole
have no relatives living in the local area, only 45
per cent of respondents living in predominantly
council rented areas have no local relatives and
these people tend to visit the local relatives they
have more frequently than other respondents. It is
also particularly important to note that 34 out of
45 respondents (76 per cent) living in private rented
accommodation have no family members in the local
area, a not unexpected finding and one which is
counterbalanced by the fact that private tenants have

the highest visiting rates with local friends of any
tenure group. While only 5 per cent of respondents
living in predominantly owner-occupied areas claim to
have no friends in their local area, as many as 16
per cent of council area respondents have no local
friends to visit and a further 10 per cent never
actually visit the friends they do have on weekdays.
There does appear, therefore, to be a definite relationship between mode of tenure and home visiting
patterns and this is confirmed by correlation coefficients of r=.11 (p=.02) between family visiting
and tenure type (taken as council-tenancy versus
other tenure mode) and r=-.12 (p=.006) between
friend visiting and type of tenure. While the former
coefficient becomes non-significant when social class
is taken into account (that is, tenure is probably
only important in influencing family visiting because
of the close association with social class), the coefficient between friend visiting and tenure type
remains significant even when considering the effect
of class; thus, mode of tenure remains as an independent influence on friend visiting. This finding
tends to support the descriptive conclusions of
previous studies which suggest that social interaction occurs on a more 'informal' basis in council-
rented areas while organised home visiting is more of
a characteristic of owner-occupied areas. (The relationship between categories of visiting frequency
with local friends and actual tenure mode of the
household is illustrated in Appendix D, Table D30.)

Extending this discussion of type of area as an
influencing factor on home visiting, it is interesting to consider also the actual type of accommodation
occupied by respondents in relation to visiting
patterns. In particular, one might expect those
living in flats to take part in more home visiting
activity than other respondents because of the space
restrictions on children imposed by the nature of
their accommodation. On the other hand, the social
isolation of people living in high blocks of flats is
a phenomenon continually referred to in the literature. Data from this survey indicate a positive
relationship between living in a flat and family
visiting (r=.08 (p=.05)) but no relationship at all
between flat-dwelling and friend visiting (r=.01
(p=.45)) (and, in fact, the former coefficient becomes
non-significant when social class is taken into
account). It is, however, interesting to note that
everyone living above first floor level in a block of
flats visits relatives living locally at least once a
week, if they have any, compared to 78 per cent of

the sample as a whole. These people are also more
likely to visit relatives outside the local area than
are other respondents. But, perhaps more important
from the point of view of comparison with previous
literature is the fact that 21 per cent of high flat
dwellers have no local friends at all (compared to 7
per cent of the overall sample) and also that another
21 per cent have no friends living outside the local
area, while those with non-local friends visit them
less frequently than do other respondents.

It was also hypothesised in Chapter 2 that
respondents living in middle-class areas of detached
housing might also tend to be socially isolated, due
to the minimal 'casual' contact which is likely to
occur in such areas. This hypothesis is not supported by the results of the survey, however. While a
lower frequency of family visiting does correlate
significantly with living in a detached house ($r=-.15$
($p=.002$)) (this relationship being entirely due to
social class differentials in family visiting),
detached house-dwelling is positively related to
friend visiting ($r=.10$ ($p=.02$)) (although this association,too,is determined largely by social class
determinants of housing type).

The mode of travel on visiting trips outside the
home is interesting to consider in some detail. The
time-budget survey of the previous day's activities
is the most useful source of data in this respect.
This shows a predominance of walking as the travel
mode employed (41 per cent of family visits and 63
per cent of friend visits) but also a high proportion
of visiting trips undertaken by car (38 per cent of
visits to relatives and 33 per cent of visits to
friends). While 67 per cent of visits to friends
involved journeys of less than ten minutes, only 53
per cent of family visits involved journeys this
short and as many as 29 per cent of visits to relatives involved journeys taking more than 20 minutes.
The main conclusion from these results would seem to
be that respondents are prepared to travel for a
longer time (and/or further) to visit relatives than
to visit friends, a conclusion which supports one of
the hypotheses on the effect of distance suggested in
Chapter 3. The results from the time-budget survey
also appear to underline the importance of car availability as a determinant of visiting activity. The
correlation coefficient between car availability and
friend visiting does prove to be significant ($r=.15$
($p=.002$)), even when the influence of social class is
taken into account but that between the availability
of a car and family visiting is non-significant.

Perhaps this is the reason (rather than the number of walk trips) why such a high proportion of friend visits involve journeys of under ten minutes.

The final hypotheses concerning home visiting relate to the importance of employment status and the number of young children which a respondent actually has in her daily care. As in previous sections of this chapter, it is reasoned here that those in paid employment will have less time to take part in home visiting activity than those who are full-time housewives, whether this work activity takes place at home or outside the home and whether during the daytime or in the evenings/at the weekend. This argument is based on the fact that women are the chief domestic workers of the household and, therefore, that those in paid employment must spend proportionally more of their 'free' time in undertaking household chores. The results of this survey do not, however, support this hypothesis, there being no statistical relationship between employment status and either family or friend visiting. At this point, it is also interesting to note the lack of relationship between the husband's assistance with domestic work and home visiting activity. Clearly, any domestic 'burden' placed on the women in this sample does not significantly influence their participation in social visiting.

Finally, the influence of the presence of young children must be considered in relation to home visiting. It was hypothesised in Chapter 2 that the number of young children which a woman has will be related to home visiting activity, since number of children serves as a surrogate for length of time spent as a mother and the latter is likely to be positively related to the formation of close social links with other mothers. Unfortunately, however, the data from this survey illustrate no such connection. The number of children under five which a woman has is not related at all to the type or frequency of home visiting activity and neither is the additional presence of a child over five in the family. The age of the youngest child is slightly related to friend visiting, in that those with a youngest child aged two or over are more likely to visit friends on a frequent basis than are those with babies and young toddlers ($r=.09$ ($p=.04$)), but the relationship with family visiting is not significant. Having at least one child at nursery school is also significantly related to friend visiting ($r=.17$ ($p=.001$)) (and is not affected by taking social class into account), which would seem to suggest the reinforcement of social interaction following contact with other young mothers 'at the nursery school gate'. Certainly, the existence of this latter relationship should not be taken to suggest that women visit each other's homes while their children are at nursery school; only an insignificant minority of visiting trips taking place on the day before interview did not involve young children along with their mothers.

Of course, home visiting is not the only relevant form of social interaction which occurs between women with young children. Shopping trips, accompanying children to school and park visiting have all been mentioned previously in this chapter as possible sources of social contact for such women. In answer to the question: 'What sort of things do you have in common with the friends you visit or chat to on the street?' - only twelve women state explicitly that they have no friends to talk to at all and one-third of these have lived in their local area for less than a year (compared to 8 per cent of the sample as a whole). The vast majority of respondents (85 per cent) cite the fact that they have young children in common as a reason for their social contacts, although 13 per cent mention common age-groups and as many as 34 per cent cite the existence of similar interests or activities. Clearly, similarity of life cycle stage (with its associated activities) is a key determinant of social interaction. Overall, most respondents consider their local area to be a friendly place (one-third say that their area is 'very friendly' and a further 45 per cent that it is 'quite friendly') and very few apparently feel totally isolated from social contact, although the quality of this contact cannot possibly be assessed by a survey of this type.

3.   Institutional/Social activities

Other 'leisure' activities, besides visiting parks and the homes of relatives and friends, are considered here in rather less detail, although the main patterns of activity can still be reasonably gauged. Respondents were asked to look at a list of possible activities and indicate which of these they took part in on a regular basis - at least two or three times a month. They were also questioned as to their mode of transport to the activity location, the length of journey involved and whether or not they took their children with them. As a separate question, they were asked if there were any activities which they would like to take part in, if not prevented from doing so. Constraints on activities listed by respondents primarily concern family (child care) commitments (227 respondents), while 66 women say they have no available time. A lack of mobility, the non-existence of facilities and a lack of information are other important constraints.

a)   Library use

121 respondents (30 per cent of the total sample) indicate that they use a library regularly on weekdays, most of them going at least once a week. As might be expected, the closest relationship of library use is with the educational level of the respondent. Table 18 illustrates this relationship clearly. There is also a strong relationship with age-group; 46 per cent of respondents aged 40 or over regularly visit a library, while only 14 per cent of those aged 20 to 24 do so and no one aged under 20. The relationship with social class is, however, negligible; although the wives of non-manual workers are more likely to use a library regularly than respondents married to men in manual occupations, the difference is not great and, for example, considering the wives of partly-skilled and unskilled manual workers, one-quarter regularly use a library. Employment status does not seem to influence library use and neither does the number of young children which a woman has despite the fact that children accompany their mothers in all but six cases. Most trips to libraries are made on foot (81 per cent) and only 11 per cent by car, thus it is not surprising that there is a lack of relationship between library use and car availability. Nor is it surprising that library visits are exclusively confined to respondents living within one mile of the nearest library (or mobile library stopping point). In all, 35 per cent of trips to libraries take only five minutes or less and 70 per cent take no more than ten minutes. Since such a relatively high proportion of respondents already visit libraries on weekdays, it is to be expected that relatively few additional respondents would include library use as a 'desired activity'. In fact, only 22 women state that they would like to visit a library regularly on weekdays if they were able to do so, most of these being fulltime housewives.

b)   Adult education

Very few respondents attend adult education

Table 18   Cross-tabulation of library use, with terminal education age

(Percentages in brackets)

	Below 16 years	16 years	17-18 years	19 years or older	Total
No regular use of library	124(85.5)	73(70.9)	55(65.5)	27(39.7)	279(69.7)
Regular use of library	21(14.5)	30(29.1)	29(34.5)	41(60.3)	121(30.2)
Total	145(100.0)	103(100.0)	84(100.0)	68(100.0)	400(100.0)

gamma = .51

173

classes on weekdays (only 21 respondents or five per
cent of the total sample) but all of these go at
least once a week. As would be expected, there is a
clear relationship with educational level, as in the
case of library use; in fact, nine out of 21 received a full-time education beyond the age of 18 years.
Attendance at adult education centres has been shown
in many studies to relate closely to middle-class
status and it is certainly true that in this study
57 per cent of those going to adult education classes
have husbands in professional and managerial occupations, compared to 31 per cent of the sample as a
whole, but the overall relationship with social class
is not as striking as that with the educational level
of the respondent.

Out of the 21 adult education students, no fewer
than 15 travel by car to the centre used, while only
two make their journeys on foot. It is, therefore,
not surprising that distance from a centre providing
daytime classes is not important in determining adult
education attendance, while car availability is definitely an influencing factor. There is no relationship with either employment status or the number of
young children in the family but those with children
at nursery school are much more likely to attend an
adult education centre than those whose children are
all at home. The latter point is emphasised by the
fact that only seven out of the 21 respondents take
their children with them when they go to their
classes and this, perhaps, explains the lack of
relationship between attendance at adult education
classes and distance from a centre with child care
facilities (of which there is only one in the borough
of Merton).

Although so few respondents actually take part
in adult education activities, it is clear from the
results of the question on 'desired activities' that
very many more would like to do so if they were able
to. No less than 131 respondents claim that they
would like to attend an adult education centre for
weekday classes and this makes attendance at classes
by far the most 'wanted' activity by the sample as a
whole. Furthermore, there is no noticeable class,
education, age or income bias in the distribution of
respondents wanting to attend adult education
classes; a genuine demand does seem to exist across
all categories of women with young children. In
many cases it became apparent during interviewing
that respondents were largely unaware of the facilities actually provided in the borough for daytime
classes and, in particular, of the creche facilities

available at one of the larger centres. There
appears to be a definite demand not only for
increased facilities of this type but also, perhaps
more importantly, for a ready availability of information regarding the existing provision of facilities
in the borough. (Similar conclusions were drawn from
a study in the Small Heath area of Birmingham - see
Richards, 1977.)

c)   'Mother and toddler' clubs

        'Mother and toddler' clubs, in various forms,
exist throughout most parts of Merton. Normally they
cater for women with very young children - under the
age of nursery schooling - and meet once or twice
each week, in Church or community halls. Their
expressed purpose is twofold: firstly, to enable
young children to establish contacts with each other
and secondly, to encourage social contact between
mothers on a weekday basis. Their catchment areas
tend to be small. Out of the 65 respondents (16 per
cent of the total sample) who attend such clubs, 55
walk to their destinations and only nine travel by
car, while 48 per cent of journeys take only five
minutes or less and 75 per cent take no longer than
ten minutes. Membership of a 'mother and toddler'
club is not associated with any particular 'social'
group; it is not statistically related to education
level, age, social class or family income. There is
a slight relationship between attendance at such
clubs and being a full-time housewife but no relationship with the number of young children which a
respondent has. An additional 40 respondents (32
being full-time housewives) would like to go to a
'mother and toddler' club if one were available in
their immediate area or if waiting lists for membership did not exist due to a shortage of supply.

d)   Sport

        Like attendance at 'mother and toddler' clubs,
participation in sports activities on weekdays does
not seem to be the province of any particular
'social' group, although there is some relationship
with car availability. The latter is presumably explained by the fact that as many as half of the
journeys to sports facilities are made by car. 42
respondents in total (11 per cent of the sample)
indicate that they take part in sports activities,
the majority of them on a weekly basis but one-
quarter at least twice a week. The majority take

their children with them, although there is some
relationship between sports participation and having
children at nursery school; some women probably use
the time while their children are at school to
engage in sports activity. A further 73 respondents
would like to take part in sport if they were able to
do so, making sport the second most 'desired
activity' by respondents as a whole (after attendance
at adult education classes).

e)   Other activities

    The remaining weekday activities considered
attract very few respondents as participants at the
present time. As noted in the Borough Plan (London
Borough of Merton, Appendix A, 1976,5), '...young
married women with young children are the least
likely sector of society to use social, cultural and
entertainment facilities'. 14 people attend some
sort of social club (not a 'mother and toddler'
club), 11 of these coming from non-manual households
and all of them travelling for less than ten minutes
to reach their club destination. Perhaps because so
many belong to professional, car-owning families,
half of them normally travel by car, while the remainder walk. Two-thirds of social club visits are
made together with young children. Only 14 additional respondents specifically mention social club
attendance as a 'desired activity' on weekdays.
    'Cultural' visiting (to museums, art galleries,
etc.) involves only eight women on a regular basis at
the present time, although a further 58 respondents
list this as a 'desired activity'. Not surprisingly,
present participants are mainly highly educated women
from professional families and they also tend to be
older than the sample as a whole. The same characteristics are evident amongst those who would like to
spend time on this type of activity but are not able
to do so at present.
    'Entertainment', in the form of cinema or
theatre visits, is enjoyed by only three respondents
in the sample, although 49 list this type of activity
as 'desired', in the absence of existing constraints.
All three are full-time housewives and the wives of
non-manual workers and they all have only one child
to take along with them. None travels for more than
ten minutes while two out of three make their journeys by car.
    In summary, 'leisure' activities outside the
home are less important, in terms of both the number
of participants involved and the frequency of

176

occurrence, than the 'unpaid work' activities of
shopping and accompanying children to school.
Amongst 'leisure' activities, home visiting stands
out as the dominant type of activity for women with
young children. Due to the differing availability
of relatives and friends in the local area, visits
to friends are more important numerically than
visits to relatives for the sample as a whole.
There is, however, a social class difference in
visiting patterns and this study supports the findings of previous work in the field which show that
working-class people are the most likely to visit
relatives frequently while middle-class people are
the most likely to visit friends. The results also
support previous assertions that visiting patterns
with friends are related to tenure mode, council
tenants being less likely than others to maintain
their friendships through home visiting. Rather
unexpectedly, no relationships are evident between
visiting patterns and either employment status or
the number of young children which a woman has. As
a determinant of social interaction, similarity of
life cycle stage appears to dominate other possible
reasons for friendship formation.

Visits to parks do not occur as frequently as
home visits but only 15 per cent of respondents say
that they never visit a park on weekdays. Amongst
the 'social status' variables considered, only
terminal age of full-time education is definitely
related to frequency of park use but, in general, it
is clear that it is the lower class, less well-
educated and lower income respondents who are the
least likely to visit parks on weekdays at all.
Practically all journeys to parks are very short(ten
minutes,travelling time or less), reflecting the
widespread distribution of open spaces throughout the
borough of Merton. The 'quality' of open space
areas appears to influence visiting patterns, whether
this is viewed in terms of areal size or the possession of a children's playground or the 'grade' of
open space concerned.

The regular use of a library and attendance at
adult education classes are both statistically
related to terminal age of full-time education. However, adult education is mentioned as a 'desired'
activity by more respondents than any other institutional or social activity and there is no education
or social class bias in this potential demand.
Relatively few respondents participate in other types
of 'leisure' activity, although attendance at 'mother
and toddler' clubs is popular where such clubs exist

and sporting activities are indicated as 'desired'
activities by a large number of respondents. The
presence of children is named as the major
constraint on participation in social and institutional activities.

General summary of survey findings

The dominance of 'unpaid work' activities (notably
shopping and taking children to school) among the
non-employment activities of respondents serves to
emphasise yet again the importance of gender-role
differentiation within society. While accompanying
children to school could be viewed simply as part of
the 'job' of child care, such a conclusion cannot so
readily be drawn in the case of shopping, particularly where the respondent (like her husband) is also
in paid employment. Both social class and car
availability influence the frequency of shopping,
while the size of shopping centre in the vicinity is
also important, since most respondents normally use
'local' shops.
      Although the weekday activities of women with
young children are primarily 'work' oriented,
certain leisure activities are widely participated
in, notably home-visiting and visits to parks.
These together with attendance at 'mother and
toddler' clubs are clearly the types of activity
most suited to the presence of young children. Other
forms of 'leisure' are constrained by child care
needs. There are definite social class differences
in 'leisure' patterns and car availability is also
an important variable in association with the distribution of social and recreational facilities.

Chapter 7

THE LOCAL ORIENTATION OF WOMEN'S LIVES

In the preceding two chapters, a number of instances
have been cited which illustrate the essentially
local nature of women's patterns of activity when
they have young children. It has been shown that
such women depend upon the existence of employment
opportunities in the very near vicinity, that the
majority of them use local shops for weekday purchases and that distances to parks visited and
friends' houses tend to be short. Chapter 8 indicates further, that for most respondents pre-school
facilities used are those provided in the local area.
    The results so far presented have been in a
generalised form, involving the subjective interpretation of the term 'local' by respondents and also
the measurement of distances in terms of journey
times. Whilst both of these methods have their value
in an overall description of activity patterns, it is
here considered useful to look in more detail at
actual activities and specific distances. Later in
this chapter the journeys to activities of a sample
of 50 respondents will be studied and interpreta-
tions suggested of the extent of their activity
space.
    However, in order to understand the constraint
of distance and the consequent local orientation of
women's lives, it is first necessary to consider the
question of mobility and transport provision. The
first part of this chapter, therefore, deals with the
questionnaire results relating to travel behaviour
and the provision of transport services.

Travel Behaviour and Service Provision

As indicated in Chapter 3, the definition of
'mobility' accepted for use in this study is that of
Hillman et al., (1976,51). They define mobility in

terms of a combination of two factors: firstly, the ability to use different methods of travel and, secondly, the availability of different travel modes. In this section both the problems involved in different forms of transport and the availability of travel alternatives in Merton will be considered in relation to actual usage patterns of respondents to the questionnaire survey.

1. Public transport

a) Provision and opinions

Map 4 shows the public transport routes contained in the borough of Merton. As in other parts of London, the bus network is relatively dense and no major area of the borough is excluded from service. There are also a number of British Rail lines serving the borough, although these vary in the frequency of service; the south-east area of the borough, in particular, is rather poorly served, having only one rail link operating at only two trains per hour in each direction. Merton as a whole is well-favoured amongst south London boroughs, so far as London Transport underground lines are concerned. The borough contains the termini of two lines serving south London: the District Line link to Wimbledon and the Northern Line which terminates at Morden.

It can be seen, therefore, that the provision of public transport in Merton is generally good and certainly of a higher standard than in many other parts of London or indeed the rest of the country. The prevailing standard of transport provision was, in fact, one of the factors employed in the selection of Merton as the study area (see Chapter 4). Because it was expected from previous research (see Chapter 3) that women with young children would have low levels of mobility compared to the population at large, it was thought useful to interview respondents in an area where at least the potential for public transport usage was good.

In the light of the actual distribution of services, it is interesting to look at respondents' opinions about public transport. In answer to the question: 'How good is the public transport service for people who live around here?'- only 66 respondents (16.5 per cent of the total sample) consider it to be 'very good' and 144 (36 per cent) 'fairly good'. If the 36 respondents who have 'no opinion' on the service are excluded, then 58 per cent of the sample think that public transport is either very

Map 4   Merton: Public transport routes

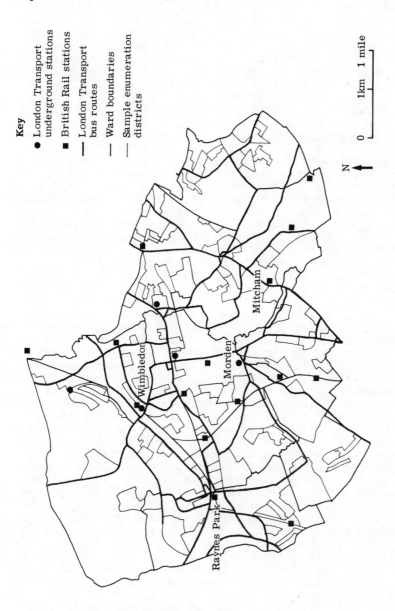

Key

● London Transport
  underground stations

■ British Rail stations

— London Transport
  bus routes

— Ward boundaries

— Sample enumeration
  districts

N ←

0   1km 1 mile

good or fairly good. This is, perhaps, a surprisingly low figure and it is instructive to reflect on how low the percentage might have been if an area with a more 'average' supply of transport facilities had been selected for study. As many as 52 respondents (13 per cent of the whole sample) consider their public transport service to be 'not good at all'.

As one would expect, there are areal variations in the perception of services; in particular, over half the respondents living in East Mitcham (see Map 1 for location of wards) think that their public transport is 'not good at all' and only 11 per cent consider it to be at all good while South Wimbledon stands out as the area with the most favourable response to this question, with three-quarters of respondents rating their public transport service as 'very good' or 'fairly good'. The variation in reply between respondents within the same area (ward) presumably reflects not only minor areal differences in supply but also differences in personal expectations and perception.

The fact that bus services are available throughout the borough while rail stations are only located in certain areas is reflected in differential opinions on the standard of public transport. Thus, there is no relationship at all between the use of bus services and respondents' opinions on public transport, while there is a definite relationship between the latter and the weekday use of trains (see Appendix D, Table D36). As will be shown later, lack of easy access to a station is an important factor in determining lack of train usage.

It might be thought that respondents' opinions on public transport would be related to length of residence in the area or whether or not the respondent grew up in the local area but, in fact, this is not the case. There is, however, one important relationship with car availability; those with weekday access to a car are very likely not to know about public transport (to have 'no opinion') or else to consider it 'very good', possibly because they have no personal evidence with which to contradict this impression.

b) The use of buses

As Map 4 shows, no area in Merton is totally isolated from bus services and this is reflected in the fact that 88 per cent of the sample respondents live within one quarter of a mile of a bus route. Given the ready availability of bus services (at

least in theory) and the fact that a majority of respondents do not have daily access to a car, it might
be expected that bus use would be prominent for this
group. However, Hillman et al., (1976) have already
documented the low frequency of journeys by bus
among women with young children (see Chapter 3) and
it is, therefore, not altogether surprising to find
that nearly half (46 per cent) of the sample respondents never travel by bus with their children during
weekdays, while only one-quarter do so as often as
once a week. Although distance from a bus route
does not appear to influence the use or non-use of
buses overall, those living within one quarter of a
mile of such a route tend to use buses more
frequently than other respondents.

One interesting relationship emerges from the
data on bus use (see Appendix D, Table D32). It
seems that a higher percentage of women who grew up
in their present local area use buses frequently
than do other respondents; in particular those
originating from outside south-west London are the
least likely ever to use buses. Presumably, in this
case, growing up in an area and a close knowledge of
local facilities are connected; those from outside
south-west London are the least likely to be
familiar with local services.

The most important determinant of whether or
not a respondent travels by bus on weekdays, however,
seems to be access or lack of access to a car.
Three-quarters of those who have effective access to
a car never use buses, compared to 31 per cent of
respondents without access to a car, while car-owners
who do use buses use them infrequently compared to
other women (see Table 19 which indicates a very
strong association between the two variables.).
Hillman et al., (1976,104) have shown that for women
without a car the most likely alternative form of
travel is walking and that public buses do not act
as car-substitutes. While the data from this survey
definitely underline the predominance of walking as
the major travel mode for women with young children,
it does seem that, at least for some activities,
buses may be used as alternatives to cars by those
for whom a car is not available.

Those respondents who, at least occasionally,
travel by bus with their children on weekdays, were
questioned regarding any problems they might encount-
er with using buses. This was because both common-
sense and previous research point to a high degree
of inconvenience for women with small children in
coping with bus travel and this is supported by the

Table 19   Cross-tabulation of weekday use of buses,
            with car availability

(Percentages in brackets)

	Car available	Car not available	Total
Once a week or more often	5(3.9)	97(35.8)	102(25.5)
Less often than once a week	27(20.9)	89(32.8)	116(29.0)
Never	97(75.2)	85(31.4)	182(45.5)
Total	129(100.0)	271(100.0)	400(100.0)

gamma = -.73

results of this survey which show a marked difference
in usage patterns of both buses and trains according
to the age of the youngest child in the family;
those with babies (under two) being much less likely to
use any form of public transport than those with
older children.
    Perhaps surprisingly, 37 per cent (80 respond-
ents) of those using buses admit to no particular
problem. Of the problems encountered, the majority
are the direct result of the presence of children;
in particular, 60 respondents complained that there is
no help on or off the buses and 49 specify various
difficulties or effort involved with children. For
40 respondents, the lack of anywhere to put the pram
or pushchair is important and ten respondents are
concerned about the problem of controlling children
on buses and the dangers involved. In contrast,
there are far fewer mentions of other problems, not
related to the presence of children; the most important of these concerns the unreliability of services
(37 respondents) or their infrequency (24 respondents). Only nine women specify the cost of fares as a
problem but this may be partly due to the wording of
the question concerned. In retrospect, it might have
been preferable to ask this question of all respondents, since the cost of fares may, in fact, act as an
important determinant of non-use of buses. However,
London Transport bus fares, especially over short
distances, were not particularly high at the time of
the survey and this, combined with the fact that a

large majority of non-car owners (who tend to come
from poorer households) do use buses, would seem to
imply that the cost of bus travel is not an overriding factor in its use in this instance, although the
actual frequency of use may be affected by cost.

c)   The use of trains

By comparison with other parts of London, the
borough of Merton is well-supplied with rail facilities but these are not widely-used by respondents on
weekdays. More than half (54 per cent) of respondents never use trains (including underground trains)
with their children during weekdays and only 40 (10
per cent) travel by train as often as once a week.
Unlike distance to a bus route, the distance to
a station (either British Rail or Underground) is
related to the actual use of trains (see Appendix D,
Table D33). While 88 per cent of respondents live
within one quarter of a mile of a bus route, only 37
per cent live within one quarter of a mile of a
station and only 3 per cent live within one quarter
of a mile of both a British Rail and an Underground
station. As far as train usage is concerned, living
near an Underground station seems to be more
important than living near a British Rail station,
although the latter is the more common case. Of
those respondents (11 per cent of the total sample)
living within one quarter of a mile of an Underground station, three-quarters use trains regularly
on weekdays, while nearly half of those living within one quarter of a mile of a British Rail station
(29 per cent of the sample) never use trains at all
on weekdays. The differences between the two types
of train service are, of course, considerable.
Underground trains run more frequently and are more
convenient to use for a woman with young children.
However, they represented (in 1977) a more expensive
form of service than the British Rail trains.
As in the case of bus use, there is a definite
relationship between the respondent's access (or lack
of access) to a car and her use of trains (see
Appendix D, Table D34). The relationship is, however, much less strong. While respondents without
cars available to them tend to use buses more often
than trains, those who have access to a car are more
likely to use trains rather than buses. (Similarly,
the wives of non-manual workers and those from
families with the highest incomes are the most likely
to use trains rather than buses.) Presumably, the
greater expense of train travel is of less importance

185

to higher income car owners than to other respondents. This finding is also of interest since it supports the suggestion, put forward previously, that bus travel acts as the primary car-substitute form of transport. Trains do not seem to act as substitutes for cars in quite the same way (see Appendix D, Table D35).

Travel by train does not appear to raise as many problems for respondents as does bus travel. Out of the 184 women using trains with their children on weekdays, more than two-thirds (68 per cent) state that they experience no problems at all with this type of travel. Of the problems mentioned by others, the most important concern children: in particular, the problem of getting pushchairs, prams and children up and down stairs or escalators without help. Problems relating to the actual services are of far less importance than in the case of bus travel, reflecting the greater reliability and convenience of trains as compared to buses.

2.   Car availability

Chapter 3 of this study has already highlighted the work of Hillman on differential personal mobility. His main emphasis is on the difference between household and individual car accessibility and he exemplifies his argument by reference to specific groups of people (having a low level of accessibility to private transport), including women with young children. Being aware of Hillman's results, it is of some interest to consider the level of access to cars amongst respondents to the present survey.

While the overall percentage of households in Merton owning at least one car is known from Census figures (and stood at 19 per cent in 1971), no data are available concerning the percentage of households with children under five having access to a car. It is, therefore, not possible to say whether the level of car ownership revealed in this study is representative of that obtaining in this type of household in the borough as a whole. The figure is, however, high (76 per cent) and may reflect over-representation of car owning households in the present sample. Of the 305 households with cars, 261 (65 per cent of the whole sample) have one car and 44 (11 per cent) have two or more cars.

Car availability comprises two distinct factors: access to a car and the ability to drive it. For the purposes of this study, access to a car was defined according to the following question: 'Is there

a car available for <u>you</u> to use during the <u>daytime</u> on
<u>weekdays</u> - that is, <u>is</u> there <u>normally</u> one <u>here</u>, <u>not</u>
<u>on special</u> occasions?' In <u>reply to this</u> question,
168 respondents (42 per cent of the total sample)
answer in the affirmative. Those from households
with two or more cars are the most likely to have
weekday access to a car, as would be expected. Respondents were next asked: 'Do you hold a current
driving licence?' In answer to this question,
just under half (193) state that they do hold such a
licence. Combining the two factors of access to a
car and licence-holding it is found that 129 respondents (32 per cent of the sample) have <u>effective</u>
use of a car on weekdays, this being defined as 'car
availability' in this study.

As anticipated, car availability is not uniformly distributed amongst the sample members; it is
strongly related to all 'social' variables. Thus,
for example, 50 per cent of the wives of professional
and managerial workers have a car available, while
only 9 per cent of those whose husbands are partly-
skilled or unskilled manual workers have effective
access to a car. Amongst tenure groups, it is owner-
occupiers who have the highest level of car availability (42 per cent) and council tenants who have the
lowest (7 per cent) while there is also a strong
relationship with family income, 68 per cent of women
from the highest income group having a car available.
The closest relationship of all is between car availability and house type; 85 per cent of those living
in detached houses, 38 per cent of those in semi-
detached houses, 28 per cent of those in terraced
houses but only 14 per cent of those living in
flats have a car available for use on weekdays.

Chapters 5 and 6 have already indicated the
extent of car usage for journeys to different
activities and those results will not be repeated
here. However, consideration of the time-budget data
for the previous day's activities allows us to identify respondents who actually <u>used</u> a car for at least
one activity on the day before interview. In fact,
107 respondents (27 per cent of the total) did so.
It is interesting that 35 per cent of women with a
car available did not use it on the previous day,
while 23 respondents without regular access to a car
did use one.

Hillman <u>et al</u>., (1976) note particularly the
differential <u>access</u> to cars by men and women but it
is an interesting point that within this sample,
respondents with husbands who travel to work by car
are only slightly less likely themselves to have used

a car on the day before interview than anyone else
(25 per cent did so), indicating the extent of
multiple car ownership. Those whose husbands walk to
work or go by bus are the least likely to have a
car available because the household is most likely
not to have a car at all. The respondents who are
most likely to have used cars on the previous day are
those with husbands travelling to work by train
(mainly to the City or West End of London) or given
a lift in someone else's car. It could not, therefore, be said that the women in this sample have a
significantly lower access to cars than their husbands, although this is mainly because such a large
proportion of men travel by train to Central London
to work and, therefore, do not use their cars on a
weekday basis. Merton may not be typical of the
country as a whole in this respect. However, in more
than half of all households with one car (59 per
cent), the husband uses this car to go to work,
whereas only 30 per cent of women daytime workers
from households with one car have access to the car
for their journey to work. Three-quarters of all
respondents using the family car to travel to work, in
fact, work only in the evenings or at weekends when
the car would be available in any case. The results,
therefore, support Hillman's contention to a limited
extent.

3.   Convenience of the local area

Problems of mobility for respondents relate very
closely to the perceived convenience of the local
area. Since most journeys within the local area take
place on foot and walking is, therefore, the predominant mode of travel for women with young children, it
is important to identify any difficulties which may
be faced in connection with walking trips. Hillman et
al., (1976,52-53) mention a number of specific
problems involved in walking with young children and
find a large percentage of women experiencing such
problems (36 to 42 per cent, depending on the age of
the youngest child). In this survey, on the other
hand, 81 per cent of respondents state that they find
no difficulties at all with walking to various places
with their children. Only 78 respondents mention any
problems specifically but for these women it is
distance which represents the important constraint.
Thus, comments made include 'places are too far
away', 'children won't walk far', 'children walk so
slowly' and 'not enough time to get to places'.
Some respondents (17) mention problems involving prams

or pushchairs. The number referring to traffic
problems and dangers (including crossing roads) is
very small (17 respondents), considering that Merton
is an urban borough with its full complement of busy
main roads and hazardous shopping streets, but this
may be partly the result of the wording of the question, which referred to 'difficulties' with walking
rather than 'dangers'.

The relatively few respondents referring to
'distance' problems in relation to walking acts as
one indicator of the convenience of local areas
generally but, in order to ascertain the direct
opinion of respondents on the convenience of their
local areas, the following question was asked:
'Thinking about the kind of things you would like to
have near where you live - places you go to fairly
often - how convenient would you say this local area
is: is it very convenient, convenient enough, not
very convenient or not convenient at all?'. In
reply, three-quarters of respondents say that they
consider their local area a 'convenient' one; 38 per
cent state that it is 'very convenient' and 38 per
cent that it is 'convenient enough'. Only 20 respondents (6 per cent) consider their area to be 'not
convenient at all'. These results serve to
emphasise the 'urban' character of the borough as a
whole, exemplified by the multiplicity of small
shopping centres (see Map 2) and the relatively easy
access to public transport. As one might expect,
perceived convenience varies between different parts
of the borough; it is highest in the Wimbledon
wards, especially South Wimbledon and is much lower
in Mitcham, especially South and East Mitcham wards.
The latter two areas are the most remote from railway
stations and major shopping centres within the
borough, although no clear relationship emerges from
cross-tabulations of perceived convenience, on the
one hand and distance from either a main shopping
centre or a station, on the other.

The perception of convenience is definitely
related to the respondents' opinion on public transport, however; that is, public transport is definitely considered to be a contributory factor in determining the convenience of the local area (see
Appendix D, Table D36). That this is most true of
rail transport is illustrated by the fact that those
who think their local area is convenient are the most
likely to use trains frequently and the most likely
to live in areas of the borough with good rail
facilities (especially South Wimbledon and West
Mitcham). As far as bus transport is concerned, the

situation is rather different. As already pointed
out, there is no relationship at all between respondents' opinion on public transport and the actual use
of buses. Similarly, it is found that those who
consider their local area to be 'not at all convenient' are the most likely to use buses frequently
(particularly those in South and East Mitcham).
Conversely, over half (52 per cent) of those who
think their area is 'very convenient', in fact, never
use buses. It seems, therefore, that while access
to a rail station represents a key element of 'convenience', access to a bus does not. What is also
implied from these findings is that, as would be
expected, 'convenience' means more than just the
existence of public transport; it also implies the
easy availability of services and facilities which
make journeys out of the local area unnecessary.
    But it is the ability to get away from the local
area which appears to remain the most important
factor in determining respondents' attitudes to
'convenience'. Those who consider their local area
to be 'not convenient at all' are the most likely
never to leave the local area on weekdays. While,
overall, 22 per cent of respondents always remain
within their local area, 45 per cent of those who
think their local area is not convenient do so. Car
availability is clearly of importance in providing a
means of access to places outside the immediate
locality and it is, therefore, no surprise to find
that those with a car available are likely to
consider their local area more convenient than those
without a car (see Table 20); only 12 per cent of
those with access to a car do not consider their
local area to be a convenient place, while 28 per
cent of those without a car speak of their local area
as lacking convenience.
    Travel outside the local area (within ordinary
walking distance of home) is found to be highly
circumscribed for this population group as a whole;
as expected from previous research, one-fifth of
respondents never leave their local area on weekdays
and less than half (47 per cent) do so as often as
once a week. Neither accessibility to bus routes nor
stations proves to be significant in determining
whether or not a respondent leaves her local area or
how frequently she does so, although the Mitcham
wards (excluding West Mitcham) stand out as the areas
where respondents are most isolated in their immediate localities and these are also the areas considered least convenient by respondents and with the
poorest public transport facilities. Car

Table 20   Cross-tabulation of perceived convenience
of local area, with car availability

(Percentages in brackets)

	Car available	Car not available	Total
Very convenient	65(51.6)	85(31.7)	150(38.1)
Convenient enough	46(36.5)	109(40.7)	155(39.3)
Not very convenient	14(11.1)	55(20.5)	69(17.5)
Not convenient at all	1(0.8)	19(7.1)	20(5.1)
Total	126(100.0)	268(100.0)	394(100.0)

gamma = .39   (6 missing cases)

availability seems to be one major influencing
factor in relation to travel outside the local area
(see Table 21); those with a car available on weekdays are much more likely to leave the area on a
frequent basis. Another interesting relationship
arises with respect to journeys away from the local
area; respondents who grew up in adjacent suburbs
to those they now live in, or elsewhere in south-west
London, tend to leave their local area more frequently than other respondents, presumably because they
still have families or friends to visit in these
relatively proximate areas.

As a final comment on local areas and getting
away from them, it is rather sad to note that a
higher percentage of respondents who consider their
local area to be an 'unfriendly' place never leave
the locality on weekdays, than those who consider
their area to be 'friendly'. This perhaps suggests
that 'friendliness' is more accurately judged by
those who are confined to an area full-time, rather
than by those who are often able to get away. (In a
very similar way, we have found that women who are
able to get away from their young children for at
least some of the time on weekdays are able to enjoy
the responsibilities of motherhood more fully during
the remaining period as a result.) Being permanently
restricted to the local area, especially if that area
offers limited services and social facilities (for
example, to enable friendships to be formed and
develop) is a major limitation on activity patterns.

It is, therefore, not surprising that this section of
the chapter has shown a close relationship between
the respondent's opinion on the convenience of her
local area, on the one hand and her level of
personal mobility and her ability to leave the local
area on weekdays, on the other.

Table 21 Cross-tabulation of weekday travel outside
the local area, with car availability

(Percentages in brackets)

	Car available	Car not available	Total
Once a week or more often	84(65.1)	105(38.7)	189(47.2)
Less often than once a week	32(24.8)	91(33.6)	123(30.7)
Never	13(10.1)	75(27.7)	88(22.0)
Total	129(100.0)	271(100.0)	400(100.0)

gamma = .47

In summary, previous research has shown that
public transport services are of relatively minor
importance to women with young children since most
journeys are carried out on foot. This study has
supported previous findings by establishing that
nearly half of the Merton sample never travels by bus
on weekdays (with their children) and that more than
half never travels by train, despite the fact that
public transport provision is generally good compared
to many other areas.
Having a car available for use and being able
to drive it are key factors in determining personal
mobility. One-third of respondents have effective
access to a car on weekdays and these women travel
more widely out of their local area than do those
without a car available. There is a strong social
class and income bias in car availability. If they
use any form of public transport, car owners are more
likely to travel by train, while non-car users are
more likely to travel by bus. Bus services appear to
act more clearly as car-substitutes than train
services, for those without access to a car, although

more problems are recorded in relation to the use of
buses than trains. These problems relate almost
exclusively to the presence of children.

Three-quarters of the sample consider their
local area to be 'convenient', reflecting the urban
'character' of the borough of Merton. Respondents'
perceptions of 'convenience' relate strongly to their
opinions on the standard of public transport provision, which vary considerably in different parts of
the borough.

The Extent of Activity Space

The first part of this chapter has considered the
use and perception of modes of transport by respondents. It has served to emphasise yet again how
'local' is the daily environment of women with young
children. The purpose of this section is to look in
more detail at a small sample of respondents; to
consider their actual out-of-home activities in terms
of journeys to activity locations and, thus, to draw
detailed conclusions about the extent of activity
space for women with young children.

1. Construction of the map

In order to produce a map which would give a
clear visual impression of activity space, a sample
of 50 respondents was selected. The sample was
selected randomly from the 400 survey respondents
but in such a way that no area of the borough would
be excluded from consideration. The precise locations of the homes of sampled respondents were plotted
on the map, using the addresses obtained by interviewers and a road atlas.

From the questionnaire responses, the following
details were obtained and Map 5 produced by joining
respondents' home locations to the following points:-

Location of paid employment (Q.A.5)
Location of shops used for weekday shopping (Q.B.2)
Location of park normally visited on weekdays (Q.C.
    1(a))
Homes visited on the day before interview (Q.C.13)
Location of library used (Q.C.11)
Location of mother and toddler club, other social
    club and/or sports facility used (Q.C.11)
Location of nursery school or supervised playgroup
    used (Q.E.2(b))
Location where children left with other person on
    weekdays (Q.E.6(b)).

Map 5   Map of weekday activities (sample of 50)

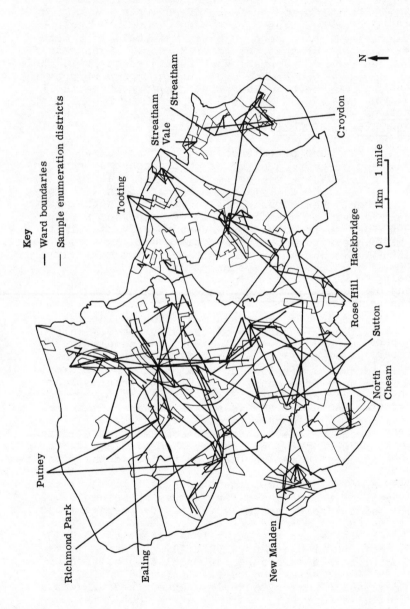

The journey lines constructed in this way refer to the activity patterns of individual women on weekdays and were selected as the most appropriate indicators of the extent of weekday activity space.

2. Discussion of findings

It must firstly be remembered that journeys on the map are shown in terms of straight line distances between origins and destinations, while actual journey lengths are unknown. Any conclusions from the information so presented should, therefore, be treated with some caution.

a) Differential journey lengths as between different weekday activities

Table 22 shows the average journey lengths to different activity locations. Median distances have been selected as the most appropriate measure of 'average' in this case because the data are very skewed in a positive direction. (In each case, the mean is considerably higher than the median figure, being influenced by a few extreme values at the upper end of the scale.) Most noticeable from Table 22 is the general shortness of journeys to activities by this small sample.

Considering the different activities separately, the shortest average journey lengths (apart from journeys to the homes of friends, which will be discussed shortly) are those to libraries, pre-school facilities, mother and toddler clubs and the locations where children are left with some other person.

Journeys to shops and parks vary greatly in length, depending on the respondent's home location in relation to existing shopping centres and to the most popular parks. Many shopping trips are very short but the importance of the main borough centres also stands out (even where weekday shopping trips are concerned), notably Wimbledon, Morden and Mitcham. This indicates a willingness to travel a greater distance to shops than to some social activities.

Journeys to different social activities vary greatly in the distance travelled. Longer journeys occur in relation to sports activities, attendance at some social clubs and visits to the homes of relatives than in connection with other social activities. So few visits to friends' homes took place amongst the small sample on the day before interview that no definite conclusion can be drawn

Table 22   Average (median) journey lengths to
            different activities (weekdays, sample of
            50)

Destination	Median distance (miles)	Number of journeys
Work	.63	8
Shops (weekdays)	.37	49
Parks	.38	42
Homes of relatives	.60	6
Homes of friends	.10	3
Libraries	.26	15
Mother and toddler clubs	.28	8
Other social clubs	.47	4
Sports facilities	.76	4
Nursery schools or playgroups	.26	27
Locations where children left	.20	23

on the difference in length of journeys to the homes
of friends, as opposed to relatives. What is clear,
however, is the predominance of home visits to the
homes of respondents by friends; had these visits
taken place in the opposite direction, a more
definite picture of the spatial occurrence of home
visiting would have become apparent.

     Journeys to the locations where respondents
leave their children with some other person on
weekdays vary most of all in their respective
lengths (note that the median figure given in Table
22 excludes children cared for in the respondent's
own home). Many women leave their children with
neighbours in the same street as their homes but
others travel considerable distances to leave their
children, at relatives' homes in particular.

b)   Weekday and evening/weekend shopping trips

     Table 23 illustrates (in average terms) the
great difference between length of journeys to shops
on weekdays and those taking place in the evenings or
at weekends ('main' shopping trips). The high median
figure for the latter type of journey is due to the
preponderance of trips to shopping centres outside
the borough. Wimbledon stands out as the only
borough centre of importance in connection with
'main' shopping trips. (Evening/weekend shopping
trips are, of course, excluded from the map of

Table 23   Average (median) journey lengths to shops
           on weekdays and evenings/weekends (sample
           of 50)

Destination	Median distance (miles)	Number of journeys
Shops (weekdays)	.37	49
Shops (evenings/ weekends)	2.25	32

weekday activities.)

c)   Journeys to work

       A tabular comparison of average distances to
work by sample respondents and their husbands is
virtually impossible because the overwhelming majority of husbands' work locations are outside the
borough and these locations are not sufficiently
precise to enable exact measurements to be taken.
However, it is quite clear that respondents travel
far shorter distances to work than their husbands
and that the majority are, in fact, employed at locations within the borough of Merton.
       With so few respondents in the small sample
being in outside employment, it was thought useful
also to look at the journeys to work of all respondents in outside employment, in order to confirm the
comparison between journey lengths of women and men.
Although approximately one-third of all respondents
in outside employment travel to work locations outside the borough, only eight out of 77 make journeys
further than adjacent suburbs. In contrast. only eight
out of 48 respondents' husbands working outside the
home (two work from home) are employed within the
borough of Merton, while 22 (nearly half) travel long
distances to work (to Central, North, East or West
London, Kent or Sussex).

d)   Differential journey lengths as between
     different respondents

       Map 5 indicates the differences in journey
lengths to activities between different respondents.
Being a composite map, it is a little difficult to
interpret visually although the overall dominance of
relatively short journeys is very apparent.
       As previously pointed out, the degree of

197

variation in journey lengths varies as between different activities. Since we are now trying to establish differences between the journey lengths of different respondents, it is necessary to select only those journeys to activities which vary considerably and exclude those where little variation is apparent. For many activities, in addition, relatively few respondents have recorded journey lengths and these activities can, therefore, also be usefully excluded. Taking both the above points into consideration, the two types of journey - to shops used on weekdays and to parks normally visited - were taken together to indicate average journey lengths for respondents. Both of these journey types display considerable variation, as between respondents and 40 respondents (out of a possible 50 in the small sample) have recorded information for both activities.

Taking the mean distance to shops and parks for each respondent and comparing these means, the range of distances is seen to extend from .13 mile to 1.67 miles. Although there is variation between different parts of the borough, this does not seem to fit any obvious pattern other than the location of facilities. Thus, middle class respondents in West Wimbledon with cars available for use on weekdays tend to travel further to shops and parks than the sample as a whole; on the other hand, so do the working class respondents in Ravensbury ward, none of whom has effective access to a car. Those with the shortest mean journey lengths live in the South Wimbledon/West Mitcham area, and near the shopping centre at Mitcham.

It was considered possible that car availability might partly determine mean journey length, despite the lack of association between journey lengths and different areas of the borough. However, this does not seem to be the case; the median of the shops/ parks distance for respondents with cars available on weekdays and the figure for those without cars are both .45 mile, while the inter-quartile range in the two cases is .33 mile and .30 mile, respectively.

Car availability, as a determinant of journey lengths, seems only to influence distances to pre-school facilities (median = .42 mile for those with cars and .23 mile for those without) and distances to social clubs, including mother-and-toddler clubs (median = .62 mile for those with cars and .28 mile for those without). For all other activities, there are no apparent differences in average journey length, related to effective car access.

<u>In summary</u>, the evidence presented by Map 5 (and supplemented by the calculation of average distances) supports the thesis that the extent of activity space for women with young children is very limited. There are differences both between different types of activity and between different respondents. The variation in journey lengths seems to be mainly a function of the differential provision of facilities, although choice decisions related to the <u>grade</u> (or type) of facilities used (in the case of shopping centres, parks and pre-school facilities) are also important determinants of distances travelled. Car availability seems to influence journey lengths only in the case of travel to pre-school facilities and social clubs.

Comparisons, both with the daily activity space of husbands (journey to work data) and with evening/weekend shopping trips, show clearly the constrained nature of women's weekday activities in a spatial sense and re-emphasise the local orientation of women's lives when they have young children.

General summary of survey findings

The analysis of data relating to mobility and distance has focused attention on the predominance of walking and the restricted spatial extent of women's activity patterns when they have young children. Car availability is seen to operate as the most important factor determining mobility since public transport is relatively little used (although buses do act as car-substitutes to some extent). Problems experienced with public transport relate far more to the presence of children than to criticisms of the services provided. Not unexpectedly, access to a car is strongly related to 'social group' characteristics of respondents.

Actual distances to activity locations reflect the differential provision of facilities within Merton to a great extent. Partly because the general provision of shopping and recreational facilities is good within the borough, the extent of activity space for respondents is very limited. Thus, the local orientation of women's lives is seen to result from a combination of a negative influence (lack of mobility) and a positive influence (local provision of facilities). Those respondents who travel further to take part in their daily activities are those with effective access to a car and/or those living at a greater distance from desired activity locations.

Chapter 8

CHILD CARE

> ...the young child needs something other than
> his home to give him the stimulus of compan-
> ionship, of space and learning experience and
> to give his mother a break and a support. We
> have to look again at the resources which we
> can devote to the youngest children. It's
> urgent that we do this now because the time
> for being a very young child is a very short
> time indeed, and every time that we miss a few
> years we have left one more young child out
>
> (Lady Plowden, 1977, 8-9).

> In developing pre-school provision...much more
> attention must be paid to changes occurring in
> society and to what people want. In other
> words the services should offer parents and
> children realistic alternatives from which to
> select those that best satisfy their changing
> needs and aspirations...if we retain an out of
> date pattern of services, we are forcing many
> families to make arrangements that are inadeq-
> uate and unsatisfactory both for children and
> parents
>
> (Tizard, Moss and Perry, 1976, 26;28).

The above quotations taken together present a reasonable summary of the types of conclusions reached
by present day researchers in the field of child
care. The first emphasises the 'educational' needs
of young children; the second, the 'day care' needs
of families. These two areas of need, though clearly
requiring different solutions, are generally considered as two aspects of the same problem. The relative weights put on these elements, however, tend to
vary with the ideological stance of the researcher.

The whole question of the inadequacy of child
care provision has been set within a historical
context in Chapter 3. Different types of child care
have been considered and the available literature
concerning the demand for child care services has
been reviewed. The aim of this chapter is to consider the provision of child care facilities in Merton
and their use by survey respondents.

Pre-School Child Care in Merton

Table 24 lists the number of places (both full-time
and part-time) which were available for children
under five in different pre-school facilities in
1976, (this being the nearest date to that of the
survey for which statistics are available), in
England as a whole and Inner and Outer London, by way
of comparison with the number of places in the London
borough of Merton. The table also indicates the percentage of each area's under five population accomm-
odated in each type of provision. As can be seen,
the percentage of children receiving some form of day
care continued to increase in the country as a whole
from 1973 (when it was approximately 23 per cent).
Greater London, however, boasts a higher percentage
than the national average, Inner London having a
higher level of provision than the Outer London boroughs. The borough of Merton has a particularly high
percentage of young children in day care (40 per
cent), compared to London as a whole. This is almost
entirely due to the large number of nursery education
places available; 23 per cent of all children under
five attend a nursery school or class in the borough,
as compared to only 14 per cent of children in
England generally and 18 per cent in Inner London.
A little over one-quarter of children receiving some
form of child care attend pre-school playgroups. The
remainder are with registered child minders or in day
nurseries. In 1975, net expenditure on day nurseries
by Merton council amounted to £7,745 per 1,000 children under five compared to a national mean for all
local authorities of £7,088. Net expenditure on pre-
school playgroups was, however, considerably lower
than the national average (£205 per 1,000 children
under five in Merton, compared with an average figure
of £467), indicating a lesser degree of subsidisation
of the private sector than in the country as a whole.
Map 6 shows the distribution of the various
types of pre-school 'institutions' in Merton in 1977.
As can be seen, there are only two public day nurseries in the borough, both of these being located in

Table 24 Day care and nursery education for children under five in 1976 (full-time and part-time)

(a = number of places, b = percentage of under five population)

	England		Inner London		Outer London (includes Merton)		London borough of Merton	
	a	b	a	b	a	b	a	b
Nursery schools and classes*	439,048	14.3	25,147	18.4	43,306	15.3	2,129	22.6
Local authority day nurseries	26,899	0.9	5,264	3.8	3,769	1.3	139	1.5
Private Day nurseries	26,079	0.9	2,324	1.7	2,823	1.0	152	1.6
Playgroups	353,845	11.6	14,331	10.5	38,283	13.5	1,001	10.6
Childminders (registered)	82,638	2.7	6,187	4.5	11,700	4.1	354	3.8
TOTAL	928,509	30.3	53,253	38.9	99,881	35.3	3,775	40.2

*Includes under five's in non-nursery classes in primary schools

Source: Calculated from figures given in Central Policy Review Staff (1978).

Map 6   Merton: Pre-school facilities

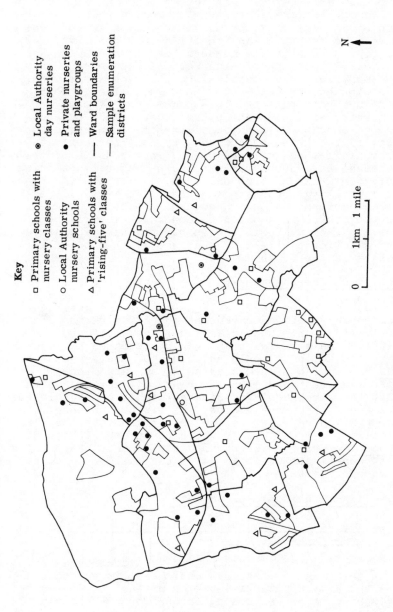

Key

□ Primary schools with nursery classes

○ Local Authority nursery schools

△ Primary schools with 'rising-five' classes

⊚ Local Authority day nurseries

● Private nurseries and playgroups

— Ward boundaries

— Sample enumeration districts

N ←

0   1km   1 mile

the eastern area (Colliers Wood and Mitcham). There
are also only two nursery schools but one of these,
at least, is more centrally located in the borough.
Out of a total of 39 primary schools in Merton, only
nine have no provision for children under five; 18
schools have separate nursery classes and a further
12 have 'rising five' classes. As can be seen from
the map, schools providing these services are widely
distributed throughout the borough, although those
with separate nursery classes are most strongly concentrated in the southern area, especially on and
around the St. Helier council estate which makes up
much of the Ravensbury ward. By contrast, only two
schools in the Wimbledon wards (in the North of the
borough) have nursery classes, the majority catering
only for 'rising five' children. Private day nurseries and playgroups have a rather different distribution pattern. Although occurring widely throughout
Merton, there is a definite concentration of such
private facilities in the (northern) Wimbledon area
and a noticeable lack of the same on the St. Helier
estate in the South.

Findings from the survey

In looking at the available data from the questionnaire survey, it is convenient to divide the subject
of 'child care' into clearly defined sections,
although this division should not be taken to imply
that the subject should not also be considered as a
whole. In fact, the reverse is the case; one of the
most important problems of pre-school services is
that they are rarely considered within a co-ordinated
framework. For the purposes of discussion here,
information relating to the use of 'institutional'
facilities, particularly those concerned with nursery
education, will be introduced first and that dealing
with non-'institutional' child care will be considered afterwards.

1.   'Institutional' child care

a)   The use and non-use of 'institutional'
      facilities

      The first questions raised by a consideration of
data relating to 'institutional' facilities concern
the actual and potential use or non-use of the latter
by survey respondents and reasons for not choosing to
send children to facilities which are available. Of
the 400 respondents to the questionnaire survey, 198

(or approximately half) have at least one child under
five at a nursery school or class, a day nursery or
supervised playgroup (that is, a playgroup where
mothers are not required to attend along with their
children). Of the remaining 202 respondents, only 21
state that they would not like their children to go
to a nursery school or supervised playgroup before
they go to school full-time, but only 63 have
actually put their children's names down for a
particular 'institution'.

By far the most important reason for not having
entered a child's name on a waiting list is the age
of the child concerned; of the 116 respondents
wanting their children to receive nursery school or
playgroup care in the future but not having put their
names down for a particular facility, 72 (62 per
cent) state their reason as the fact that their
children are too young for the question to have been
seriously considered at this stage. Other reasons
are of far less importance and, in fact, 16 per cent
state that there is 'no particular reason' for their
not having entered their children's names on a waiting list. Perhaps the need to do so has not been
made clear to these women. Certainly, the provision
of 'institutional' care for pre-school children -
even of state nursery education - is not an automatic
occurrence. Even where there is no shortage of
places (and this is rare even in a local authority
area with very good nursery provision, such as
Merton), children under the age of full-time schooling will not be 'summonsed' to attend a particular
school or class; the parent concerned must register
a desire for the child to take up a place which has
been provided before the child will be satisfact-
orily 'placed'. In addition, private playgroups and
nursery schools often have long waiting lists and
the prior entry of a name is often an essential pre-
condition for obtaining a place at all before the age
of five, let alone at two and a half or three. It is
therefore perhaps a little surprising that so few
women who definitely want their children to attend a
nursery school or supervised playgroup have actually
got as far as putting their names down for a particular 'institution', even if their children are very
young. It is perhaps significant, from a geographical point of view, that those respondents who
already have their children's names entered on a
waiting list (63 women) tend to live nearer to the
chosen facilities than other respondents. The apparent locational bias in the decision to put down children's names is not, however, so evident in the case

of private 'institutions', where only 58 per cent
intend to send their children to the nearest playgroup in any case.

As previously mentioned, 21 respondents state
that they would not like their children to go to a
nursery school or supervised playgroup before they
go to school full-time. Compared to the sample as a
whole, these women tend to be working-class and from
low income families (but not lone parents). They
were also younger at the birth of their first
children. The most predominant relationship is, however, with education level; out of only 23 respondents in the whole sample who left school before the
age of 16, ten fall into the group who do not want
their children to go to nursery school. Women who
want their children with them at home tend to lead
rather isolated lives; one-third live in flats and
only two respondents have access to a car on weekdays; 15 take part in no social activities and the
remainder only participate in one activity; none of
them left their homes many times on the day before
interview. The children of respondents with this
type of life-style would, objectively, appear to be
more in need of pre-school education than others.
The reasons given by their mothers for not sending
them to nursery school at all are primarily self-
oriented (13 state that they prefer to keep the child
at home with them) or a matter of personal belief
(two consider that children are too young to go to
school before the age of five and four assert that
children do not need pre-school education). Financial reasons are certainly not dominant and this is
presumably because of the widespread distribution of
state nursery schools and classes in Merton, particularly in areas with a predominance of lower income
families. These women are clearly not constrained by
a lack of provision of facilities but their whole
life-style echoes the dominance of the gender-role
constraint.

Having studied the future intentions of respondents with respect to nursery education, it is relevant to stress that probably not all those who now
state that they want their children to attend nursery
schools will, in fact, send them when the time comes,
either because they have changed their minds or because a place is not made available. It is, therefore, perhaps more relevant to look at actual use and
non-use of facilities, taking only those respondents
with a youngest child aged three or four (of whom
there are 113 in the present sample).

Table 25 shows the correlation coefficients

Table 25   Correlation of use of nursery schools with other variables

	Terminal education age	S.e.g. of husband	Family income	Age of respondent	Car availability
Use of nursery school	r=.24* (p=.006)	r=.16* (p=.05)	r=.05 (p=.29)	r=-.22* (p=.009)	r=.21* (p=.01)

	Employment Status	Children over 5	Length of residence	Within $\frac{1}{4}$ mile of nursery school	Attitude to motherhood
Use of nursery school	r=.04 (p=.35)	r=-.00 (p=.5)	r=.01 (p=.47)	r=-.02 (p=.44)	r=-.04 (p=.32)

*Relationships significant at the .05 level of significance

N.B.   See Appendix C for specification of variables.

between the use of nursery schools on the one hand
and a range of variables considered as potential determinants on the other. As can be seen, only four of
the relationships described in the table prove to be
significant at the .05 level of significance. The
degree of association is greatest in the case of the
terminal education age and present age of the respondent. It is no surprise that sending children to
nursery school should be related to the mother's
education level, especially since this relationship
has already been noted with respect to future
intentions of nursery school use. The fact that the
use of nursery schools is related to an older age-
group is less clearly comprehensible, especially
since there is no relationship at all between nursery
school use and having children over five in addition
to a child aged three or four. Although social class
is also related to the use of nursery schools (as is
car availability), it is clear from partial correlation analysis that the two variables, education level
and age of the mother, are the dominant statistical
correlates.

The lack of relationship between nursery school
use and family income is interesting since it is
often assumed that poorer families are hindered from
sending their children to nursery school by a lack of
ability to pay fees. In the case of Merton this
factor is obviously of much less importance since
state nursery classes and schools are widely distributed throughout the borough. (It will be seen later
that the use of private facilities is closely related
to higher family income).

Table 25 also indicates a lack of relationship
with other variables hypothesised to influence
nursery school attendance. The fact that women in
paid employment are not more likely to send their
children to nursery schools is not entirely unexpected, considering the facts discussed in Chapter 5.
As previously noted, nursery schools and playgroups
do not provide ideal opening hours from the point of
view of the employed mother. It was hypothesised
that people living in the local area for less than a
year would be less likely to send their children to
nursery schools because of the need to put children's names down on a waiting list some time in
advance. No relationship of this type is apparent,
however. There is, similarly, no relationship with
distance from a nursery school or playgroup, despite
the fact that primary and nursery schools generally
have small catchment areas and also that a locational bias has already been shown to exist in the case

of entering children's names on waiting lists.
Finally, it is interesting that no relationship
exists between nursery school use and the woman's
attitude to motherhood. It might have been thought
that an expressed desire to be free from the responsibilities of motherhood, at least occasionally,
would be related to sending children to nursery
school. Such is obviously not the case; perhaps
the lack of nursery school attendance itself contributes to a desire to be free from motherhood responsibilities for some women.

b)   The type of nursery school used

Having looked at questions relating to the use
or non-use of all 'institutional' facilities, it is
now important to distinguish between different types
of nursery care. Table 26 lists the actual numbers
of respondents with children in different types of
nursery schools (or with their names down for future
attendance). As can be seen, respondents are almost
equally divided between patronage of state and private pre-school facilities. Comparison with Table 24
shows that, while the level of attendance at state
'institutions' is fairly representative of the
borough as a whole, the sample over-represents
private playgroup and nursery school use. This is
partly because the sample also tends to over-repres-
ent professional and managerial households in the
population, which are the families most likely to
send children to private nursery schools and playgroups (65 per cent of such households using pre-
school facilities send their children to private
nursery schools compared to 50 per cent of skilled
manual households, for example).

Table 26   Respondents with children at nursery
             schools (including those with names on
             waiting lists).

	Number of respondents	
State nursery class	64)	
State nursery school	39)	
'Rising five' class	16)	122
Day nursery	3)	
Private playgroup/nursery school	138	
Total	260	

The varying types of nursery facilities are characterised by different features. In the first place, private playgroups tend to cater for children at a younger age than state schools; while no children under three years old in the sample at present attend state nursery schools or classes (or even day nurseries), 32 per cent of those attending private playgroups or nursery schools are under three. Amongst three year olds, a majority of those in outside child care (65 per cent) go to private playgroups but by the age of four, 85 per cent of children are attending state schools, the majority (53 per cent) in state nursery classes. Hours of attendance are closely related to type of facility; almost all state 'institutions' offer all-week or half-week schooling, while most private playgroups are open for less than five half-days per week. Of respondents with children at state schools, only three out of 89 send them for less than five half-days each week, while three-quarters of those with children at private 'institutions' do so.

The differing ages of children attending pre-school facilities and the different hours of opening are both reflected in the relationship between attendance at private or state 'institutions' and the respondent's attitude to nursery education. Of the sample as a whole (excluding those who do not intend their children to go to nursery school at all), 52 per cent agree with the statement that: 'The benefit to my children of nursery school is the most important reason for sending them there', while 47 per cent believe that: 'Having some free time myself is important but the benefit to my children of nursery school is equally important too'. Only three respondents (1 per cent) state that: 'Having some free time myself is the most important reason for sending my children to nursery school'(and none of these actually has a child at nursery school at the present time). Those who consider their children's benefit to be the most important reason for sending them to nursery school are more likely to have children attending state schools, while those who value their own free time away from the children equally as much are more likely to have children at playgroups or private nurseries (r=-.15 (p=.02)).

It has already been noted that some relationship exists between the type of pre-school facility used and social class. The relationship is not, however, as clear-cut as one might expect; in particular, while 65 per cent of respondents with husbands in professional and managerial occupations send their

Table 27   Cross-tabulation of type of pre-school facility used, with family income

(Percentages in brackets)

	Under £3000	£3000-£5000	£5000-£7000	£7000+	Total
State	21 (67.7)	45 (47.4)	28 (49.1)	11 (28.9)	105 (47.5)
Private	10 (32.3)	50 (52.6)	29 (50.9)	27 (71.1)	116 (52.5)
Total	31 (100.0)	95 (100.0)	57 (100.0)	38 (100.0)	221 (100.0)

Gamma = .28   (179 missing cases)

children to private playgroups, nearly as many (59
per cent) in the partly-skilled and unskilled manual
household group also use private facilities. The
clearest socio-economic relationship is with family
income (see Table 27). The relationship with terminal education age is more complex but equally comprehensible. Respondents with the highest and lowest
education levels are the most likely to send their
children to state schools, the latter presumably because they are easily available at no cost and the
former because of a concern for the educational quality of pre-school child-care; highly educated respondents are over-represented amongst those using
state nursery schools, as opposed to classes in
primary schools. The nursery schools are generally
considered to have the highest educational standards
and this belief is reflected in longer waiting lists
for these 'institutions' than any other (either state
or private) in the borough and also in the fact that
respondents using these schools travel further to get
to them than those taking children to other types of
pre-school facility.
    Apart from the special case of nursery school
use referred to above, in general it is true to say
that social characteristics of respondents are important in determining the type of facility used, only
in so far as social areas are related to the geographical distribution of different types of 'institutions'. It has already been noted that private
playgroups and nurseries are concentrated more in
the northern part of the borough while state schools
offering nursery education are predominant in the
South (see Map 6). Practically the whole of Ravensbury ward, in the southernmost part of Merton, is
occupied by the St. Helier estate, a large area of
(mainly) single-family houses built by the Greater
London Council in the inter-War period. Occupants
of this estate fall predominantly into the 'skilled
manual worker' social group. While all state
schools in this area offer nursery places, there are
no private facilities within easy reach. (63 per
cent of respondents in this area live more than half
a mile from the nearest private playgroup). In the
northern part of the borough the majority of respondents live more than half a mile away from a state
nursery school or class but in Ravensbury ward, 88
per cent of respondents live within one quarter of a
mile of state provision and all of them live within
half a mile.
    It is this distribution pattern of nursery fac-
ilities which largely accounts for the 'social'

212

differences between users of different types of
school since distance to facilities is important in
determining their use. This is clearly shown in
Table 28. While 65 per cent of those living within
one quarter of a mile of a state nursery school or
class send their children to state facilities, only
one-quarter of those living more than half a mile
away do so. It is interesting, however, that there
is a variation in usage pattern between different
types of state school; all but one respondent using
a state nursery class live within half a mile, four
out of five with children at nursery schools do so,
but only one-quarter of those who send their children to a 'rising five' class. Respondents using
private playgroups or nursery schools live, in
general, much further away from state facilities
than those who actually use state schools.

In contrast, there is much less relationship
between the use of private facilities and distance
to be travelled than is the case with state nursery
places (although there is still a moderate association between the variables - see Appendix D, Table
D37). In most areas of the borough, private playgroups or nursery schools are to be found within a
short distance of home; two-thirds of all respondents live within one quarter of a mile and 93 per
cent within half a mile of such facilities. It is
interesting that, while 88 per cent of respondents
using state nursery schools or classes send their
children to the nearest facility of that type, only

Table 28   Cross-tabulation of type of pre-school
           facility used, with distance to the near-
           est state nursery school/class
           (Percentages in brackets)

	Under $\frac{1}{4}$ mile	$\frac{1}{4}-\frac{1}{2}$ mile	Over $\frac{1}{2}$ mile	Total
State	60(65.2)	41(50.0)	21(24.4)	122(46.9)
Private	32(34.8)	41(50.0)	65(75.6)	138(53.1)
Total	92(100.0)	82(100.0)	86(100.0)	260(100.0)

gamma = .52   (140 missing cases)

60 per cent of users of private 'institutions' actually send their children to the nearest one. As
well as reflecting differences in standards and hours
of opening, this fact also underlines the widespread
distribution of private nursery schools and the
general ease of access to one or more facilities of
this type.

Having elucidated the relationship between the
distribution of nursery places and actual usage patterns, it now becomes possible to 'explain' the relationships between state/private facility use and different 'social' variables in terms of this distribution pattern of facilities. A low negative association is evident between distance to the nearest state
nursery facility and social class; in particular, 45
per cent of professional and managerial families live
more than half a mile from the nearest state provision, while less than one-quarter of working-class
families do so (see Appendix D, Table D38). The relationship between social class and distance to the
nearest private nursery facility is negligible but it
is interesting that nearly 80 per cent of partly-
skilled and unskilled manual households in the sample
live within one quarter of a mile of the nearest
playgroup, the highest percentage of any social class
group. This presumably helps to explain the large
percentage of respondents from this group sending
their children to private, rather than state, facilities. It is interesting that a much higher percentage of working-class, than middle-class, respondents
send their children to the nearest nursery provision.

The relationship between family income and type
of pre-school facility used (see Table 27) is also,
at least partly, explicable in terms of location
patterns. Again, the clearest relationship concerns
the distribution of state facilities (Table 29).
While 80 per cent of the lowest income group live
within half a mile of the nearest state nursery
school or class, less than half of the highest income
group do so. It is very interesting, however, that
higher income respondents are not more likely to live
near to a private nursery facility than other respondents (in fact, they are slightly less likely to do
so), despite the fact that they have the greatest
tendency to use such facilities. This fact highlights the general point that distance is a more
important constraint for some groups in the population than for others. The highest income group
consists of respondents who not only can afford to
send their children to private nursery facilities but
also have access to private transport which overcomes

Table 29   Cross-tabulation of distance to the nearest state nursery school/class
with family income

(Percentages in brackets)

	Under £3000	£3000-£5000	£5000-£7000	£7000+	Total
Under ¼ mile	22 (44.0)	58 (38.2)	23 (28.8)	7 (14.9)	110 (33.4)
¼-½ mile	18 (36.0)	53 (34.9)	26 (32.5)	15 (31.9)	112 (34.0)
Over ½ mile	10 (20.0)	41 (27.0)	31 (38.7)	25 (53.2)	107 (32.5)
Total	50 (100.0)	152 (100.0)	80 (100.0)	47 (100.0)	329 (100.0)

gamma = .30

the problem of distance (see Chapter 7). Thus,
journey times to nursery schools are no longer
amongst this group than for any other respondents.
It can, therefore, be concluded that the type of
nursery facility used is most closely related to what
is available in the local area concerned, although
this constraint of provision has much less effect on
higher income, higher class households than it does
upon others.

In summary, the data from the Merton survey
emphasise the part-time nature of the provision of
pre-school child care, only nine respondents having
their children in full-time care. In contrast to
previous 'official' predictions, very few respondents
are found who do not want their children to attend
some sort of nursery school before the age of full-
time schooling. Actual usage patterns of pre-school
facilities relate strongly to the education level
and age of respondents but not to income (Merton had
a very good standard of state nursery education
provision at the time of the survey).

Within the sample there is an almost equal division between those using state facilities and those
using private playgroups or nursery schools. The
use of different types of facilities relates most
strongly to the distribution pattern of these facilities, which itself is related to both social class
and income distribution patterns. Distance to a
state nursery school or class is important in determining its use, while distance to private facilities
is less important, reflecting the lower level of
constraint on higher income car-using respondents.

2.   Non-'Institutional' child care

Young children not only attend nursery schools
or playgroups outside the home; many of them are
cared for by a person (or persons) other than their
mother on at least some occasions during weekdays.
It was suggested to respondents that: 'It's often
difficult or impossible to take children with you to
various places - to work or to social meetings or on
main shopping trips, for instance. Do you ever
leave your child(ren) with anyone else, during the
daytime on weekdays, so that you can do those sort
of things on your own?' In answer to the latter
question, 261 respondents state that they do sometimes leave their children with another person,
while 139 (35 per cent) say that they do not. Of
the reasons given for not leaving children with
someone else. the most important are that there is

'no need' or 'no particular reason' (40 per cent)
that there is no suitable person available (23 per
cent) and that the mother concerned does not like
leaving her child with someone else (20 per cent).
In addition to this last figure, 12 per cent of
respondents state that their children will not be
left with anyone else and 10 per cent consider their
children too young to be left. Apart from the 32
respondents who are not able to find a suitable substitute carer for their children, it appears that
the women who never leave their children with anyone
else on weekdays have simply accepted the full-time
child care role which has devolved upon them, without questioning its total involvement to any great
extent.

Those respondents who do leave their children,
at least occasionally, with someone else, most commonly rely on friends (114 respondents) or on their
mothers (or mothers-in-law) (89 respondents) or other
relatives (21 respondents). Having a relative living
in the respondent's household (22 cases) is, as
would be expected, related to child care arrangements
but no pattern is visible concerning the presence of
'other adults' in the household since only six respondents fall into this category. Mothers and other
relatives are most commonly used as substitute child
carers when it is necessary for respondents to be
away from home for long hours during the day or
where younger children are involved. Although the
majority of respondents request this kind of child
care only once a week or less often, it is also true
that women who go out to work are over-represented
amongst those leaving their children with mothers.
Compared with the 100 respondents who leave their
children in the care of mothers or other relatives,
the number relying on their husbands for daytime
child care is very small - only 18 respondents - and
of these, only two are in outside employment. As
might be expected, half of the husbands concerned are
shift-workers and a further three are unemployed.
It is interesting, however, that considering all
respondents with husbands at work, there is no relationship evident in the data between the husband's
hours out of the home each day and the extent of his
assistance with child care responsibilities in
general.

As previously stated, friends provide the most
numerically significant child care service but they
are rarely used frequently and almost never for a
whole day at a time. 90 per cent live in the same
local area as the respondent concerned. Only six

respondents leave their children with friends every day while they are at work but many other friends probably look after children in out-of-nursery school hours to accommodate part-time working mothers. It is possible that at least some of the 'friends' referred to by respondents are, in fact, paid child- minders; although respondents were asked by inter- viewers whether this was the case, it is likely that those leaving their children with unregistered minders would not want to identify their 'friends' in this way. Consequently, only 17 respondents openly state that they leave their children with paid child- minders and of these only four are in outside paid employment on every weekday. It does not seem likely, in view of what is known about the extent of childminding nationally, that this very small number of respondents really represents all those who use childminding services in one form or another. Amongst the 17 respondents leaving their children with childminders, twelve are full-time housewives and it is clear that the 'minders' referred to are, in fact, daily nannies/au pairs who look after the children in the respondents' own houses; the resp- ondents concerned all being the wives of professional or managerial workers and most of them falling in the highest income group represented in the sample as a whole.

In summary, two-thirds of respondents leave their young children with some other person on weekdays, at least occasionally. Friends are the most commonly used child carers, especially for in- frequent or shorter time periods. Mothers (or mothers-in-law) are the most important substitute carers for longer periods of time or younger child- ren. Relatively few respondents apparently use childminders, although this number may in fact be under-recorded.

General summary of survey findings

The standard of provision of pre-school child care is particularly high in Merton and this is reflected in the large proportion of respondents either at present using such facilities or intending to do so in the future. However, this provision is primarily in the form of part-time nursery education, which may not always satisfy the needs of individuals for day care. Since pre-school facilities tend to have small catchment areas, it is to be expected that the use of state or private facilities will reflect the distribution pattern of such services within the

borough, although the use of private pre-school
facilities is also related to higher 'social group'
characteristics.

Clearly, 'institutional' services do not
provide for all the child care needs of respondents
and most women regularly leave their children with
at least one other person on weekdays (even if only
infrequently). Paid employees are particularly
likely to leave their children with their mothers,
although in general friends are the most commonly
used substitute carers. Few respondents leave their
children regularly with their husbands and, of those
who do, most are married to men on shift-work or who
are unemployed.

The most obvious finding which emerges from
this study of child care is the dominance of women
as child carers, whether one considers the respondents themselves, the nursery school or playgroup
teachers and helpers, mothers or friends. No other
type of data could more clearly point to the
continuing strength of gender-role differentiation
within society.

Chapter 9

THE QUALITY OF LIFE

It is impossible to study the daily lives of women
with young children without becoming involved in some
measure of judgement concerning the quality of those
lives. If it is true, as has been asserted throughout this study that women with young children find
their daily activities (and, indeed, their whole lives)
constrained by specific societal and physical constraints, then it becomes important to assess whether
or not their sense of well-being is thereby dimini-
shed. If it can be shown that women with young
children tend to suffer a poor quality of life, then
the focus on specific constraints and their remedies
is more obviously justifiable. This chapter considers various data from the questionnaire survey relating to 'quality of life' measures. In order to
introduce the subject area, it is necessary briefly
to consider background literature in the field at the
outset.

Studies of the 'Quality of Life'

Smith (1977,31) notes that,'The idea of trying to
measure an abstraction like the quality of life is
anathema to many people...'. However, recent years
have seen a great explosion in the number of studies
directed to that end (see, for example, the many
pieces of research quoted in Szalai and Andrews
(ed.), 1980) and many have been undertaken by geographers concerned, in particular, with the spatial
aspects of social well-being. It is unnecessary here
to list all of these studies but excellent biblio-
graphies are to be found in Smith (1977) and Pacione
(1980).
        The most important element of this work to be
brought out here is the division into two groups of
studies: those employing 'objective' indicators of

social welfare   and those using 'subjective'
measures. It is the former group into which most
geographical work has fallen;   a notable example
being Smith's (1973) study of social well-being in
the United States, which uses seven primary criteria
operationalised in terms of objective indicators to
assess the spatial variation in quality of life at
different spatial scales.
The development of suitable objective criteria
has been a dominant task of those working within the
'social indicators movement'. On the other hand,
many writers have suggested that such objective
elements may give only a very limited indication of
actual satisfaction with life   and instead that '...
it is people's perceptions of their own well-being...
or lack of well-being, that ultimately define the
quality of their lives' (Pacione, 1980,195). A
number of researchers have, therefore, sought to establish 'subjective' indicators of social welfare
through direct social research methods. A leading
British proponent of this approach is Hall, who in
1973 and 1975 carried out national surveys designed
to measure the quality of life and assess changes
over time (see, Hall, 1976). The results of this
work are discussed later.
In seeking to explain statistical variation in
'subjective' quality of life measures, different
researchers have suggested different aspects (or life
concerns) as being of importance. Pacione (1980),
looking at the results of 13 British and American
studies found five areas to be common to all the
studies;   these being housing, health, job satisfaction, standard of living   and leisure. In his own
research he found 'standard of living' to be the most
important predictor of overall quality of life measures, with job satisfaction and the availability of
consumer services also ranking as important elements.
While many researchers have accepted the close
connection between objective and subjective measures
of social welfare, there is apparently no necessary
correlation between the two (see, Kuz, 1978). In
this study attempts will be made to view 'quality of
life' from both subjective and objective viewpoints,
in order to offer a broader perspective on the problems of the particular group being studied. The
extent to which these measures are correlated will
also be discussed below.

'Satisfaction with life'

As recorded above, the practice of using respondent-reported data as indicators of quality of life is now well-established among social researchers. One source of such data is 'satisfaction with life', an overall measure derived from bipolar semantic scales. The construction of this indicator is discussed below. The justification for considering 'satisfaction with life' as a suitable subjective measure of quality of life rests on the same criteria as the use of any subjective indicator; namely, that the perception of well-being held by the individual is an accurate representation of actual well-being.

The derivation of the 'satisfaction with life' measurement will first be discussed together with the results obtained from individual contributing scales. The overall indicator will then be correlated against a range of variables predicted as influences of life satisfaction.

1.   Derivation of the semantic differential test and previous results

The bipolar adjectival scales used in the semantic differential test for 'satisfaction with life' are indicated in Figs. E1 to E3 in Appendix E. The semantic differential is really a type of Likert scale, providing a means of measuring several different semantic dimensions (or different kinds of meaning) which we use in conceptualising any object or idea (Elms, 1976,27). The technique was developed in 1957 by Osgood as a general measuring instrument, the selection of actual items for use being determined by the nature of the problem under study. In administering the semantic differential test, some items are reversed in a random manner in order to avoid response bias tendencies (Kerlinger, 1969, 564-579). The items are scored from 1 to 7, with 7 at the positive end. The scores on each scale are summed and the total is divided by the number of scales, in order to produce a single figure which can represent overall 'satisfaction with life'. It is, therefore, of great importance that the scales contribute to a unidimensional structure.

The particular scales chosen for this research were developed and used jointly by American and British quality of life studies conducted in the mid-1970's (see, Campbell, Converse and Rodgers, 1976; Hall, 1976). The British studies were carried out by the former Social Science Research Council (S.S.R.C.) Survey Unit under the direction of Abrams and Hall. A wide variety of subjective measures were derived from the four individual studies carried out by the

S.S.R.C. Survey Unit, of which the present 'satisfaction with life' measure is but one. The two
national surveys carried out in 1973 and 1975 each
covered nearly one thousand respondents. One
important result to emerge from these studies was
that, in general, women tended to experience greater
'satisfaction with life' than men and married women
greater 'satisfaction with life' than non-married
women (Hall, personal communication).

    Access to additional special data from these two
national surveys was granted in the form of results
on 'satisfaction with life' for women with children
under five only; there were 98 respondents in this
category in 1973 and 84 respondents in 1975. The
1973 survey used all ten bipolar scales chosen for
the Merton study, while in 1975 only eight of the
scales were employed. The data derived from the two
national surveys (relating to women with young
children) are shown in Figs. E1 and E2 (Appendix E).
By comparison with the overall data from the surveys,
women with children under five were shown to have low
satisfaction levels, despite the fact that married
women in total experienced the highest levels of
'satisfaction with life'. This fact alone says a
great deal about the emotional stresses of caring for
young children.

2.   'Satisfaction with life' from the Merton sample

    As mentioned previously, the semantic differen-
tial test for 'satisfaction with life' employed in
the Merton study used the ten bipolar scales developed for the 1973 national Quality of Life Study. The
overall results are shown in Fig. E3 in Appendix E,
and these can be compared with the results from the
national studies for women with children under 5,
shown in Figs. E1 and E2. The results are remarkably
similar; indicating a relatively low level of
'satisfaction with life' among members of this group
in general.

    Table 30 gives a comparison of the mean scores
on each individual scale for each of the three
studies, together with the related standard derivat-
ions. The same features are evident in each case.
In all three studies, the highest mean score occurs
on the Happy/Unhappy scale and the lowest on the
Free/Tied down scale. The former scale also shows
the most internal consistency overall, having low
standard deviations in all three cases. Unfortunately, one of the interesting scales from the point of
view of this research project - the Under my control/

Table 30   Semantic differential test : mean scores

Scale	1973 national study*		1975 national study*		1977 Merton study	
	Mean	s.d.	Mean	s.d.	Mean	s.d.
Interesting/Boring	4.99	1.44	4.90	1.41	4.77	1.44
Enjoyable/Miserable	5.59	1.36	5.17	1.50	5.44	1.35
Free/Tied down	3.22	1.57	3.46	1.47	3.38	1.63
Smooth/Rough	4.94	1.60	4.66	1.33	4.88	1.49
Rewarding/Disappointing	5.32	1.57	−		5.60	1.44
Easy/Hard	4.30	1.74	4.18	1.59	4.08	1.69
Fulfilling/Frustrating	4.98	1.53	4.72	1.63	4.60	1.70
Full/Empty	5.94	1.24	5.25	1.62	5.73	1.44
Under my control/Controlled by others	4.50	1.71	−		4.55	1.85
Happy/Unhappy	6.17	1.26	5.72	1.39	6.00	1.21

*Women with children under 5 only

Controlled by others scale - is not available for the
1975 study. Both the Merton study and the 1973 national study produced a fairly low mean score for this
scale (which is certainly to be expected considering
the nature of the samples) but also, interestingly, a
high standard deviation, indicating a wide range of
response to this scale.

The results obtained from the present study were
subjected to common factor analysis in order to check
the unidimensionality of the semantic differential
measure. After iteration of the two principal factors, only one factor emerged with an eigen-value
greater than 1 (in fact, 3.59) and this explained 82
per cent of the variation in the data. It was, therefore, accepted that the data represent overwhelmingly
a unidimensional structure and can be accepted as
forming one clear measure of 'satisfaction with life.'

Looking in more detail at the correlation matrix
formed from the individual scales' inter-relationships, high inter-correlations are evident in the
case of all scales except the Under my control/Cont-
rolled by others scale, which has low correlations
with all other scales and low loadings on both Factor
1 and Factor 2. Compared to the other nine scales in
the analysis, this scale has a very low communality
figure and, in general, appears to detract from the
validity of the overall measure. It was, therefore,
decided to omit this scale from the calculation of
'satisfaction with life' scores. Overall satisfaction scores for all respondents were computed by adding the scores on the remaining nine scales and dividing the result by nine.

3. Relationships between 'satisfaction with life'
   and other variables

Despite the existence of a generally low self-
reported 'satisfaction with life' among women with
young children, variations within the group are
naturally to be expected, dependent on numerous
different influences. This section will attempt to
summarise the relationships between satisfaction
levels and other variables within the Merton data,
which are hypothesised to be influencing factors (for
specification of variables, see Appendix C).

Tables 31 and 32 present these relationships in
summary form. The most important influences on satisfaction level, as indicated by correlation coefficients and mean scores of categories, are those
involving attitudes to motherhood and employment,
socio-economic characteristics (social class, income
and housing), the presence of a husband, age of the

Table 31   Summary of significant influences on 'satisfaction with life' (p≥.05)

Positive Influences	r	Negative Influences	r
Attitude to motherhood	.37	Employment status preference	-.36
Enjoyability of motherhood	.43	Attitude to work	-.24
Owner-occupation	.28	Attitude to position of women	-.14
Predominant owner-occupation in area	.15	Council tenure	-.26
Family income	.18	Flat dwelling	-.13
Car availability	.15	Age of the youngest child	-.12
Socio-economic group of husband	.12	Age at birth of first child	-.10
Age of husband	.19	Health problems	-.23
Husband present in household	.20		
Sufficient help with house-work from husband	.16		
Sufficient help with child care from husband	.14		
Child left with other person	.16		
Number of social activities	.18		
Home visit (friend) at least once a week	.10		
Friendliness of area	.13		

Table 32   'Satisfaction with life' mean scores for
            categories of major influencing
            (categorical) variables

Variable	Category	Mean score	No. in category
Attitude to motherhood	Never wished to be free	5.30	204
	Sometimes wished to be free	4.71	162
	Often wished to be free	3.93	33
Enjoyability of motherhood	Always	5.50	80
	Nearly always	5.08	175
	Usually	4.59	104
	Sometimes	4.19	39
	Hardly ever	2.00	1
Employment status preference	Prefer to work now	4.47	95
	Happy at home	5.22	215
Tenure of household	Own outright	5.27	17
	Own mortgage	5.12	253
	Council rent	4.39	70
	Private rent (unfurnished)	4.74	35
	Private rent (furnished)	4.59	10
	Free with job	5.06	8
	Lodger/with relatives	4.57	6
Flat dwelling	Lives in flat	4.66	64
	Lives in house	5.00	335
Family income	£7000 or more	5.15	47
	£5000-7000	5.04	80
	£3000-5000	4.95	151
	£3000	4.53	50
Car availability	Car available	5.16	128
	Car not available	4.84	271
Socio-economic group of husband	Professional and managerial	5.18	123
	Other non-manual	4.96	79
	Skilled manual	4.96	137
	Partly-skilled and unskilled	4.64	32

Table 32 cont.

Variable	Category	Mean score	No.in category
Husband present in household	Husband present	4.99	380
	Husband not present	4.08	19
Help with housework from husband	Too much	5.06	10
	About right and fair	5.07	266
	Not really enough	4.74	99
Help with child care from husband	Too much	5.46	7
	About right and fair	5.04	309
	Not really enough	4.69	62
Child left with other person	Never left	4.88	139
	Husband	4.42	18
	Mother/mother-in-law	4.91	89
	Other relative	5.35	21
	Friend	5.03	113
	Childminder	5.22	17
	Day nursery	3.78	2
Age of the youngest child	Under 1 year	5.13	101
	1 year	4.94	96
	2 years	4.87	90
	3 years	4.95	66
	4 years	4.67	46
Health problems	No problems	5.03	349
	Do almost anything	4.41	18
	Cannot do certain things	4.72	25
	Cannot do lots of things	2.92	7

youngest child and health problems.
    The highest correlation coefficients of all are
those relating to motherhood attitudes. The highest
mean score on 'satisfaction with life' is that related to respondents who state that 'being a mother has
always been enjoyable'. A very high mean score also
relates to those who have 'never' wished to be free
from the responsibilities of motherhood. In
contrast, very low scores represent those with negative attitudes to motherhood. Attitudes to work also
correlate strongly with 'satisfaction with life' and,
indeed, appear to be simply the 'other side of the
coin' from attitudes to motherhood. In particular,

there is a large difference in mean score between
those housewives and home-workers who would prefer
to be out at work now and those who are 'happy at
home'.

It is interesting that the relationship between
'attitude to work' (for derivation, see Chapter 5)
and satisfaction level is <u>negative</u>; that is, respondents who hold more traditional attitudes to the
question of women's employment tend to be more satisfied with life. The same is also true of the relationship with the general 'attitude to the position of
women'. However, perhaps these results are to be
expected. Harper and Richards (1979,58) remind us of
the strength of old norms of behaviour; even when
these are rejected openly, they still cause guilt and
confusion. It might, therefore, be expected that
those who hold 'progressive' attitudes but find themselves 'tied to women's role' would experience lower
satisfaction levels. In contrast, those whose attitudes and way of life are 'in concordance' (those with
'traditional' views) might be expected to experience
higher levels of 'satisfaction with life' as they
suffer no conflict of ideas. Table 33 looks at the
relationship between satisfaction levels and attitudes in more detail, combining the two attitude
variables into one variable. It is clear that those
who hold 'progressive' attitudes to work for women
are the most likely to achieve low scores on the
'satisfaction with life' rating.

It was to be expected that socio-economic characteristics would act as important determinants of
life satisfaction. In particular, it was expected
that working class women would tend to have lower
satisfaction scores than middle class women (see
Chapter 2). Table 32 indicates this to be the case,
with mean scores varying quite widely but an especially low mean score for the wives of partly-skilled
and unskilled manual workers, as compared to other
groups. 'Standard of living' has also been previously identified as a useful indicator of quality of
life. Approximating this factor as 'family income',
we can see from Table 32 that there is a close
connection between income levels and satisfaction
scores; those with low incomes ( )elow £3000 per
annum) having particularly low scores.

Housing issues have also assumed importance in
previous studies of life quality. In this study two
aspects of housing are clearly related to 'satisfaction with life'; tenure of the household and flat-
dwelling. Being a council tenant seems quite definitely to relate to lower satisfaction levels, as does

Table 33   Cross-tabulation of 'satisfaction with life', with attitude variables (categorised)

(Percentages in brackets)

	'Traditional' attitude to work and position of women	'Traditional' attitude to position of women / 'Progressive' attitude to work	'Progressive' attitude to position of women / 'Traditional' attitude to work	'Progressive' attitude to work and position of women	Total
High (scores 5-7)	46(66.7)	38(55.9)	53(49.5)	63(41.2)	200(50.4)
Neutral (scores 4-4.99)	18(26.1)	22(32.4)	47(43.9)	67(43.8)	154(38.8)
Low (scores 1-3.99)	5(7.2)	8(11.8)	7(6.5)	23(15.0)	43(10.8)
Total	69(100.0)	68(100.0)	107(100.0)	153(100.0)	397(100.0)

chi-square = 17.12   (p=.008)   (3 missing cases)

living in a flat. In contrast, owner occupiers
appear to enjoy greater 'satisfaction with life'
and even those renting their homes from a private
landlord generally experience higher satisfaction
levels than council tenants (see Table 32). While
flat dwelling is associated with lower satisfaction
scores, there is little apparent variation related to
height above ground; in fact, those living in ground
floor flats have a <u>lower</u> mean score than those in
first floor flats and also lower than those living
at least five floors from the ground.

There are three remaining variables which seem
to act as important determinants of 'satisfaction
with life'; these being, the presence of a husband
in the household, the age of the youngest child and
health problems. Lone parents score particularly low
figures on the satisfaction rating, as compared to
women with a husband present in the household (see
Table 32). This was to be expected when one considers the importance of companionship in dealing with
the constant problems associated with child-rearing
and also the low social and financial status of lone
parents.

The age of the youngest child has an interesting
relationship with satisfaction levels. It seems that
women are most satisfied with life when they have a
baby (under one year old). Markedly lower satisfaction levels are associated with having a youngest
child aged four years (see Table 32). Perhaps this
indicates a growing dissatisfaction with the allotted
role of mother over time or simply more role-
involvement where there is a young baby.

The final variable to be discussed here is that
relating to health problems. Physical health has
been identified in previous studies as an important
determinant of life quality. In the Merton sample,
50 respondents indicate that they have some problem
with their health although only seven state that this
problem prevents them from doing 'a lot of things'.
The mean satisfaction scores in Table 32 clearly
indicate low 'satisfaction with life' for these seven
respondents and, overall, there is an important correlation between the existence of health problems and
low satisfaction levels (see Table 31).

Table 34 lists the variables hypothesised to
influence life satisfaction but (at least in this
study) not found to be closely correlated with satisfaction scores. Amongst these, important examples
are employment status, the number of young children
which a respondent has and most of the environmental
variables relating to access to facilities and type

Table 34   Variables hypothesised to influence
            'satisfaction with life', but not
            significantly related at p>.05

	r
Employment status	-.04
Terminal education age	.06
Total number of children	-.03
Number of children under 5	-.07
Child at nursery school	-.08
Home visit (family) at least once a week	.07
Distance to local shops	-.00
Distance to main shopping centre	-.05
Distance to local park	.07
Percentage professional and managerial households in e.d.	-.01

of area. It may be that objective 'geographical'
variables are less important in determining overall
satisfaction levels than previously thought. However, 'satisfaction with life' is only one of many
possible indicators of 'quality of life' and objective spatial criteria must later be considered as
independent indicators, in addition to their relationship with this subjective variable.

In summary, the generally low scores on the
semantic differential test for 'satisfaction with
life', for the sample as a whole, are comparable with
those obtained from two national surveys (women with
children under five only). Variation in satisfaction
scores within the sample is related most closely to
differences in attitudes to motherhood and to employment. It is those who hold 'traditional' views on
the question of work for women and/or have very
positive attitudes to motherhood who score highest on
the 'satisfaction with life' measure.

'Satisfaction' can also be related to 'social
group' characteristics. Those from higher social
class, higher income households are very likely to
have a high 'satisfaction with life' score, while
lone parents, in particular, have low scores on this
measure. Respondents with a young baby have higher
scores than others. Health problems are seen to be
linked to lower 'satisfaction with life'. Perhaps
surprisingly, there is no relationship between
'satisfaction' scores and actual employment status,
while the number of children in the family and
distance to facilities also do not seem to influence

life satisfaction.

'Quality of life' as Measured by Activities Outside the Home

As discussed previously, measures of the 'quality of life' may encompass both subjective and objective indicators. The use of the term 'objective'does not, of course,imply that the choice of such indicators is value-free. In all cases, the subjective judgement of the researcher is involved in the choice of indicators, where this is not the result of questioning the respondents directly. It is up to the individual researcher concerned to select 'appropriate' measures to illustrate life quality and the choice may vary widely from study to study and between different client groups.

One of the premises of the present research is that the study of out-of-home activity patterns can help in the definition of 'quality of life' (see Chapin, 1971). It is suggested, in fact, that levels of social well-being may be related to the 'richness' (or otherwise) of activity patterns. This section aims to illustrate the point by considering the results of the time-budget study in the Merton survey, referring to the previous day's activities and also taking into account material on social activities in general. However, it is clear that the extent of out-of-home activity patterns may be closely related to the amount of assistance with work in the home given by husbands. Therefore,this limiting factor will first be discussed. In addition to acting as a constraint on activity patterns, lack of assistance from husbands can also be thought of directly as a factor in lowering the quality of life for women with young children.

1.   Help by husbands

It has already been well-documented in Chapter 2 that the general amount of assistance with housework and child care received from husbands is small, even where the wife is also employed full-time. Harper and Richards (1979,189) note that child-centred tasks tend to be more often shared than household jobs and that middle class husbands tend to do more housework than working class husbands. Tolson (1977, 70) attempts to explain the position of the working class man in this respect:

...what is fundamentally at stake, in the

working-class family, is a man's 'conjugal
right' to reproduce the <u>authority</u> he faces
at work. Because the insistence on domestic
'harmony' is, at root, a defence of male
supremacy, the balance of a man's identity
hangs upon the demarcation of domestic responsibilities. Any challenge to the status
quo is taken personally, as a confrontation.
And because, in its origins, the sexual
division of labour is irrational, such a
confrontation encounters deeply unconscious
barriers of resistance'.

If one views the male position in these terms, the
actual evidence of lack of domestic assistance which
can be seen is entirely comprehensible.
    Previous studies have detailed the number of
hours spent by men and women on household and child
care tasks (see Szalai, 1975; Harper and Richards,
1979). However, it was beyond the scope of the
present study to obtain explicit information in this
area. Instead, the subjective judgement of the respondent concerning her husband's helpfulness was
relied upon to provide relevant evidence. The
questions (derived from a previous questionnaire used
in the Protective Legislation Survey [O.P.C.S.,1977])
asked respondents whether, firstly, the amount of
housework and secondly, the amount of day-to-day
care of the children carried out by husbands was
'too much, about right and fair or not really
enough?'. The vast majority of women in the sample
consider the help received to be 'right and fair' in
both cases. Harper and Richards (1979,211) note the
same tendency among their respondents, pointing out
that the level of assistance probably fitted in well
with previous low expectations.
    In the Merton study, however, 100 women state
that their husbands do not do enough housework and
62 feel they participate too little in the care of
their children. As might be expected from previous
literature, these are predominantly the wives of
working class men and, in particular, those whose
husbands have a low terminal age of full-time education. It is important to note that perceived lack
of assistance with housework and child care are both
significantly correlated with lower 'satisfaction
with life' scores (see Tables 31 and 32) and that
these relationships remain significant when social
class differences are taken into account (in partial
correlation analysis).
    It is useful at this point to compare the

Table 35   Husbands' assistance with domestic tasks (N.O.P. survey, 1977)

(Percentages in brackets)

'In general, do you think you are helpful around the house?'

	Very helpful	Fairly helpful	Not very helpful	Not at all helpful	Total
Total sample of husbands	165(40)	176(43)	50(12)	21(5)	412(100)
Sample of husbands with children under five	35(36)	42(43)	12(12)	8(8)	97(100)

results from a national survey, also conducted in
1977, on the subject of Women in Britain (National
Opinion Polls). Table 35 shows the response from
husbands themselves in relation to their own helpfulness. It is notable that only 20 per cent of those
with young children feel themselves to be insuffic-
iently helpful. However, in answer to the question:
'Would you like to change places with your wife?' -
90 per cent of husbands with non-employed wives say
'no' and 92 per cent of husbands with children under
five would not want to do so . Clearly, husbands do not
rate the quality of life of their wives very highly,
despite the professed 'helpfulness' which they themselves display! In contrast, nearly one-third of
non-employed wives with young children favour changing places with their husbands, which is a surprisingly high figure considering the strength of social
norms.

As mentioned earlier, domestic assistance from
husbands may not only raise the overall satisfaction
level of women with young children directly but also
allow wives to take part in more varied and interesting activities both inside and outside the home. In
contrast, the husband who demands that all housework
be completed, meals cooked and children be in bed on
his return from work each day is clearly placing a
real constraint on his wife in terms of possible non-
domestic activities during the daytime and, thus,
severely limiting her 'quality of life'.

2. Out-of-home activity patterns (time-budget
    information)

The form of the time-budget information collected in the Merton survey is described in Chapter 4.
(It is important to remember that home visits undertaken by relatives and friends to the respondent's
home are included in 'out-of-home' activities since
they are clearly non-domestic and reciprocal,
activities.) As an attempt to consider the varied
'richness' of out-of-home activity patterns, four
sets of information were derived from the data
collected:-
   a) the number of different 'activity periods'
       (or times out of home) on the time-budget
       day,
   b) the lengths of time spent on different types
       of out-of-home activity,
   c) the number of different types of out-of-home
       activity experienced on the time-budget day,
   d) the total length of time spent out of home

on the time-budget day.

a)   The number of different 'activity periods'

The study of the previous day's activities indicates that only 21 respondents did not leave home at all (or have a relative or friend to visit them) on the day before interview. These tend to be people with young babies, 'traditional' attitudes and high 'satisfaction with life' scores. However, a subset of five respondents in this group are lone parents, whose characteristics do not match those of the majority group.

For the remainder of the respondents (379), the number of different 'activity periods' in the time-budget day varies between one and four. It was hypothesised that those with a larger number of young children would leave the house on fewer occasions because of the inconvenience involved in taking them all out but this does not prove to be correct. However, the age of the youngest child is important; 22 per cent of respondents with a youngest child aged three or four went out of the home four times compared to only 7 per cent of those with a child under one year old, while 42 per cent of the latter group went out only once or not at all. This result clearly reflects the need to take children to and from school or nursery school; 52 per cent of respondents with a child over five had three or four activity periods out of home, compared to 28 per cent of those without an older child.

Since the number of times out of home is most closely related to the need to take and collect children from school, it can not be considered as a suitable index of 'quality of life' for women with young children. It is interesting, however, that there is also a relationship with family income; in particular, respondents in the highest income group seem to experience more activity periods away from home than other women. So it is possible that, in the case of some respondents at least, the number of times out of home is an indicator of activity 'richness'.

b)   Time spent on different activities

Taking single-purpose activity episodes only, the mean length of time spent away from home for different types of activity is as shown in Table 36. Apart from paid employment, which occupies the longest periods of time away from home (but which itself may also act as a constraint on other out-of-home activities), respondents tend to spend longer out of home on individual social rather than 'unpaid work' activities.

Table 36   Mean length of time spent on different types of activity (time-budget data)

Activity	Length of time out-of-home for individual activity periods (hours)
a) Paid employment	5.05
b) 'Unpaid work'	
Shopping	1.38
Taking children to school	0.43
Accompanying other family members	1.25
c) 'Leisure' activities	
Home visit to relatives	2.90
Home visit to friends	2.38
Home visit from relatives	2.05
Home visit from friends	1.43
Park visiting/recreation	1.93
Other institutional/social activity	1.57

c)   The number of different types of activity experienced

The rationale for abstracting this information was the premise that the degree of variety of activity may be used as an indicator of 'quality of life'. As shown above, a large overall number of activities out of home may indicate nothing more than the need to take and collect children from school several times each day. In order to measure 'richness' of activity pattern, it is necessary to count only those types of activity which differ from each other.

The number of different types of activity varies from nought to six, with two as the mode. Correlation analysis indicates a significant relationship with age ($r=.18$ ($p=.001$)), older women undertaking more varied activities than younger women. While social class (measured in terms of the socio-economic group of the husband) is unexpectedly not related to variety of activity pattern, there is a significant relationship with the social class status of the

area (e.d.) in which the respondent lives (measured
in terms of the percentage of employed residents who
are in professional or managerial occupations) (r=.16
(p=.001)). Car availability is, surprisingly, not
significantly related to variety of activity pattern.

It was hypothesised that the number and age of
the respondents' children would be important
influences on activity patterns. As in other
instances, the actual number of young children does
not seem to be a major determinant in this case but
there is a relationship with the age of the youngest
child (r=.16 (p=.001)). This relationship, considered in more detail in tabular form, shows an interesting pattern; the modal number of different
activities for those with a baby under one year old
is one, for those with a child aged one or two years
old is two and for those with a youngest child aged
three or four is three (see Appendix D, Table D39).
Related to this is the fact that respondents with a
child at nursery school have a wider range of
activities than those with all young children at home
full-time (r=.29 (p=.001)). It is also important to
note that those who have a child over five in addition
to a younger child tend to undertake more varied
activities than those without (r=.16 (p=.001)).

Respondents who regularly leave their children
in the care of some other person are more likely to
have a wider variety of activities (r=.14 (p=.003)).
It is not suggested that these people are leaving
their children in order to undertake these activities
(since almost all activities are undertaken with
children in tow) but it seems that the same sort of
people who do not leave their children with anyone
else also do not have very varied activity patterns.
There is also a slight relationship between number of
different activities and help with child care from
husbands.

One of the most interesting findings related to
variety of activities is the unimportance of variables concerned with employment. Repeatedly in this
study it has been assumed (and to some extent proven
- see Chapter 6) that paid employment itself acts as
a constraint on other types of activity. However,
here we find that employment status is completely
unrelated to variety of activity. This indicates
that women who undertake paid employment are still
expected to be responsible for other activities of
an 'unpaid work' nature. The type of paid work
undertaken is also not related to variety of activities; even the number of working days each week
does not influence activity variety. There is a

slight relationship with the number of hours worked
each week, with longer hour workers having fewer
different activities than shorter hour employees but
there is no relationship with the location of employment.

Finally, it is important to note that there is
no relationship evident between 'richness' of activity pattern and any of the attitude variables contained in the data, nor indeed with the 'satisfaction
with life' measure. In relation to the latter, it is
possible, therefore, that the number of different
activities undertaken (whether or not this represents
a 'quality of life' variable) is not of great importance in determining the subjective well-being of
women with young children.

d)   Total length of time spent out of home

If neither the number of different 'activity
episodes' nor the number of different types of
activity can be definitely identified as indicators
of life quality, it is possible that the total length
of time spent out of home (as measured from the time-
budget information) will provide a better guide. The
time-budget record of the previous day's activities
shows the following information:-

Mean length of time out of home - 3.33 hours
Standard deviation   - 2.23 hours
Minimum length of time out of
  home   -   0 hours
Maximum length of time out of
  home   - 9.75 hours

As previously mentioned, 21 respondents did not leave
home at all; 54 respondents (13.5 per cent of the
total) were out for six or more hours.

Before considering the relationships between
length of time away from home and different social
and environmental variables, it must not be overlooked that activities outside of home may vary considerably according to other, completely different
criteria, such as the weather or the day of the week.
During the interview period a record of the weather
was kept in two locations within the borough. There
was very little variation in conditions during the
three weeks although the second week had two partly
wet days and there were three quite cloudy days in
total. The remaining days were all fine and sunny.
Analysis of the data shows that weather conditions
on the time-budget days are not a significant determinant of total length of time spent out of home. In
contrast, the day of the week for which the

information was collected does seem to be related to length of time out of home. In particular, those with activities recorded for Mondays seem to leave their homes for significantly shorter periods than other respondents. However, the mode of data collection employed meant that whole areas were covered by interviewers on particular days. Taking into account both social class and education level, the relationship between day of the week and the length of time spent out of home disappears, indicating that different types of people tended to be interviewed on different days. Therefore, it was not considered necessary to control for day of the week in considering other relationships.

We have already seen that paid employment occupies the longest periods of time out of home. Therefore, it would be expected that a close relationship would exist between total time spent away from home and employment status. Table 37 shows this relationship to be as predicted. Those out at work spend significantly longer away from home than other respondents, while home-workers spend most time at home. Because of the importance of this relationship it was decided to control for employment status by taking only those respondents who are full-time housewives for consideration in the rest of this section.

The most notable finding regarding time spent out of home by housewives is the relative lack of obvious predictor variables. As in the case of the number of types of activity undertaken, very few significant relationships emerge from the analysis. It was expected that women of higher social class/ education/income would spend more time away from home than other respondents (reflecting wider choice patterns of behaviour) but this is not statistically proven from the time-budget data. However, in the case of family income, it is notable that 72 per cent of those in the highest income group (£7000 per annum or more) were out of home for three or more hours during the preceding day, compared to only 38 per cent of women in the lowest income group (less than £3000 per annum) and only one housewife in the highest income group was away from home for less than one hour, compared to 14 per cent overall.

Those who actually used a car to undertake any activity on the previous day were more likely to have spent a longer time away from home (r=.20 (p=.001). This is an interesting finding since it suggests that a car is viewed as a means of undertaking more time-consuming activities and not simply as an aid in

Table 37   Cross-tabulation of total length of time spent out of home on previous day, with employment status (and work location)

(Percentages in brackets)

	Out at Work	Work at Home	Not in Employment	Total
Up to 1 hour	13(16.9)	9(24.3)	41(14.3)	63(15.8)
1-2.99 hours	18(23.4)	18(48.6)	116(40.6)	152(38.0)
3-5.99 hours	27(35.1)	6(16.2)	98(34.3)	131(32.7)
6 or more hours	19(24.7)	4(10.8)	31(10.8)	54(13.5)
Total	77(100.0)	37(100.0)	286(100.0)	400(100.0)

chi-square = 20.32   (p=.002)

saving time. From this perspective it does seem justifiable to consider the length of time spent away
from home as an indicator of activity 'richness'.

The total length of time out of home, spent by
full-time housewives, is not related to number or age
of young children but the relationship with use of a
nursery school is significant (r=.13 (p=.01)). Of
course, respondents with a child at nursery school
may also have a younger child at home, so it was
interesting to see that the relationship between
length of time out of home and nursery school use
disappears when only those housewives with one child
under five are considered separately. It is not easy
to explain why this occurs but it is clear that the
relationship between child care and time spent away
from home is by no means a straightforward one.

As far as other predicting variables are
concerned, there is some tendency for respondents who
have lived in their local areas for less than one
year to go out less than other women (in fact, 10 per
cent did not leave home at all) and there is also a
slight tendency for respondents to be out less if
their husbands are away from home for longer hours
each day and also if their husbands provide insufficient help with housework. It is impossible to
assess the effects of shift-working amongst husbands
since the majority of shift-systems encountered in
this survey were of the 'rolling' or 'alternating'
kind and answers would,therefore,be likely to vary
depending on the precise shift being worked by husbands at the time of interview.

Perhaps most important to consider here is the
total lack of relationship between length of time
spent away from home and all the attitude variables,
including 'satisfaction with life'. This exactly
mirrors the situation with respect to the variety of
activities undertaken (considered earlier) and
suggests that the total length of time out of home
may also not be of importance in influencing subjective 'quality of life'. There is, however, no logical
reason why it should not be included as an objective
indicator of activity 'richness', especially when the
relationship with car use (already discussed) is
taken into account.

3.   Social activities

a)   Number of different types of regular social
      activity

In Chapter 6 all non-employment activities

normally undertaken were considered, including
'social' activities. Here it is suggested that the
number of different types of social activities taken
part in on a regular basis may be used directly as an
indicator of 'activity richness' and, therefore,
possibly as an indicator of 'quality of life'. It
must be remembered, however, that nearly half of all
respondents (195) list no social activities at all
(these exclude activities such as park visiting and
visiting friends or family which were referred to
separately and which nearly all respondents take part
in), while only 21 per cent of the sample name more
than one type of social activity.
    Table 38 summarises the results of correlation
analysis designed to illustrate the influences on
number of different types of social activity. The
most important influences seem to be those related to

Table 38   Summary of significant influences on number
            of different types of social activity
            (p≥.05)

Positive Influences	r	Negative Influences	r
Child at nursery school	.20	Employment status preference	-.13
Child left with other person	.18	Attitude to work	-.17
Attitude to position of women	.13		
Age of respondent	.23		
Percentage of professional and managerial households in e.d.	.18		
Socio-economic group of husband	.24		

social and personal characteristics, attitudes to
work and the general position of women and the
ability to leave children elsewhere on a regular
basis. In particular, there is a definite relationship with age, perhaps because older women have had
more time to develop social activities. The clear
relationship with social class variables is not at
all unexpected, given the class bias involved in such
participation (see Chapters 2 and 6).
    Those who are 'happy to be at home' at present

take part in more social activities than those who
would prefer to be out at work. Perhaps this is one
reason why they are 'happy to be at home'.
Certainly those taking part in social activities
tend to favour 'traditional' attitudes to the question of work for women while, at the same time,
asserting 'progressive' attitudes to the general
position of women in society. There is a slight
relationship between number of social activities and
help with housework from husbands. The ability to
leave children is, of course, crucial as so many
social activities are more easily undertaken without
children. Therefore, it is not surprising that
there is a relationship between the number of social
activities taken part in, on the one hand and
having a child at nursery school and also leaving
children with some other person on a regular basis,
on the other. There is, however, no relationship
evident with either the number of children which a
woman has or the age of the youngest child.
     Cross-tabulations relating to employment
variables indicate that women working in manual jobs
are much less likely to take part in social activities than those in non-manual employment. As might
be expected, three-quarters of full-time workers
have no weekday social activities while amongst all
those working for more than 21 hours each week, no-
one takes part in more than one activity. So weekday working does seem to act as a constraint on
participation in social activities, although it
should be mentioned that home workers are as likely
as housewives to take part in such activities outside
the home.
     Other cross-tabulations (not reproduced here)
reveal two further relationships: firstly, those who
had their first child at an older age are more
likely to take part in varied social activities,
perhaps because they had already established these
activities before the birth of their children and
simply continued them subsequently. In the second
place, the tenure characteristics of the local area
seem to be related; people who live in predominantly
council-rented areas take part in the fewest social
activities, although this may possibly represent a
spurious correlation.
     The relationship between the number of different
social activities participated in and 'satisfaction
with life' is significant and positive (r=.18 (p=
.001) suggesting that a more varied social life may
be definitely a contributing factor in determining
life satisfaction. This variable, therefore,

represents the only one of the activity measures
(used in this study as objective indicators of
quality of life) which can be significantly related
to the subjective 'satisfaction with life' measure.

b)   People with very few social or recreational
     activities

     In Chapter 5 the construction of a new variable
relating to social and recreational activities was
mentioned briefly. This variable was created by
counting the number of times a respondent replied
'never' to questions concerning the frequency of
activities (park visiting, home visiting, social
activities and so on). Those respondents (44 in
total) who received a score of between five and
seven on this variable (maximum being seven) were
considered as a group to be 'people with very few
social or recreational activities' and hence a low
degree of activity 'richness'.
     Looking at the characteristics of this group,
there is a predominance of women in paid employment
which is to be expected. On the other hand, there is
also a subgroup of housewives with only one child,
this child being under the age of one. Mobility
constraints may be important in deterring respondents
from out-of-home activities, since very few have a
car available for use. Related to this is the fact
that members of this group have lower family incomes
than the sample as a whole.
     Of most importance here is the indication that
those with very few social or recreational activities
tend to have lower scores on the 'satisfaction with
life' measure than respondents as a whole and this
especially is true of those in paid employment. A
related finding is that members of the group are more
likely to 'prefer to stay at home', in general, than
other women, especially those who are out at work
now. This possibly indicates a reaction against the
situation of constraint felt by those who are not
able to participate in social activities.
     The results considered here serve to support
the conclusion of the previous section that the
variety of social activities appears to be an important factor in contributing to life quality. Those
who do not participate in social and recreational
activities, for whatever reasons, seem to experience,
both subjectively and objectively, a lower level of
'quality of life' than other respondents.
     In summary, both the 'richness' of activity pat-
terns in general and the extent of social activity,

in particular, have been considered as potential
contributors to 'quality of life' for respondents.
The number of different 'activity periods' during
the course of a day has been shown to be most closely
connected to the need for children to be accompanied
to and from school. However, the number of different
types of activity undertaken is, perhaps, a better
measure of life quality; certainly relationships
with the age of the youngest child, having a child at
nursery school and leaving children in the care of
some other person indicate an association between
variety of weekday activity and some lessening of the
gender-role constraint on activities. However, there
is no relationship between any of the general
'activity' variables and 'satisfaction with life'.
Despite this fact, it is clear that higher income,
car-using respondents are more likely to spend longer
hours out of home than other housewives. Various
aspects connected with the influence of husbands also
seem to be important in affecting length of time away
from home.

Unlike the general 'activity' variables, the
number of different social activities taken part in
by respondents on weekdays is significantly related
to 'satisfaction with life'. It is older, higher
social class women who have most social activities
while respondents in employment outside the home take
part in very few such activities.

'Quality of Life' as Measured by Access Capability

Access to resources has been identified by many
researchers in geography as a major determinant of
'quality of life' (see Chapters 2 and 3). The degree
of access to different facilities and services varies
widely according to particular constraints. Some of
these constraints may be subjective rather than
objective: access may be limited as much by lack of
information as by geographical location. However,
it is the spatial distribution of opportunities which
is the subject under consideration here. Much of
the material used has been previously dealt with in
other contexts in Chapters 5,6, 7 and 8, so detailed
discussion will be restricted to only the most
salient points.

1. Access to paid employment

It has already been mentioned, in Chapter 5,
that there are no data available at district level to
show variations in job supply across the borough of

Merton. It is, therefore, not possible to correlate
distance to potential employment with any other
variables from the survey. However, Merton is fairly
well-placed as a whole with respect to employment,
being situated close to inner London and having major
suburban centres of retailing and industry within
relatively easy reach. In addition, there is considerable local employment, both manual and non-manual,
such that '...in most cases the supply of jobs can
equal the demand by women'(Anon., 1978). Bearing
these points in mind, it is not surprising to find
that of the 286 full-time housewives in the sample,
only 17 mention a lack of suitable jobs (either in
terms of the type of work or in terms of the hours
of work) as a reason for not being in employment.

Most employed women with young children work
either at home or within the immediate local area,
their location of employment being very largely
dictated by their need (or desire) to fulfil gender-
role expectations (see Chapter 2, Fig. 1). This
being so, the women in paid employment outside the
home in this sample could be said to represent a
'fortunate' group, in that the vast majority have
found jobs locally (70 per cent travel for no longer
than ten minutes to work). In addition, three-
quarters of all respondents who want to go out to
work after their children are at school expect to
find employment in their local areas. (Whether, in
fact, they will be able to do so, in the light of the
changing situation of employment and unemployment
since this survey was carried out, is another issue
altogether. In whatever way the position changes in
the near future, it remains true that the women of
Merton are relatively favoured with local employment
opportunities.)

Ready access to paid employment, particularly
part-time, is of great importance to women with
young children since it provides a valuable choice
of activity, both at the present time and for the
future. It should, therefore, be defined as one
factor contributing to a greater 'quality of life'
for Merton residents than for women in many other
geographical situations.

2.   Access to shopping facilities

The borough of Merton is generally well-placed,
not only with respect to employment opportunities
but also with respect to shopping and service facilities, as a result of its location within the metropolitan area of Greater London. Easy access to such

facilities is considered to contribute towards a
good 'quality of life' for women with young children
since it is women who are predominantly the household shoppers (see Chapter 6).

Although Merton as a whole is well-supplied
with shopping centres, compared to many other places,
there are considerable differences in access potential between different parts of the borough. Respondents living close to larger centres are clearly at
an advantage since these are the most favoured locations for shopping. There is certainly a close relationship between the grade of centre used for weekday shopping and whether or not the shops actually
used are the closest to home. While those living
near larger centres have ready access to good shopping facilities, those living further away have to
travel to use these facilities. Local shops are seen
by many as being too costly and providing too limited a range of goods but, on the other hand, there are
considerable problems involved in visiting more
distant centres. The availability of a car often
appears crucial in determining the ability of a
respondent to use a larger shopping centre but, of
course, access to this personalised form of transport
is also not distributed evenly within the population.

The quality of life of respondents, therefore,
varies with respect to shopping access. Such access
may be of great importance in influencing activity
'richness' since shopping is a predominant 'unpaid
work' activity undertaken by women with young children; some 60 per cent of respondents actually went
shopping on the day before interview (see Chapter 6).
Distance to shops does not, however, correlate
significantly with the 'satisfaction with life'
variable.

3.   Access to parks

Access to parks may be important in influencing
'quality of life' in two respects; firstly, open
space provides a visual amenity, a generally pleasant
environment in which to live and, secondly, parks
comprise a useful recreational resource. As in the
case of shopping centres, Merton is also well-placed
with regard to parks. Map 3 illustrates the distribution of parks in the borough, indicating their
widespread occurrence. In fact, very few areas of
Merton are remote from a park, and 82 per cent of
respondents live within one quarter of a mile's
of such a facility (see Chapter 6). This is, presumably, the reason why distance from a local park does

not appear to influence 'satisfaction with life' (see Table 34).

Proximity to a park seems to be important in determining the use made of it, since respondents living within five minutes travelling time of a park are more likely to visit it on a daily basis. However, the quality of open space is also an important factor and it is interesting that one-third of the sample do not visit the park which is closest to their home. In particular, it seems that the provision of a children's playground influences the use made of a park (see Chapter 6).

It has been argued in other research that park use is a class-biased activity and that working class people do not visit parks or value their proximity. If this is so, then access to parks cannot be presumed to contribute to the quality of life of women with young children in general. However, it has been shown that no relationship exists between park use and social class, for the Merton sample, so allowing us to include proximity to parks as a valuable objective indicator of life quality. In particular, ready access to open space may be of great importance to people living in flats and it is interesting that in this sample flat-dwellers are more likely to use parks than other respondents, especially if they live in high blocks of flats.

4. Access to friends and relatives

The importance of social interaction in enhancing mental health and its lack in promoting loneliness and depression is a recurring theme in social science literature. Therefore, it is considered justifiable to include access to friends and relatives as one element of total life quality. As might be anticipated, very few respondents were found to be without friends in their immediate local areas; in fact, only 7 per cent report a lack of local friends and many of these are new residents in their areas (see Chapter 6). On the other hand, a majority of respondents state that they have no relatives living near them (57 per cent of the sample) and this is especially true of middle class women. The latter, however, appear to compensate for this lack of family interaction by a higher level of visiting with friends.

Overall, social visiting proves to be the most important 'leisure' activity undertaken by respondents (as has been shown in Table 36). Most state that their contact with friends and neighbours is

promoted by the fact that they have children in
common. Respondents living in high flats are found
to have a lower level of visiting activities than
others, indicating that the often-reported social
isolation of flat-dwellers appears to hold true in
the case of this research also. If social interaction is considered to be an important contributor to
'quality of life', there is clearly an onus on archi-
tects and planners to produce housing which does not,
so effectively, cut off residents from each other's
company.

Most members of the Merton sample consider their
local areas to be 'friendly' in character and this
apparently contributes to their overall 'satisfaction
with life' (see Table 31). It is also notable that
frequent visiting with friends correlates significantly with the life satisfaction measure.

5. Access to transport

In one major respect access to transport is a
very important contributor to 'quality of life' and
that concerns car availability. Chapter 7 has detailed the extent to which access to private transport
is class-and income-related and also its relationship
to activities undertaken. In this sample, 32 per
cent of respondents were found to have effective
access to a car on weekdays; that is, there was a
car available for their use and they were able to
drive it. This is a relatively high percentage compared to previous studies in other areas but it is
important to remember that 68 per cent of respondents
do not have access to a car and are, therefore, limited in the scope of their out-of-home activities as
a result. The availability of a car is positively
correlated with 'satisfaction with life', (see Table
31).

Access to public transport is of much less importance to women with young children, mainly because
the chief alternative form of travel to car use is
walking. Being an urban area, the borough of Merton
is well-supplied with public transport routes and 88
per cent of respondents live within one quarter of a
mile of a bus route (see Map 4). In contrast, a
large area in the south-east of the borough is remote
from a railway station and, in fact, only 37 per cent
of respondents live within one quarter of a mile of a
station. Distance to the nearest railway station is
significantly related to train use and respondents
report fewer problems involved with the use of trains
(accompanied by young children) than with the use of

buses. It seems, therefore, that access to a railway station should probably be included as an indicator of life quality, whereas access to buses is of less importance.

6. Access to child care

A major tenet of this research work is that access to child care is a predominant influence both on activities and on 'quality of life'. Women who are unable (or unwilling) to leave their children in the care of some other person or institution, at least occasionally, are effectively denied access to many types of activity and have their access to other activities severely restricted.

The borough of Merton is well-supplied with pre-school facilities compared to most other areas (see Table 24) and these are widely distributed throughout the whole borough (see Map 6). However, not all respondents live sufficiently close to a nursery school or playgroup to be able to take their children there and distance to such facilities does seem to influence use (Table 25), especially in the case of state schools. There is also the problem of lack of places and the subsequent need for waiting lists, especially in the private sector; it must be remembered that there is almost total dependence on the private sector for the 'institutional' care of children under the age of three years.

The majority of respondents tend to view nursery schooling as an aspect of the education needs of their children rather than as 'child care' for their own benefit, so it is perhaps not surprising that having a child at nursery school is not significantly correlated with the 'satisfaction with life' measure (see Table 34). However, there is a relationship between 'satisfaction' and leaving children with some other person on a regular basis and it may be this aspect of child care which should most seriously be considered as contributing to a woman's 'quality of life'.

In summary, access to services and facilities required by women with young children has been examined in relation to 'quality of life' determination. It has been shown that good access to most facilities is available for respondents although there are spatial differences in the supply of shops, parks and pre-school services. Car availability has been emphasised as of great importance in permitting access to services outside the local area. Access to trains probably also contributes to the 'quality of life' of respondents. The availability of friends and relatives is of great importance to women with young children, not only because of the statistical dominance of home visiting amongst 'leisure' activities but also because of the significance of non-'institutional' child care in providing opportunity for women to undertake desired activities without their young children.

General Summary of Survey Findings

The purpose of this chapter has been to investigate the 'quality of life' for women with young children, in order to assess the importance of constraints on activities. It was felt that if the quality of life could be demonstrated to be poor among the sample members, then there would be more justification for focusing on policies to remove or lessen these constraints.

Consideration of the relevant literature has indicated that 'quality of life' can be viewed both subjectively and objectively. In this study, data relating to the subjective assessment of life quality are contained in the 'satisfaction with life' measure, based on a semantic differential test. The results show low levels of life satisfaction among respondents in general. In particular, those in lower social class and income groups, those living in council housing or in flats and lone parents or those receiving little help from their husbands experience less 'satisfaction with life'.

Two types of measure have been used as objective indicators of 'quality of life'. In the first place, the extent of out-of-home activity patterns has been viewed as an important predictor. The time-budget data provide a depth of information not otherwise obtainable and illuminate the bare facts on activities derived from other sources in the questionnaire. However, these data cannot be said to make available any concrete evidence concerning 'quality of life' influences. Different aspects of time spent out of home have been discussed in relation to activity 'richness' and 'satisfaction with life' and some useful relationships have been indicated. But it must be remembered that each individual person's activity pattern on any one day is subject to many random influences. Therefore, it is perhaps not surprising that no clear picture has emerged and that the existence of out-of-home activities should remain only tentatively as a predictor of life quality. Looking particularly at <u>social</u> activities out of home, there is a significant correlation with 'satisfaction with life' and participation in this type of activity is considered definitely to contribute towards life quality.

The second objective measure of 'quality of life' concerns the question of access to facilities and services. Most environmental variables have been shown not to correlate with 'satisfaction with life' but this may be because of the generally good access to facilities enjoyed by all respondents. The borough of Merton is located sufficiently near to inner London to experience predominantly 'urban' characteristics. Consequently, employment opportunities, shopping centres, parks and bus routes are all widely available to residents and there are no real problems of access, although some areas are relatively remote from a major shopping centre. Easy access to rail transport is less universally available and respondents living in areas distant from a station are considerably disadvantaged with regard to mobility. However, it is car availability which is the most crucial factor in determining personal mobility, and this also correlates significantly with 'satisfaction with life'.

In conclusion, 'quality of life' has been shown to vary between different groups of respondents. The implications of this variation stretch beyond the scope of this study into questions of the redistribution of wealth but the implications also include the need for a change in social attitudes towards single parents and towards family roles. In addition, 'quality of life' as measured by life satisfaction has been shown to be generally low for women with young children as a whole. Major societal change may be essential before life quality can really be improved and this point is taken up in Cahpter 10, following.

Chapter 10

CONCLUSIONS AND A LOOK TO THE FUTURE

It is traditional (and necessary) to complete the discussion of a research project by summarising the principal findings of the empirical study undertaken and relating these findings to previous literature in the field. The 'conclusion' is, therefore, a finishing-point, a summary of work to date.

However, geography has long since been transformed from a subject concentrating solely on the descriptive study of spatial processes and patterns as they exist to one equally concerned with ways and means of changing existing patterns and altering the operating forces which produce these patterns. It is, therefore, to be expected that a study aimed at the criticism of existing structures should be concluded by a consideration of possibilities for future change.

This final chapter, thus, has a two-fold purpose. It will seek both to summarise the main findings of the research project concerning constraints on the spatial activities of women with young children and also to suggest policy, legal and social changes necessary for such constraints to be lessened or eliminated.

Research Findings

1. Principal conclusions from the literature

The chief conclusions from the literature study fall under two headings; (a) constraints (of different kinds) can be readily identified and have a definite impact on activity patterns and (b) the gender-role constraint acts as the predominant influence on the daily lives of women, especially with young children.

CONCLUSIONS AND A LOOK TO THE FUTURE

a)   **The impact of constraints**

i.   Constraints may be identified as <u>societal</u> (that
     is, implicit within the structure of society) or
     <u>physical</u> (relational elements with activity
     patterns as the products of societal structure).
ii. The gender-role constraint is the major influ-
     ence on employment status and conditions of work
     for women with young children. It also influe-
     nces the character of social and other non-
     employment activities.
iii. Socio-economic constraints determine the extent
     to which the gender-role constraint is operative
     in the case of the individual woman. There is
     differential access to resources (in social
     terms) and those with low incomes have less
     access to participatory activities, transport,
     child care facilities and a reasonable 'quality
     of life' in general.
iv. Social class norms of behaviour act as a
     constraint on activities, although there is
     evidence of change towards a more socially
     'neutral' pattern of behaviour for women with
     young children, especially in the case of social
     visiting patterns.
v.   The type of area in which a woman lives (in
     social terms) influences certain activities,
     particularly home visiting.
vi. Differential personal mobility is itself the
     result of societal structures. Lack of mobility
     influences activity patterns by restricting the
     extent of activity space and encouraging the
     local orientation of activities.
vii. The actual provision of services and facilities
     in different areas is a reflection of patterns
     of <u>social</u> inequality. Women with young children
     without access to facilities in their local
     areas are severely constrained in their activit-
     ies.
viii. The lack of adequate child care facilities is
     particularly important in relation to the empl-
     oyment of mothers.

b)   **The predominance of the gender-role constraint**

i.   Gender-role ideology remains a strong influence
     on individual behaviour patterns despite
     apparent changes in role expectations in recent
     years. The 'myth of motherhood' maintains its
     grip on social theory and policy.
ii. The growing importance of employment roles for

women does not negate the predominance of
traditional 'female' roles; in fact, the
nature of women's work roles tends to <u>reinforce</u>
the traditional division of labour by <u>sex and</u>
the female responsibility for domestic and
child care duties.
iii. The gender role constraint influences <u>all</u> women
with young children, regardless of soc<u>ial</u> class
background (although the influence may be
modified to some extent by social/income
status).
iv. The constraint acts as the predominant
influence on the daily lives of women with
young children (virtually by definition) since
<u>all</u> activities must be co-ordinated with child-
<u>ren</u>'s needs.
v. Loneliness and isolation may be the result of
the overwhelming importance of the gender-role
constraint. Certainly, depressive illness is
disproportionately associated with this population sub-group.

2. <u>Principle conclusions from the empirical study</u>

The major conclusions from the empirical study
will be considered in relation to the hypothesised
relationships set forward in the first part of
Chapter 4 and Fig.˙ 2 (page 80).

a) <u>The direct influence of societal constraints</u>
    <u>(Influence numbered 2).</u>

1. <u>Gender-role</u>

i.   The gender-role constraint directly influences
     employment status (in particular, through the
     age of the youngest child in the family and
     reasons given for not being in employment) and
     conditions of employment (location, hours and
     'status').
ii. The gender-role constraint prescribes the dom-
     inance of 'unpaid work' activities in non-
     employment, out-of-home activity patterns - in
     particular, the statistical predominance of
     taking children to and from school or nursery
     school.
iii. The constant presence of children militates
     against participation in social and institut-
     ional activities on weekdays and promotes home
     visiting as the chief 'leisure' activity.
iv. Personal mobility is restricted by various

aspects of the gender-role constraint, especially for those who do not have effective access to a car on weekdays.

v. The influence of the gender-role constraint on the activities of women with young children has, as one important outcome, low 'satisfaction with life' levels in general and, in particular, low satisfaction levels for women who are lone parents or who receive inadequate domestic help from their husbands (that is, those for whom the gender-role constraint is physically most restrictive).

2. Socio-economic structures

i. The constraint of low income influences participation in paid employment, ensures low mobility levels and deters the use of private pre-school facilities.

ii. The income constraint has, as one result, low 'satisfaction with life' levels for those from families with low incomes.

iii. The social class constraint is a direct influence on differential shopping and home visiting patterns.

iv. Those in lower social class groups experience less personal mobility, are less likely to use pre-school facilities at all and are subject to lower satisfaction levels than those in higher class groups.

v. A lower level of personal education is associated with the non-use of parks, libraries and adult education facilities on weekdays and also with the lack of use of pre-school facilities.

vi. The predominant tenure mode of the local area is the only 'type of area' measure which seems to act as an independent influence on home visiting patterns.

b) The influence of physical constraints (Influence numbered 3).

i. The constraint of a low level of personal mobility is related to problems of public transport use and distance to railway stations. Car availability is a key factor in determining personal mobility but effective access to a car is not available for two-thirds of sample members.

ii. Those without cars shop more frequently, consider their local area to be less convenient

and suffer lower 'satisfaction with life'
levels than respondents with access to a car.

iii. The provision of opportunity constraint
structures patterns of shopping and the use of
parks and pre-school facilities, both in terms
of the quantity and the quality (or grade) of
facilities proximate to home.

iv. The survey area is, in general, well-supplied
with employment, shopping, park, transport and
pre-school facilities and the provision of
opportunity constraint is not, therefore, of
great importance to women with young children
in this particular case.

c) Restrictions on activities (Influence numbered
   4).

i. The various constraints jointly act to modify
activity preferences and, thus, influence
activities in the ways considered in sections
a) and b) above. Constraints can be seen to be
operative both in the case of long-term (normal)
activity patterns and short-term (time-budget)
activity patterns.

ii. The time-budget data illustrate particularly
the general dominance of 'unpaid work' activities for women with young children and also,
the importance of home visiting as the major
'leisure' activity.

iii. Weekday activities can be seen to take place
within a very limited activity space (compared
to the activities of men and non-weekday
activities).

d) The influence of attitudes (Influence numbered
   5).

i. Attitudes to work are a major influence on
actual employment status and on employment
status preferences.

ii. Attitudes to motherhood, the general position of
women in society and work are important in
influencing activity preferences and subsequent
patterns in general, and are closely linked to
levels of 'satisfaction with life'.

e) Quality of life (Influences numbered 7 and 8).

i. 'Satisfaction with life' is one (subjective)
measure of quality of life. This is positively
related to attitudes to motherhood and

negatively related to work attitudes (the latter
indicating a situation of personal conflict for
respondents holding 'progressive' attitudes to
work but restricted to non-employment or to
poor employment conditions, by gender-role
considerations).

ii. Actual employment status does not appear to
influence 'satisfaction with life' but higher
satisfaction levels are related to other
activity criteria - notably the number of social
activities undertaken, home visiting with
friends and leaving children regularly with
some other person on weekdays.

iii. The number and extent of specific (time-budget)
out-of-home activities are not very clearly
related to quality of life considerations, due
to the statistical dominance of 'unpaid work'
activities for women with young children. However, there seems to be an association between
variety of weekday activity and some lessening
of the gender-role constraint (through increasing age of children, leaving children with some
other person and sending children to nursery
school).

iv. Access to services and facilities is generally
good in the survey area but variations in such
access provide one objective measure of quality
of life differences amongst respondents.

3. Discussion

The conclusions from the empirical study are
generally in accordance with previous research findings and theoretical premises. In particular, this
study has illustrated the importance of gender-
differentiation in society in determining activity
patterns. Evidence relating to employment indicates
that women's work roles are structured by the gender-
role constraint, an empirical conclusion which helps
to strengthen earlier more theoretical work. Similarly, non-employment activities are influenced by
role considerations and there is an emphasis on
'unpaid work' activities in the results from the
time-budget survey; this, too, has previously been
suggested by the literature. It was not possible
for the present study to measure the extent of depressive illness amongst the sample but there is
evidence of low 'satisfaction with life' levels in
general.

Socio-economic structures have been shown to be
of importance in influencing activities.

Respondents from households with low incomes have
lower mobility levels than others, as expected, but
in this study were not shown to have much lower
access to most types of facility. In particular, the
good standard of provision of state pre-school
facilities, especially in lower income areas of
Merton, means that respondents are not denied access
to 'institutional' child care on the grounds of cost.
No real evidence was found in this survey to support
the contention that patterns of behaviour are becoming more socially 'neutral'; in fact, significant
differences were discovered between members of
different social classes in terms of shopping and
home visiting patterns, while education level clearly
influences the use of parks, libraries and adult
education classes and also the use of pre-school
facilities. This expected effect of education level
has, however, also been discussed in previous literature. Most of the assertions made concerning
differences between types of area were found to be
not relevant to the present study.
 This research has stressed the importance of
lack of personal mobility as a physical constraint
on activities and this accords with previous research
on differential access to personal transport. However, the findings related to provision of opportunity (the actual provision of services and facilities
in different areas) as a constraint on activity
patterns are largely inconclusive. Where real differences in distribution patterns exist, these clearly
affect activities, for example, in the case of grades
of shopping centres or parks or in the case of types
of pre-school facilities. However, the survey area
is generally well-supplied with services and facilities and with employment opportunities, so in this
case it seems that the provision of opportunity does
not operate as a very important constraint. However,
previous indications of a constraint on employment
due to lack of child care facilities is supported by
the finding that very few children referred to in the
survey occupy places in anything other than part-
time nursery education.
 One of the most interesting (and disturbing)
findings of this study concerns the inter-relationships between actual behaviour, attitudes and satisfaction levels. Previous theoretical work has
stressed the continuance of gender-role ideology as
a major constraint on behaviour patterns, despite
changes in the law and apparent changes in society.
This research has underlined the importance of gender
role differentiation in influencing the daily lives

of women with young children and has linked the
notion of 'constraint' with generally low levels of
'satisfaction with life' (and possibly with other
measures of 'quality of life'). However, results
also show the 'progressive' outlook of respondents in
terms of their attitudes to work and to the general
position of women in society. Clearly, attitudes
held are in many cases not in accordance with actual
situations experienced. It is primarily this
conclusion which has led the author on, from a
summary of previous findings, to a consideration of
ways to introduce change; in particular, to a review
of possibilities for introducing choice elements into
women's activity patterns by the lessening or elimin-
ation of constraints. This review forms the subject
of the next section.

Possibilities for the Future

This section, although developing from the conclusions of the empirical study based in Merton, must of
necessity range further afield in its consideration
of future change. Possibilities for the future have
been considered by a wide variety of writers and
many of their ideas will be referred to here. It is
important to remember that, when considering the
future, there is no right answer or completely
accurate scenario. Future change depends so critically upon complex and unknown elements. The emphasis
throughout is, however, clearly upon the provision of
alternatives in order to create choice situations
and not upon the imposition of a new set of constraints.

1.   The lessening of physical constraints

a)   Mobility and the provision of service centres

One of the major conclusions, both of this
empirical study and also of previous research,
concerns the spatially limited nature of women's
activity patterns on weekdays. The restricted
activity space occupied by women is partly the result
of mobility limitations; especially, it has been
shown that access to a car is a key element in im-
proving personal mobility. The 1976 Transport Policy
Document (Department of the Environment, 1976,35)
recognises that,'The most crucial social problem to
emerge from the transport review is lack of mobility
for those without access to a car. The first priority among the objectives of transport policy,

therefore, is to ensure the existence of effective
local public transport to meet the needs of those
dependent on it'. The words are apparently sincere
but no specific policies are proposed to ensure
social equality of access. Apps (1975,44) notes the
acceptance of the production-consumption split in
the economy and states that the bias towards production '...explains why the journey to work is regard-
ed as the major aspect of "the transport problem"
rather than the trips made by housewives, children,
pensioners (or alternatively, the absence of these
people on the roads,' (see also, Jones et al.,
1983). It seems unlikely that public transport
facilities will be significantly improved in the
future (except possibly in specific local areas) to
ensure greater mobility for daytime users such as
women with young children (groups which wield very
little power within society).

In any event, it is debatable whether improved
public transport provision would have a great impact
on the extent of activity space for women with young
children. It has been clearly demonstrated that
public transport use is not an important factor,
even where a car is not available on weekdays and
where public transport networks are already very
good. Public transport will probably never operate
as a real alternative to cars because of the
problems associated with using buses and trains
(especially buses) in the company of young children.

It would seem, therefore, that location with
respect to desired activities is of greater importance to the carless than access to public transport
facilities (Paaswell, 1976,41). In addition, it is
essential to remember that, while car availability
may enable women to take part in more activities
more easily, this does not mean that the distances
travelled to activities are necessarily much longer
for car users than for others (see Chapter 7). It
is clear, therefore, that constraints other than
those relating simply to mobility are also important
in restricting the extent of activity space for
women with young children - constraints relating
directly to the presence and needs of children.
Therefore, it is not only those without access to a
car who need to find all necessary services and
facilities within their local area.

However, '...specialisation and changing market
conditions have increased the size and reduced the
number of a whole range of local service facilities'
(Mitchell and Town, 1977,1) and it seems idealistic
to suppose that the trend towards centralisation of

services would simply be reversed in the interests of greater social equity. Although the approval given by planners to large scale, nucleated developments, at the expense of local provision of facilities, can be attacked as encouraging the upward redistribution of resources, it is nevertheless true that a large number of respondents (including those with fairly low incomes) use major shopping and service centres in preference to local facilities because of their undoubted advantages in providing a wider range of goods at lower prices.

The optimum solution would, therefore, seem to be a combination of two supply situations; firstly, a minimum level of provision of services and facilities at the local scale and, secondly, the provision of higher-grade services at nodal points, easily accessible by public transport routes as well as by car. The London borough of Merton exemplifies such a pattern of provision at present and most respondents are not severely constrained in their activities by a lack of provision of services and facilities. Non-urban areas would obviously present a much greater challenge to such a policy on provision; it is in these areas that the lack of local services acts as a more important constraint on activity patterns.

b) The provision of child care

> ...Government policy is contradictory. It gives with one hand by passing legislation to encourage and facilitate employment for women with young children; and it takes away with the other by limiting the amount of day care provision on the basis of doubtful evidence
> (Whicheloe, 1977, 14).

The demand for daytime child care continues to increase while the supply remains static; indeed, if it were not for expansion in the private sector there could well be an overall decline in total provision in the near future, as local education authorities review their spending on nursery education in the light of current economic circumstances. Results from the Merton survey show how few women with young children do not want their children to attend some type of pre-school facility before the age of five. State nursery school and nursery class provision (especially the latter) is particularly good in Merton but this type of facility is not ideal for the children of working mothers without

some complementary day care provision. Legislation
on equal pay and opportunities is largely meaningless
unless significant improvements are made in child
care facilities, so that women have a real choice in
relation to employment status (Ellis, 1978,116). A
report by the Trades Union Council recommends the
integration of all types of pre-school provision
into one comprehensive programme for child care to be
under the control of local authorities (Ellis, 1978,
117). A similar proposal has been put forward by the
Central Policy Review Staff (1978) and by the
National Union of Teachers (1977), the latter laying
stress on the needs of children for pre-school
education (an approach supported by considerable
research evidence on the value of 'headstart'
programmes in the United States [Lazer et al.,1977]).
Very recently, there have been some attempts at the
co-ordination of nursery services by a number of
local authorities in response to such recommendations
(see Ferri et al., 1981; Bradley, 1982).

In the light of the situation in Britain as
regards child care provision, it is interesting and
useful briefly to consider the parallel situation in
other countries. Daytime child care provision varies
widely in type and extent in different parts of the
world, from a heavy dependence on 'institutional'
care in such countries as Israel, the U.S.S.R. and
China, to complete reliance on 'extended family'
care in most developing countries. Between different
Western countries there are also great differences in
child care provision. In the United States, nearly
half of all three to five year olds attend nursery
schools, but it is estimated that only 11 per cent
of the pre-school children of working mothers are in
day care centres, most of the remainder being looked
after by relatives or informally by friends and
neighbours. (David, 1978,447-448). In Australia,
27 per cent of pre-school children have two working
parents but only 3 per cent are attending recognised
child care centres (14 per cent of the children with
full-time working mothers) (Apps, 1975,72). These
situations can be compared with the much more adequate provision of facilities in such countries as
France and Sweden. In France, for example, 25 per
cent of two year olds, 70 per cent of three year
olds and practically all four year olds attend pre-
school facilities; nurseries are often open from
8 a.m. to 6.30 p.m. and full day care is much more
common than it is in England. In addition to providing better facilities, France also has '...the
best system of family benefits in Western Europe and

265

perhaps the world...'   (Tizard, 1976,43) which
enable women to choose to remain at home with their
children if they prefer not to work. Sweden, too,
has considered child care issues in relation to total
family needs;   parents of young children have the
right to work a six hour day with their incomes
boosted through National Insurance and also are
eligible for long-term, paid maternity and paternity
leave. At the same time, both group day care centres
and family-based child care, paid for by the state,
are highly developed and there is great concern for
the quality of provision: 'Day nurseries and in-
family day care should not merely serve as parking
lots for children but also as good environments for
them' (Martensson, 1977,114).

Fogarty et al., (1971,251) state that,'The
population is prepared to accept excellent but not
merely adequate day-care facilities for its young
children'. A recent Gallup Poll survey (Social
Surveys (Gallop Poll) Limited, 1979) has shown that
only a small minority of women would prefer their
young children to be cared for in an 'institutional'
setting while they themselves worked;   most would
prefer their children to be looked after informally
by friends or relatives (not childminders). This
conclusion,while emphasising the great value of such
informal child care, also reflects seriously on the
quality of day care at present available in this
country. Nor is the overall quality likely to
improve in the near future, given the current
government emphasis on childminding (a form of care
where standards are very difficult to control) as a
cheap alternative to state provision.

Even considering only the quantity of 'institutional' provision of child care, Britain clearly
falls towards the poorer end of the spectrum amongst
other nations. Not only is there inadequate provision of facilities compared with the demand for such
services, particularly by working mothers, but there
is also no official recognition (in the form of
family benefits) of the financial constraints which
in some cases force both parents to go out to work.
It is essential that the provision of outside child
care should be viewed as part of total family
policy;   otherwise it simply serves to reinforce
discriminatory views. As David (1978,440) asserts,
in the case of the United States, 'Policies for pre-
school children especially highlight the fact that
the state assumes a sexual division of labour in
child care and the economy'. Firestone (1971,233)
goes further and stresses that '...radical goals

must be kept in sight at all times. Day-care
centres buy women off. They ease the immediate
pressure without asking why that pressure is on
women'. So long as the care of young children
continues to be viewed as 'women's role', both by
governments and by society as a whole, there can be
no real development of the system of child care
provision in this country.

2.   The elimination of societal constraints

It has been shown above how very limited is the
potential for lessening the impact of physical
constraints on the activities of women with young
children. It is unlikely that mobility can be significantly improved other than by increased car
availability, a factor outside the normal scope of
planning agencies to control. The provision of
services and facilities, although more directly the
concern of planners, has become increasingly centra-
lised in recent years and again it seems very unlikely that access to service centres for relatively
immobile groups, such as women with young children,
will improve substantially in the future, except
perhaps in certain localities (such as New Towns).
The provision of child care facilities, in particular, is now considered with disfavour in government
circles; pre-school provision is, if anything,
likely to decrease rather than increase in the near
future.
It may be, therefore, that the only way in
which change can come about is through the eliminat-
ion of societal constraints, rather than through the
lessening of physical constraints. It is not within
the field of this study to argue the case for the
destruction of existing socio-economic structures
through political revolution. This section will
consider only the possible means of eliminating
gender-role discrimination. It should, however, be
pointed out that many writers consider gender-role
differences to be so embedded in (and determined by)
socio-economic structures, that changes in the one
area could only be envisaged through overall political and social change. If it is true that '...
women's oppression under capitalism arises from the
fact that the reproduction of this society takes the
form of the family' (Smith, 1978,11), then clearly
this 'oppression' can only be relieved by the
capitalist society not being reproduced - in effect,
by the ending of capitalism, (see also, Lane, 1983).
However, it is difficult to hold completely to

such a rigid and deterministic view, when it seems
that,'Gender differentiation is more ancient, more
stable and more widespread than any other type of
social differentiation. It appears under all known
economic systems and political orders' (Holter, 1971,
5). A more optimistic view of the future could,
therefore,be presented, suggesting that changes can
be brought about to undermine gender-role differences in society without the necessary pre-condition
of political revolution.

a)   Changes in the law

Possibilities for future change involve two
inter-related aspects;   firstly, changes in the law,
and secondly, ideological change. It is not
possible for one set of changes to work effectively
without the other. This has already been demonstrated in the case of Equal Pay and Sex Discrimination
legislation in the 1970's. Legislation alone does
not alter the system of gender differentiation in
society, since it does not remove the prior responsibilities women have for domestic work and child-
rearing (see Oakley, 1979;   Counter Information
Services, no date;   Bland et al., 1978;   Wekerle et
al., 1980,8;   Buswell, 1983). The whole system of
social security which operates in this country is
predicated on the continued acceptance of traditional family roles (Wilson, 1977;   Land, 1978) and
this is perhaps the area where legislative change is
most needed. As Nandy (1978,690) says, 'A social
security system which facilitates rather than hind-
ers equality for women will have to be based on a
wholly different and more realistic basis'.   In
particular, it is necessary to take into account
demographic change. The conventional nuclear family
is no longer necessarily the standard model for
society (see Lenero - Otero (ed.), 1977);   greater
consideration must be given to the needs of women
bringing up children on their own. Whether it will
be or not is highly debatable;   after all, '...the
one-parent family lobby is mainly women fighting for
benefits in a world where the serious politics are
played and the major decisions taken by men' (Turner,
1978,12).

Legislative change is needed but it can only be
really effective if societal attitudes and norms are
altered as well. The relatively low level of achievement of the Equal Opportunities Commission, set up
to 'police' the Sex Discrimination Act (1975), is
illustrative of the meagre impact of legal change

without a corresponding will to change society
(Coote, 1978). However, changes in the law do have
some influence, if only in raising the consciousness of women concerning their rights; such changes
are a necessary element of the movement towards
equality between women and men. But, as Rowbotham
(1980) reminds us, '...if we are to achieve genuine
equality, we shall need a very wide-ranging cultural
revolution indeed - one which transforms the very
nature of sexuality.'

b)   Ideological change

        As we have noted in earlier chapters, women
have been entering the labour force in increasing
numbers in recent years but they are limited in
their freedom to develop significant careers by their
gender-role commitments to home and children. The
point is neatly summarised by Harper and Richards
(1979,11): 'When a woman has a baby in our society,
she acquires with it a role - she is now a mother.
Should she also be in paid employment, she takes on
a further role - working mother. There is no equivalent second role for the male parent. Whoever
heard of a working father?' It is simply assumed
that a man should act as breadwinner for his family
and be the one to aim at the development of a long
term career (Tolson, 1977,48). This is the other
side of the gender-role constraint and is equally
invidious and arbitrary. As Fogarty et al., (1971,
34) state, '...in the long run the needs both of
individual men and women and of the community...are
likely to be best met if women and men base their
career and family choices principally on their
abilities and needs as individuals and not on sex-
typed or other group stereotypes or norms'. If
women demand special consideration as employees on
the basis of their home responsibilities, this can
only lead to an intensification of gender differences within society. What is needed instead is a
total reformulation of occupational roles, such that
men and women are more easily able to share in the
upbringing of their children (Young, 1977; see also,
Jeffries, 1977; Pleck, 1984).
        It will never be enough simply to provide more
'institutional' child care to enable women to go out
to work; '...our present day-care arrangements
probably contribute as much to traditional stereotypes as they provide options. In particular, the
employment of women in paid as well as unpaid child-
care arrangements probably substantiates the

occupational segregation which is the strongest
source of economic discrimination' (Rowe, 1977,183).
While such externally-provided care may be of the
highest standard and meet the needs of young children
very well, it is nevertheless true that '...the
private spaces of the home and the private shapes of
individual lives cannot be fully mass-serviced.
Something remains that individuals must do. Must
these individuals always be women?' (Boulding, 1977,
71).

The acceptance of what has been termed
'androgynous' child care lies at the basis of possibilities for future ideological change. Traditional
gender-roles can only be eliminated if social policy
(and subsequent legislation) is directed towards
helping men and women to develop inter-related roles.
The simple 'reversal' of traditional roles, although
welcome in providing another choice dimension in
society, does little or nothing to alter the underlying assumptions of the division between production
and consumption. The real importance of child-
rearing must be recognised and the over-emphasis on
'production' at the expense of 'reproduction' be
evaluated. 'Having and bringing up children are only
burdens in a society that makes them so' (Oakley,
1979,393). A new attitude to the value of child
caring would highlight the important fact that,'The
care of children is not in itself an isolating nor
demeaning activity' (Mackie and Pattullo, 1977,21).
It is an occupation which can and possibly should
be shared equally by men and women, to the greater
benefit of men, women and children.

However, there is very little sign at present of
such a shift in ideology. Harper and Richards (1978,
221), writing of their women respondents, note that
'such ways out were occasionally dreamed about,
seldom experimented with. There was a deep fear of
disturbing social structures by stepping outside
prescribed roles and there was often distrust of
those who had tried to clear the way to new paths.'
Bernard (1971,15) makes the point that '...most women
would reject any radical reorganisation of the social
structure required for the achievement of full
equality.' However, the apparent support given by
many women to traditional roles must be viewed in the
light of societal convention and attitudes which are
obviously important in shaping ideas; '...we must
beware of confusing acquiescence with contentment;
the impossibility of remedy can inhibit action without inhibiting the sense of grievance' (Runciman,
1972,30).

CONCLUSIONS AND A LOOK TO THE FUTURE

Within a truly just society where all individuals were given a completely free choice of dominant activity many women (and many men) would choose a domestic and child care role for themselves, especially if the true importance of such a role were recognised in society and in the law. Increased efforts must be made through education and government policy to free individuals from ideological constraints on behaviour. It has <u>not</u> been argued here that all women should be <u>removed</u> from the domestic sphere but it has been argued that women (and men) should be able to choose their major sphere of activity. Such a choice can only come about if the whole basis of gender-role differentiation in society is re-examined, both at a personal level and at a national level. This re-evaluation of societal goals is a future <u>possibility</u> but it remains no more than that at the <u>present time</u>.

Allen, S. & Barker, D.L. (1976), Sexual divisions and
     and society, in Sexual Divisions and Society:
     Process and Change (London: Tavistock).
Alexander, S. & Taylor, B. (1980), In defence of
     'patriarchy', New Statesman, 1 February, 161.
Ambrose, P. (1974), The Quiet Revolution (London:
     Sussex University Press).
Anderson, J. (1971), Space-time budgets and activity
     studies in urban geography and planning,
     Environment and Planning, 3, 353-368.
Anderson, T.R. & Zelditch, M. (1975), A Basic Course
     in Statistics with Sociological Applications
     (New York: Holt, Rinehart and Winston).
Anon. (1978), Demand for part-timers, Midweek, 52, 1.
Angrist, S.S. (1967), Role Constellation as a Varia-
     ble in Women's Leisure Activities, Social
     Forces, 45, 423-431.
Apps, P. (1975), Child Care Policy in the Production-
     Consumption Economy, Public Policy Paper No. 2
     (Victorian Council of Social Service, Victoria,
     Australia).
Arregger, C.E. (1966), Graduate Women at Work
     (Newcastle upon Tyne: Oriel).
Athanasiou, R. & Yoshioka, G.A. (1973), The Spatial
     Character of Friendship Formation, Environment
     and Behavior, 5, 43-65.
Balmer, K. (1974), Urban Open Space and Outdoor
     Recreation, in P. Lavery (ed.), Recreational
     Geography (Newton Abbot, Devon: David &
     Charles).
Banister, D. (1977), Car availability and usage: a
     modal split model based on these concepts,
     Geographical Paper No. 58 (Department of Geog-
     raphy, University of Reading).
Banz, G. (1976), Life Style Mapping - A New Planning
     and Programming Tool, Urban Ecology, 2, 109-118.

Becker, E. (1964), The Revolution in Psychiatry (New York: The Free Press).

Bell, C. (1970), Mobility and the Middle Class Extended Family, in C.C. Harris (ed.), Readings in Kinship in Urban Society (Oxford: Pergamon).

Bell, C. & Healey, P. (1973), The family and leisure, in M. Smith, S. Parker and C. Smith (eds.), Leisure and Society in Britain (London: Allen Lane), 159-170.

Bernard, J. (1971) The status of women in modern patterns of culture, in C.F. Epstein and W.J. Goode (eds.), The Other Half: Roads to Women's Equality (New Jersey: Prentice-Hall).

Birrell, D. (1972), Relative Deprivation as a Factor in Conflict in Northern Ireland, The Sociological Review, 20 N.S., 317-343.

Blackstone, T. (1976), The Education of Girls Today, in J. Mitchell and A. Oakley (eds.), The Rights and Wrongs of Women (Harmondsworth, Middlesex: Penguin), 199-216.

Bland, L. et al., (1978), Women 'inside and outside' the relations of production in Women's Studies Group, Women Take Issue : Aspects of Women's Subordination (London: Hutchinson), 35-78.

Bollman, S.R., Moxley, V.M. & Elliott, N.C. (1975), Family and Community Activities of Rural Nonfarm Families with Children, Journal of Leisure Research, 7, 53-62.

Bolton, B. (1975), An end to homeworking? (Fabian Tract 436, London: The Fabian Society).

Bone, M. (1977), Pre-school Children and the Need for Day Care (London: O.P.C.S.).

Bott, E. (1957), Family and Social Network (London: Tavistock).

Boulding, E. (1977), Women in the Twentieth Century World (New York: Sage).

Bowlby, J. (1951), Maternal Care and Mental Health (Geneva: World Health Organisation).

Bowlby, J. (1953), Child Care and the Growth of Love (Harmondsworth, Middlesex: Penguin).

Bowlby, S.R., Foord, J. & MacKenzie, S. (1982), Feminism and Geography, Area, 14, 19-25.

Bracey, H.E. (1964), Neighbours: On New Estates and Subdivisions in England and U.S.A. (London: Routledge).

Bradley, M. (1982), The Coordination of Services for Children under Five (Windsor: NFER/Nelson).

Brail, R.K. & Chapin, F.S. (1973), Activity Patterns of Urban Residents, Environment and Behavior 4, 163-190.

British Broadcasting Corporation (1978), The People's

Activities and Use of Time (London: B.B.C.).

Brown, G.W., Bhrolohain, M.N. & Harris, T. (1975). Social class and psychiatric disturbance among women in an urban population, Sociology, 9, 225-254.

Brown, G.W. & Harris, T. (1978), Social Origins of Depression: A Study of Psychiatric Disorder in Women (London: Tavistock).

Bruce, A. (1974), Facilities required near home, Built Environment, 3, 290-291.

Brunsdon, C. (1978), It is well-known that by nature women are inclined to be rather personal, in Women's Studies Group (ed.), Women Take Issue: Aspects of Woman's Subordination (London: Hutchinson).

Bullock, N., Dickens, P., Shapcott, M. & Steadman, P. (1974), Time Budgets and Models of Urban Activity Patterns, Social Trends, 5, 45-59.

Burtenshaw, D. (1973), Relocated Wives, New Society, 24, 688.

Buswell, C. (1983), Women, Work and Education, Social Policy & Administration, 17, 220-231.

Campbell, A., Converse, P.E. & Rodgers, W.L. (1976), The Quality of American Life (New York: Russell Sage).

Carey, L. & Mapes, R. (1972), The Sociology of Planning: A Study of Social Activity on New Housing Estates (London: Batsford).

Carlstein, T., Parkes, D. & Thrift, N. (eds.), (1979), Timing Space and Spacing Time in Socio-Economic Systems, Vol. 2, Human Activity and Time Geography (London: Edward Arnold).

Carney, J.G. & Taylor, C. (1974), Community Development Projects: review and comment, Area, 6, 226-231.

Carnforth, M. (1963), Dialectical materialism: An Introduction, Vol. 3. The Theory of Knowledge (London: Lawrence & Wishart).

Central Advisory Council for Education (England) (1967), Children and their Primary Schools (Plowden Report) (London: H.M.S.O.).

Central Policy Review Staff (1978), Services for Young Children with Working Mothers (London: H.M.S.O.).

CES Ltd., (1984), The Outer Estates in Britain; A Preliminary Comparison of Four Estates, Interim Report (London: CES Ltd.).

Chapin, F.S. (1971), Free time activities and quality of urban life, Journal of the American Institute of Planners, November, 411-417.

Chapin, F.S. & Hightower, H.C. (1965), Household

Activity Patterns and Land Use, Journal of the American Institute of Planners, 31, 222-231.

Chapin, F.S., & Logan, T.H. (1969), Patterns of time and space use, in H.S. Perloff (ed.), The Quality of the Urban Environment: Essays on "New Resources" in an Urban Age (Washington D.C. : Resources for the Future, Inc.), 305-332.

Chapman, J.R. (1976), Economic Independence for Women: The Foundation for Equal Rights (Beverly Hills, California: Sage).

Chisholm, M. & Manners, G. (1971), Geographical space: a new dimension of public concern and policy, in M. Chisholm and G. Manners (eds.), Spatial Policy Problems of the British Economy (London: Cambridge University Press), 1-23.

Cicchetti, C.J. (1971), Some Economic Issues in Planning Urban Recreation Facilities, Land Economics, 47, 14-23.

Coates, B.E. & Rawstron, E.M. (1971), Regional Variations in Britain (London: Batsford).

Coates, K. & Silburn, R. (1970), Poverty: the Forgotten Englishmen (Harmondsworth, Middlesex: Penguin).

Committee on Local Authority and Allied Personal Social Services (1968), Report of the Committee (Seebohm Report) (London: H.M.S.O.).

Consultative Committee on Infant and Nursery Schools (1933), Report of the Committee (Hadow Report) (London: H.M.S.O.).

Coote, A. (1978), Equality and the curse of the Quango, New Statesman, 1 December, 734-737.

Counter Information Services (no date), Women under attack, Crisis Special Report, 15.

Coverman, S. (1983), Gender, domestic labor time, and wage inequality, American Sociological Review, 48, 623-637.

Cullen, I., Godson, V. & Major, S. (1972), The Structure of Activity Patterns, in A.G. Wilson (ed.), Patterns and Processes in Urban and Regional Systems (London papers in Regional Science 3, London: Pion Limited), 281-296.

David, M.E. (1978), Women caring for pre-school children in the U.S.A., International Journal of Urban and Regional Research, 2, 440-462.

Davidson, R.N. (1976), Social Deprivation: An Analysis of Intercensal Change, Transactions of the Institute of British Geographers, 1 N.S., 108-117.

Davies, B. (1968), Social Needs and Resources in Local Services (London: Joseph).

Daws, L.F. & McCulloch, M. (1974), Shopping activity

patterns: a travel diary study of Watford,
Current Paper 31/74 (Building Research Establishment, Watford, Herts.).

Deakin, N.D. (1970), Colour, Citizenship and British
Society (London: Panther).

Deakin, N.D. (1977), Inner area problems: positive
discrimination revisited, Greater London
Intelligence Journal, 37, 4-8.

Dennis, N., Henriques, F. & Slaughter, C. (1956),
Coal is our Life (London: Tavistock).

Department of Education and Science (1972),
Education: A Framework for Expansion (London:
H.M.S.O.).

Department of the Environment (1976), Transport
Policy: A Consultative Document (London:
H.M.S.O.).

Dowling, S. (1977), The inter-relationship of child
health clinics and day care facilities in the
pre-school years, in Voluntary Organisations
Liaison Council for Under Fives, 0-5: A Changing
Population, papers from a Seminar, Institute of
Child Health.

Drake, C., & Horton, J. (1983), Comment on editorial
essay: Sexist bias in political geography,
Political Geography Quarterly, 2, 329-337.

Duncan, S.S. (1976), Research directions in social
geography: housing opportunities and constraints, Transactions of the Institute of British
Geographers, 1 N.S., 10-19.

Elias, P., & Main, B. (1982), Women's Working Lives:
Evidence from the National Training Survey
(University of Warwick Institute for Employment
Research).

Eliot-Hurst, M.E. (1969), The Structure of Movement
and Household Travel Behaviour, Urban Studies,
6, 70-82.

Ellis, V. (1978), The under-fives: report of a TUC
working party, State Service, April, 116-118.

Elms, A.C. (1976), Attitudes, Social Psychology,
Block 10, Milton Keynes: Open University Press).

English, J. (1976), Housing Allocation and a Deprived
Scottish Estate, Urban Studies, 13, 319-323.

Everitt, J.C. (1976), Community and Propinquity in a
City, Annals of the Association of American
Geographers, 66, 104-116.

Eversley, D.E.C. (1973), The Planner in Society,
(London: Faber & Faber).

Eyles, J. (1968), The Inhabitants' Perception of
Highgate Village (London), Discussion Paper 15
(London School of Economics, Department of
Geography).

Eyles, J. (1971), Pouring New Sentiments into Old Theories: How Else Can We Look at Behavioural Patterns?, Area, 3, 242-250.

Eyles, J. (1974), Increased Spatial Mobility: A Minor Social Indicator?, Area, 6, 305-308.

Ferri, E., Birchall, D., Gingell, V. & Gipps, C. (1981), Combined Nursery Centres: A New Approach to Education and Day Care (London: Macmillan).

Festinger, L., Schachter, S. & Back, K. (1950), Social Pressures in Informal Groups: A Study of Human Factors in Housing (Stanford: Stanford University Press).

Field, D.E. & Neill, D.G. (1957), A Survey of New Housing Estates in Belfast (Department of Social Studies, Queen's University of Belfast).

Finch, J. (1983), Married to the Job: Wives Incorporation in Men's Work (London: Allen & Unwin).

Firestone, S. (1971), The Dialectic of Sex: The Case for Feminist Revolution (London: Jonathon Cape).

Firth, R., Hubert, J. & Forge, A. (1969), Families and their Relatives: Kinship in a Middle Class Sector of London (London: Routledge).

Fodor, R., (1978), Day-care policy in France and its consequences for women, International Journal of Urban and Regional Research, 2, 463-481.

Fogarty, M.P., Rapoport, R. & Rapoport, R.N. (1971), Sex, Career and Family (London: Allen & Unwin).

Foley, D.L. (1950), The Use of local facilities in a metropolis, American Journal of Sociology, 56, 238-246.

Forrest, J. (1974), Spatial Aspects of Urban Social Travel, Urban Studies, 11, 301-313.

Galbraith, K. (1974), Economics and the Public Purpose (London: Andre Deutsch).

Gans, H.J. (1961a), Planning and Social Life: Friendship and Neighbor Relations in Suburban Communities, Journal of the American Institute of Planners, 27, 134-140.

Gans, H.J. (1961b), The Balanced Community: Homogeneity or Heterogeneity in Residential Areas, Journal of the American Institute of Planners, 27, 176-184.

Gans, H.J. (1962), Urbanism and suburbanism as ways of life, in A.M. Rose (ed.), Human Behaviour and Social Processes (Boston: Houghton, Mifflin), 625-648.

Gans, H.J. (1967), The Levittowners: Ways of Life and Politics in a New Suburban Community (Harmondsworth, Middlesex: Penguin).

Gans, H.J. (1972), Planning for People, not Buildings, in M. Stewart (ed.), The City: Problems

of Planning (Harmondsworth, Middlesex: Penguin),
363-384.

Garbrecht, D. (1978), The utilisation of inner-city
open space, II, Parks and Recreation, 43, 13-16.

Gavron, H. (1966), The Captive Wife: Conflicts of
Housebound Mothers (London: Routledge).

Ginsberg, S. (1977), Women, work and conflict, in
N. Fonda & P. Moss, (eds.), Mothers in Employ-
ment (Uxbridge, Middlesex: Brunel University
Management Programme).

Gittus, E. (1976), Flats, Families and the Under-
Fives (London: Routledge).

Glazer, N. (1967), Race in the City, in B.J.L. Berry
& J. Meltzer (eds.), Goals for Urban America
(New Jersey: Prentice-Hall), 85-98.

Glennerster, H. & Hatch, S. (1974), Positive Discrimination and Inequality, Fabian Research Series,
No. 314.

Godkin, M. & Emker, I. (1976), Time-space Budget
Studies in Sweden: A Review and Evaluation, in
B.P. Holly (ed.), Time-Space Budgets and Urban
Research: A Symposium (Department of Geography,
Kent State University).

Gove, W.R. (1972), The relationship between sex
roles, marital status, and mental illness,
Social Forces, 51, 34-44.

Gove, W.R., & Tudor, J.F. (1973), Adult sex roles
and mental illness, American Journal of Sociology, 78, 812-835.

Gray, F. (1975), Non-explanation in urban geography,
Area, 7, 228-235.

Gray, F. (1976), Selection and Allocation in Council
Housing, Transactions of the Institute of
British Geographers, 1 N.S., 34-46.

Greater London Council, Intelligence Unit (1974),
1971 Census Data for London (London: G.L.C.).

Greater London Council Planning Department (1968),
Surveys of the Use of Open Space Vol. 1,
Research Paper No. 2 (G.L.C.).

Gutenschwager, G.A. (1973), The Time-Budget -
Activity Systems Perspective in Urban Research
and Planning, Journal of the American Institute
of Planners, 39, 378-387.

Hagerstrand, T. (1970), What About People in Regional
Science, Papers of the Regional Science Association, 24, 7-21.

Hakim, C. (1980), Homeworking: some new evidence,
Employment Gazette, 88, 1105-1110.

Halkett, I. (1974), Private gardens, private worlds,
Community (Canberra, Australia: Department of
Urban and Regional Development) No. 6.

Hall, J. (1976), Subjective measures of quality of
    life in Britain: 1971 to 1975, Some develop-
    ments and trends, Social Trends, 7, 47-60.
Hall, J. & Perry, N. (1974), Aspects of Leisure in
    Two Industrial Cities, Occasional Papers in
    Survey Research No. 5 (London: Social Science
    Research Council Survey Unit).
Hall, P., Thomas, R., Gracey, H., & Drewett, R.
    (1973), The Containment of Urban England
    (London: Allen and Unwin).
Hannon, P. (1978), Minders of our future?, New
    Society, 11 May, 304-305.
Hanson, S. & Hanson, P. (1980), Gender and Urban
    activity patterns in Uppsala, Sweden, Geograph-
    ical Review, 70, 291-299.
Hardy, D. (1973), Recreation Space and Social Plann-
    ing, in J. Rees & P. Newby (eds.), Behavioural
    Perspectives in Geography, Monographs in Geog-
    raphy No. 1 (London: Middlesex Polytechnic),
    81-93.
Harper, J. & Richards, L. (1979), Mothers and Work-
    ing Mothers (Melbourne, Australia: Penguin).
Harris, M. (1973), Some Aspects of Social Polariza-
    tion, in D. Donnison & D. Eversley (eds.),
    London: Urban Patterns, Problems and Policies
    (London: Heinemann), 156-189.
Harvey, D. (1975), Social Justice and the City
    (London: Edward Arnold, paperback edition).
Hayford, A.M. (1974), The Geography of Women: An
    Historical Introduction, Antipode, 6, 1-19.
Healy, P. (1977), Childminding has become fashion-
    able, but it can't be done on the cheap, The
    Times, 10 May, 10.
Hedges, B.M. (1974), Time budgets, Social Trends, 5,
    35-44.
Hemmens, G.G. (1970), Analysis and Simulation of
    Urban Activity Patterns, Socio-Economic
    Planning Sciences, 4, 53-66.
Herbert, D.T. & Williams, W.M. (1964), Some new
    techniques for studying urban sub-divisions,
    Geographia Polonica, 3, 93-117.
Higgs, G. (1975), An assessment of the action compo-
    nent of action space, Geographical Analysis, 7,
    35-50.
Hillier Parker May & Rowden (1974),London Borough of
    Merton Shopping Study.
Hillman, M. (1970), Mobility in New Towns (unpub-
    lished Ph.D. thesis, University of Edinburgh).
Hillman, M., Henderson, I., & Whalley, A. (1973),
    Personal Mobility and Transport Policy (London:
    P.E.P., Broadsheet No. 542).

Hillman, M., Henderson, I., & Whalley, A. (1976), Transport Realities and Planning Policy (London: P.E.P.).

Hiro, D. (1971), Black British, White British (London: Eyre & Spottiswoode).

Hitchcock, J.R. (1972), Daily Activity Patterns: an exploratory study, Ekistics, 34, 323-327.

Hoggart, R. (1973), Changes in Working-Class Life, in M. Smith, S. Parker & C. Smith (eds.), Leisure and Society in Britain (London: Allen Lane), 28-39.

Holland, J. (1981), Work and Women (Bedford Way Papers 6, University of London Institute of Education).

Holter, H. (1971), Sex roles and social change, Acta Sociologica, 14, 2-12.

Horton, F.E. & Reynolds, D.R. (1971), Effects of Urban Spatial Structure on Individual Behavior, Economic Geography, 47, 36-48.

Hubback, J. (1957), Wives Who Went to College (London: Heinemann).

Hunt, P. (1980), Gender and Class Consciousness (London: Macmillan).

Hurstfield, J. (1978), The Part-Time Trap : Part-Time Workers in Britain Today (London: Low Pay Unit).

I.B.G. Women & Geography Working Party (1981), Perspectives on Feminism and Geography.

Jary, D. (1973), Evenings at the Ivory Tower; Liberal Adult Education, in M. Smith., S. Parker, & C. Smith (eds.), Leisure and Society in Britain, (London: Allen Lane), 263-277.

Jeffries, M. (1977), A man's place is in the home, The Sunday Times Magazine, 20 March, 19.

Jephcott, P. (1962), Married Women Working (London: Allen & Unwin).

Jephcott, P. (1971), Homes in High Flats (Edinburgh: Oliver & Boyd).

Jones, P.M., Dix, M.C., Clarke, M.I., & Heggie, I.G. (1983), Understanding Travel Behaviour (Aldershot Hants: Gower).

Jowell, R. & Airey, C. (eds.), (1984), British Social Attitudes : the 1984 Report (London: Social and Community Planning Research).

Kennedy, F.R. (1967), Policies to Combat Negro Poverty, in B.J.L. Berry & J. Meltzer (eds.), Goals for Urban America (New Jersey: Prentice-Hall).

Kenny, M. (1977), Love's labours lost, The Sunday Times Magazine, 4 September, 70.

Kerlinger, F.N. (1969), Foundations of Behavioral

Research (London: Holt, Rinehart & Winston).

Knox, P.L. (1975), Social Well-Being: A Spatial Perspective (London: Oxford University Press).

Koutsopoulos, K.C. & Schmidt, C.G. (1976), Mobility constraints of the carless, Ekistics, 42, 29-32.

Kuz, T.J. (1978), Quality of life, an objective and subjective variable analysis, Regional Studies, 12, 409-417.

Land, H. (1978), Who cares for the family?, Journal of Social Policy, 7, 257-284.

Lane C. (1983), Women in socialist society with special reference to the German Democratic Republic, Sociology, 17, 489-505.

Lazar, I., Hubbell, R., Murray, H., Rosche, M., & Royce, J. (1977), Preliminary findings of the developmental continuity longitudinal study, paper presented at Office of Child Development 'Parents, Children and Continuity' Conference, El Paso, Texas,

Lee, T. (1966), A Null Relationship between Ecology and Adult Education, The British Journal of Educational Psychology, 36, 100-102.

Lee, T. (1968), Urban Neighbourhood as a Socio-Spatial Schema, Human Relations, 21, 241-267.

Leigh, A. (1980), Policy research and reviewing services for under fives, Social Policy & Administration, 14, 151-163.

Lenero-Otero, L. (ed.), Beyond the Nuclear Family Model: Cross-Cultural Perspectives (Beverly Hills, California: Sage).

Lenntorp, B. (1979), A Time-geographic simulation model of individual activity programmes, in T. Carlstein., D.N. Parkes & N.J. Thrift (eds.), Timing Space and Spacing Time in Socio-economic Systems (London: Edward Arnold).

Lindsay, J.J. & Ogle, R.A. (1972), Socio-economic Patterns of Outdoor Recreation Use Near Urban Areas, Journal of Leisure Research, 4, 19-24.

London Borough of Enfield (1975), Household Interview Survey - Borough Development Plan, Background Paper (London Borough of Enfield).

London Borough of Merton (1974), Borough Plan - Appendix B (Interim Report on Open Space and Recreation) (London Borough of Merton).

London Borough of Merton (1976), Borough Plan - Appendix A (Report on Indoor Recreation and Leisure) (London Borough of Merton).

London Borough of Southwark (1970), Recreation in Southwark: Leisure Survey (Department of Architecture and Planning, London Borough of Southwark).

London Council of Social Service (1977), Childmind-
    ing in London: A Study of support services for
    childminders (London: L.C.S.S.).
Lopata, H.Z. (1971), Occupation : Housewife (New
    York: Oxford University Press).
Mackie, L. & Pattullo, P. (1977), Women at Work
    (London: Tavistock).
Macmurray, T. (1971), Aspects of Time and the Study
    of Activity Patterns, Town Planning Review, 42,
    195-209.
Manley, P., & Sawbridge, D. (1980), Women at work,
    Lloyds Bank Review, 135, 29-40.
Mann, P.H. (1965), An Approach to Urban Sociology
    (London: Routledge).
Martensson, S. (1977), Childhood interaction and
    temporal organisation, Economic Geography, 53,
    99-125.
Martin, J., & Roberts, C. (1984), Women and Employ-
    ment: A Lifetime Perspective (London: Depart-
    ment of Employment/O.P.C.S.).
McDowell, L. (1983), Towards an understanding of the
    gender division of urban space, Environment and
    Planning D: Society and Space, 1, 59-72.
McDowell, L., & Bowlby, S. (1983), Teaching feminist
    geography, Journal of Geography in Higher
    Education, 7, 97-107.
Meltzer, J., & Whitley, J. (1967), Social and
    Physical Planning for the Urban Slum, in B.J.L.
    Berry & J. Meltzer (eds.), Goals for Urban
    America (New Jersey: Prentice-Hall), 133-152.
Melville, J. (1983), Mothers in the front line, New
    Society, 10 March, 372-374.
Meyerson, M. (1967), National Urban Policy Approp-
    riate to the American pattern, in B.J.L. Berry,
    & J. Meltzer (eds.), Goals for Urban America
    (New Jersey: Prentice-Hall), 69-84.
MIL Research Ltd., (1976), Exploratory Study on
    Transport For The Disadvantaged: Report.
Miller, R. (1982), Household activity patterns in
    nineteenth-century suburbs: a time-geographic
    exploration, Annals of the Association of
    American Geographers, 72, 355-371.
Miller, S.M., & Roby, P.A. (1970), The Future of
    Inequality (New York: Basic Books, Inc.).
Mills, E.S. (1967), An Aggregative Model of Resource
    Allocation in a Metropolitan Area, American
    Economic Review, 57, 197-210.
Milton Keynes Development Corporation (1970), The
    Plan for Milton Keynes Vol. 1.
Milton Keynes Development Corporation (1974), Milton
    Keynes Household Survey 1973: Summary.

BIBLIOGRAPHY

Ministry of Housing and Local Government, Sociolog-
    ical Research Section (1966), Home and Environ-
    ment: A Pilot Study in Reading.
Mitchell, C.G.B., & Town, S.W. (1977), Accessibility
    of various social groups to different activit-
    ies, T.R.R.L. Supplementary Report, 258,
    (Department of the Environment).
Mitchell, J. (1966), Women: the Longest Revolution,
    New Left Review, 40, 11-37.
Mitchell, J. (1971), Women's Estate (New York:
    Penguin).
Mitchell, J. (1976), Women and Equality, in J.
    Mitchell & A. Oakley (eds.), The Rights and
    Wrongs of Women (Harmondsworth, Middlesex:
    Penguin), 379-399.
Mitchell, L.S., & Lovingood, P.E. (1976), Public
    Urban Recreation: An Investigation of Spatial
    Relationships, Journal of Leisure Research, 8,
    6-20.
Momsen, J.H., & Townsend, J. (eds.), (1984), Women's
    Role in Changing the Face of the Developing
    World (Papers, Women and Geography Study Group
    Session, Institute of British Geographers,
    Durham).
Morgan, B.S. (1976), The Bases of Family Status
    Segregation: A Case Study in Exeter, Transact-
    ions of the Institute of British Geographers,
    1 N.S., 83-107.
Moser, C.A., & Kalton, G. (1971), Survey Methods in
    Social Investigation (London: Heinemann, second
    edition).
Moser, C.A., & Scott, W. (1961), British Towns - A
    Statistical Study of their Social and Economic
    Differences (London: Oliver & Boyd).
Moss, P. (1978), Child care, New Society, 45, 693.
Moss, P., & Plewis, L. (1976), Who wants nurseries?,
    New Society, 43, 188.
Muller, P.O. (1976), The Outer City; Geographical
    Consequences of the Urbanisation of the Suburbs,
    Resource Paper No. 75-2 (Washington D.C.:
    Association of American Geographers).
Myrdal, A., & Klein, V. (1956), Women's Two Roles:
    Home and Work (London: Routledge).
Nandy, L. (1978), Double bind for women, New Society,
    45, 689-690.
National Opinion Polls (1977), Women in Britain
    (London: N.O.P.).
National Union of Teachers (1977), The Needs of the
    Under-Fives (London: N.U.T.).
Noordhoek, J., & Smith, Y. (1971), Family and work,
    Acta Sociologica, 14, 43-51.

Nursery Action Group/Benwell C.D.P. (1977), Work and
    Play in Benwell.
Oakley, A. (1974a), The Sociology of Housework
    (London: Martin Robertson).
Oakley, A. (1974b), Housewife (London: Allen Lane).
Oakley, A. (1979), The failure of the movement for
    women's equality, New Society, 49, 392-394.
Oakley, A. (1980), Women Confined (London: Martin
    Robertson).
Oberg, S. (1976), Methods of describing physical
    access to supply points, Lund Studies in Geog-
    raphy Ser. B., No. 43 (University of Lund,
    Sweden).
Office of Population Censuses and Surveys (1977),
    Protective Legislation Survey (London:O.P.C.S.).
Oppenheim, A.N. (1968), Questionnaire Design and
    Attitude Measurement (London: Heinemann).
Osborn, A.F. (1983), Maternal employment, depression
    and child behaviour, E.O.C. Research Bulletin,
    8, 48-67.
Paaswell, R.E. (1976), Problems of the Carless
    (Washington D.C.: U.S. Department of Transport-
    ation).
Pacione, M. (1980), Quality of life in a metropolitan
    village, Transactions of the Institute of
    British Geographers, 5, 185-206.
Pahl, R.E. (1962), Adult Education in a Free Society
    (London: New Orbits Group Publication 10).
Pahl, R.E. (1968), Spatial Structure and Social
    Structure, C.E.S. Working Paper No. 10 (London:
    Centre for Environmental Studies).
Pahl, R.E. (1971a), Patterns of Urban Life (London:
    Longman).
Pahl, R.E. (1971b), Poverty and the Urban System, in
    M. Chisholm, & G, Manners (eds.), Spatial
    Policy Problems of the British Economy (London:
    Cambridge University Press), 126-145.
Pahl, R.E. (1975), Whose City? (Harmondsworth,
    Middlesex: Penguin).
Pahl, R.E. (1977), Inner City Jobs, letter to 'The
    Times' (1st March).
Pahl, J.M., & Pahl, R.E. (1971), Managers and their
    Wives (Harmondsworth, Middlesex: Penguin).
Paige, D., & Jones, K. (1966), Health and Welfare
    Services in Britain in 1975 (London: Cambridge
    University Press).
Palm, R., & Pred, A. (1974), A Time-Geographic
    Perspective on Problems of Inequality for Women,
    Working Paper No. 236 (Institute of Urban and
    Regional Development, University of California,
    Berkeley).

Peet, R. (1975), Inequality and Poverty: A Marxist-Geographic Theory, Annals of the Association of American Geographers, 65, 564-571.

Pine, V.R. (1977), Introduction to Social Statistics (Englewood Cliffs, New Jersey: Prentice-Hall).

Pirie, G.H. (1976), Thoughts on revealed preference and spatial behaviour, Environment and Planning A, 8, 947-955.

Pleck, J.H. (1984), The work-family role system, in P. Voydanoff (ed.), Work and Family: Changing Roles of Men and Women (Palo Alto, California: Mayfield), 8-19.

Plowden (Lady) (1977), Children and parents: self help and the voluntary role, in Voluntary Organisations Liaison Council for Under Fives, 0-5: A Changing Population (papers from a Seminar, Institute of Child Health).

Pritchard, N. (1967), Planned Social Provision in New Towns, Town Planning Review, 38, 25-34.

Rapoport, R., & Rapoport, R.N. (1975), Leisure and the Family Life Cycle (London: Routledge).

Reid, I. (1977), Social Class Differences in Britain: A Sourcebook (London: Open Books).

Richards, M. (1977), Birmingham project creates interest in adult education, Times Educational Supplement, 23 December, 8.

Richman, N. (1976), Depression in mothers of pre-school children, Journal of Child Psychology and Psychiatry, 17, 75-78.

Roberts, K. (1970), Leisure (London: Longman).

Robinson, J.P., Converse, P.E., & Szalai, A. (1972), Everyday life in twelve countries, in A. Szalai (ed.), The Use of Time: Daily activities of urban and suburban populations in twelve countries (The Hague: Mouton), 113-143.

Rose, C. (1977), Reflections on the Notion of Time Incorporated in Hagerstrand's Time-Geographic Model of Society, Tijdschrift voor Economische en Sociale Geografie, 68, 43-50.

Rothblatt, D.N., Garr, D.J., & Sprague, J. (1979), The Suburban Environment and Women (New York: Praeger).

Rowe, M.P. (1977), Child care for the 1980's: traditional sex roles or androgyny?, in J.R. Chapman & M. Gates (eds.), Women into Wives: The Legal and Economic Impact of Marriage (Beverly Hills, California: Sage).

Royal Commission on the Distribution of Income and Wealth (1975), Report No. 1: Initial Report on the Standing Reference (London: H.M.S.O.).

Runciman, W.G. (1972), Relative Deprivation and

Social Justice (Harmondsworth, Middlesex: Penguin).

Rushton, G. (1969), Analysis of spatial behaviour by revealed space preferences, Annals of the Association of American Geographers, 59, 391-400.

Scheuch, E.K. (1972), The time-budget interview, in A. Szalai (ed.), The Use of Time: Daily activities of urban and suburban populations in twelve countries (The Hague: Mouton), 69-87.

Sessoms, H.D. (1963), An Analysis of Selected Variables affecting Outdoor Recreation Patterns, Social Forces, 42, 112-115.

Shepherd, J., Westaway, J., & Lee, T. (1974), A Social Atlas of London (London: Oxford University Press).

Simmie, J.M. (1974), Citizens in Conflict: The Sociology of Town Planning (London: Hutchinson).

Smith, D.M. (1973), The Geography of Social Well-Being in the United States (New York: McGraw-Hill).

Smith, D.M. (1977), Human Geography: a Welfare Approach (London: Edward Arnold).

Smith, J. (1978), Women and the family, International Socialism, 104, 11-16.

Smith, P.K. (1979), How many people can a young child feel secure with?, New Society, 48, 504-506.

Social Surveys (Gallop Poll) Limited (1979), Work and Mothers Survey (London: Gallop).

Speakman, S. (1983), Women and shiftwork: a study of the effects of shiftworking patterns on work opportunities and family life, E.O.C. Research Bulletin, 8, 37-47.

Sullerot, E. (1971), Woman, Society and Change (London: Weidenfeld & Nicolson).

Szalai, A. (ed.), (1972), The Use of Time: Daily activities of urban and suburban populations in twelve countries (The Hague: Mouton).

Szalai, A. (1972), Introduction. Concepts and practices of time-budget research, in A. Szalai (ed.), The Use of Time: Daily activities of urban and suburban populations in twelve countries (The Hague: Mouton), 1-12.

Szalai, A. (1975), Women in the light of contemporary time-budget research, Futures, 7, 385-399.

Szalai, A., & Andrews, F.M. (eds.), (1980), The Quality of Life: Comparative Studies (Beverly Hills, California: Sage).

Talbot, M. (1979), Women and Leisure (London: Sports Council/S.S.R.C.).

Tallman, I. (1969), Working-class wives in suburbia: fulfilment or crisis?, Journal of Marriage and the Family, 31, 65-72.

Teitz, M. (1968), Toward a Theory of Urban Public Facility Location, Papers of the Regional Science Association, 21, 25-52.

Thompson, B., & Finlayson, A. (1963), Married Women who Work in Early Motherhood, British Journal of Sociology, 14, 150-168.

Thorns, D.C. (1972), Suburbia (London: MacGibbon & Kee).

Thrift, N. (1976a), An Introduction to Time-Geography (University of East Anglia: Geo Abstracts Ltd., CATMOG No. 13).

Thrift, N. (1976b), A reply to Brian Holly's paper: some more problems and a Utopian perspective, in B.P. Holly (ed.), Time-Space Budgets and Urban Research: A Symposium (Department of Geography, Kent State University).

Thrift, N., & Pred, A. (1981), Time-geography: a new beginning, Progress in Human Geography, 5, 277-286.

Tivers, J. (1976), Open Space in the City: An Analysis of Open Space Provision in London and Sydney (unpublished M.Sc. dissertation, University of London).

Tivers, J. (1978), How the other half lives: the geographical study of women, Area, 10, 302-306.

Tivers, J. (1979), Commercial development and women's employment, Slate (The Radical Paper on Architecture and the Building Industry).

Tizard, J. (1976), Ten comments on low cost day care for the under fives, in DHSS/DES, Low Cost Day provision for the under fives (papers from a Conference, London), 43-44.

Tizard, J., Moss, P., & Perry, J. (1976), All Our Children: Pre-school services in a changing society (London: Temple Smith/New Society).

Tolson, A. (1977), The Limits of Masculinity (London: Tavistock).

Toomey, D.M. (1970), The Importance of Social Networks in Working Class Areas, Urban Studies, 7, 259-270.

Tulpule, A.H. (1974), Characteristics of Households With and Without Cars in 1970, Supplementary Report 64 UC (Transport and Road Research Laboratory).

Turner, J. (1978), One-parent families: the undeserving poor?, New Society, 6 July, 11-12.

Ullman, E.L. (1974), Space and/or Time: Opportunity for Substitution and Prediction, Transactions of the Institute of British Geographers, 63, 125-139.

U.K. Central Housing Committee (1967), The Needs of New Communities (London: H.M.S.O.).

Urben, E. (1977), A case study of child-minders in the London Borough of Camden, in M. Mayo (ed.), Women in the Community (London: Routledge), 45-51.

Vickery, C. (1977), The time-poor: a new look at poverty, Journal of Human Resources, 12, 27-48.

Walters, M. (1977), Men and children are still put first, The Sunday Times, 27 February, 13.

Ward, B., & Dubos, R. (1974), Human Needs, in A. Blowers, C. Hamnett & P. Sarre, (eds.), The Future of Cities (London: Hutchinson), 131-140.

Watts, J. (1980), After the event, The Observer.

Webber, M.M. (1964a), Culture, Territoriality, and the Elastic Mile, Papers of the Regional Science Association, 13, 59-69.

Webber, M.M. (1964b), The Urban Place and the Non-place Urban Realm, in M.M. Webber et al., (eds.), Explorations into Urban Structure (Philadelphia: University of Pennsylvania Press).

Wekerle, G.R., Peterson, R., & Morley, D. (1980), New Space for Women (Boulder, Colorado: West-view).

Wheeler, J.O. & Stutz, F.P. (1971), Spatial Dimensions of Urban Social Travel, Annals of the Association of American Geographers, 61, 371-386.

Whicheloe, U. (1977), Factors affecting the provision of day care for children under three years old: a critique of government policy (project submitted as a course requirement of the CNAA B.Sc. degree in social sciences, Polytechnic of the South Bank, London).

White, M.J. (1977), A Model of residential location choice and commuting by men and women workers, Journal of Regional Science, 17, 41-52.

Wigan, M.R., & Morris, J.M. (1979), The Transport Implications of Activity and Time Budget Constraints (Australian Road Research Board Research Report ARR 93).

Williams, A. (1966), The Optimal Provision of Public Goods in a System of Local Government, Journal of Political Economy, 74, 18-33.

Willis, M. (1969), Sociological Aspects of Urban Structure, Town Planning Review, 39, 296-306.

Willmott, P. (1973), Some Social Trends, in J.B. Cullingworth (ed.), Problems of an Urban

Society, Vol. 3 (London: Allen & Unwin), 94-119.

Wilson, E. (1977), Women and the Welfare State (London: Tavistock).

Women and Geography Study Group of the IBG (1984), Geography and Gender : An Introduction to Feminist Geography (London: Hutchinson).

Young, M. (1977), Towards a new concordance, New Society, 17 November, 351-352.

Young, M., & Willmott, P. (1957), Family and Kinship in East London (London: Routledge).

Young, M., & Willmott, P. (1973), The Symmetrical Family (Harmondsworth, Middlesex: Penguin).

COPY OF THE QUESTIONNAIRE

WOMEN WITH YOUNG CHILDREN

	E.D. Code	Respondent No.		6
				7

Q.1 Household

First of all, could you tell me who else lives here, as part of your household? Could you tell me how old your child(ren) is/are?

		8

Husband   1   9

Other relative(s) (16 or over)   2

Other adult(s) (e.g. lodger) (16 or over)   3   10

No. of children (under 16) (write in ages)..........Ages.....   11

SECTION A - EMPLOYMENT

QA.1. ASK ALL RESPONDENTS

I'd like to start with some questions about paid employment. Do you do any paid work at all?   Yes -> QA.1.(a)
                                           No 3 -> QA.13
                                                 (Page 5)

QA.1(a)   (IF 'YES' TO QA.1.)

Do you go out to work, or do you work at home?
(n.b. If both, ring CODE 1)   12

                              Out to work 1]->QA
                              Home-worker 2]   2

2

IF CODE 1 OR 2 AT QA.1. - CONTINUE:

QA.2.	What work do you do? Could you describe what you <u>actually</u> do in your job? (n.b. If 'child-minder', note total number of children cared for, full-time or part-time)....................................	13

QA.3.	Do you <u>normally</u> work on Monday to Friday, or do you only work on certain days of the week? (n.b. Disregard length of time worked on any one day).	

On Monday - Friday (daytime)	1
On 4 weekdays (daytime)	2
On 3 weekdays (daytime)	3
On 2 weekdays (daytime)	4
On 1 weekday (daytime)	5
On weekdays, but less than once a week (Specify)...............	6
Evening/weekend only	7

14

QA.4.	How many hours each week do you spend at work on average?

Less than 8 hours	1
8 hours but less than 12 hours	2
12 hours but less than 18 hours	3
18 hours but less than 21 hours	4
21 hours but less than 24 hours	5
24 hours but less than 30 hours	6
30 hours or more	7

15

IF 'HOME-WORKER' (CODE 2 AT QA.1.) GO TO QA.8.

ASK ONLY THOSE WHO GO <u>OUT</u> TO WORK (CODE 1 AT QA.1.)

QA.5.	Where exactly do you work? (n.b. Obtain <u>name</u> of factory, firm etc. and <u>address</u> of workplace (street and suburb).......	16

QA.6.	What is your <u>main</u> means of travel to work? (n.b. Code ONE only; for travel mode covering the greatest distances)

Walking	1
Cycling	2
Public Bus	3
Firm's Bus	4

17

3

Train/Tube	5	
Lift in car/motor bike	6	
Own car/motor bike	7	
Other (specify).................	8	

QA.7. About how long does it usually take you to get from home to the main place you work, door to door?

................minutes (1 way trip) □ 18

ASK ALL IN PAID EMPLOYMENT (CODE 1 OR 2 AT QA.1.)

QA.8. Some women say that by far the most important reason they work is for the money they earn and the things it buys. While others say that other reasons are as important or even more important than the money. Which of these statements comes closest to your own view: (SHOW CARD A:1) □ 19

(a) Money is by far the <u>most</u> important reason I <u>work</u>   1-> QA.9. □ 20
(b) Money is important but other reasons are equally important   2
(c) Other reasons are more important than money   3 ->QA.8. (a)

QA.8.(a) (IF CODE 2 OR 3 AT QA.8.)

What are the 'other reasons' which are important to you in deciding to work? □ 21
.... □ 22
(TAKE BACK CARD A:1)

ASK ALL IN PAID EMPLOYMENT

QA.9. Do you think of yourself primarily as a housewife who has a job or as a working woman who also runs a home?

Housewife who has a job	1	
Working woman who runs a home	2	□ 23
D.K.	3	
(Doesn't run a home)	4	

FULL-TIME WORK (CODE 7 AT QA.4.), GO TO QA.11.

APPENDIX A - COPY OF THE QUESTIONNAIRE

4

ASK THOSE WORKING LESS THAN 30 HOURS PER WEEK

QA.10. Are there any particular reasons why you don't work full-time?
(n.b. Code 1, 2 and 3 CAREFULLY)
RING NO MORE THAN 3 CODES

'Duty to children/bad for children to be away full-time — 1
Desire to be with children while young — 2
Lack of suitable child care facilities — 3
Difficulty of school hours/ holidays — 4
No time/too many other (social) commitments — 5
Housework/problem of combining work with housework — 6
No suitable full-time work available — 7
Don't need money/not worth it — 8
Husband doesn't allow — 9
Don't want/prefer not to — *10

(*n.b. Don't code this no. until after probing for specific reasons)

Other (specify).................. 11
D.K. — 12

24
25
26

ASK ALL IN PAID EMPLOYMENT

QA.11. Were you employed full-time before you were married or had children?

(30 hours or more each week)

Yes   1 -> QA.11(b)
No   -> QA.11.(a)

27

QA.11.(a) (IF 'NO' TO QA.11.)

Were you employed part-time?

Yes   2 -> QA.11(b)
No   3 -> QA.17 (but present 'home-workers' GO TO QA.15)

QA.11.(b) (IF CODE 1 OR 2 ABOVE)

Where exactly did you work in your last full-time job before you married or before you had children? (or in

293

5

your last part-time job, if no previous full-time job)
(n.b. Obtain name of factory, firm,
etc. and address of workplace (street,
suburb)).............................
.... | 28

IF CODE 1 OR 2 AT QA.11., CONTINUE:

QA.12. What sort of work did you do at that
time? Was it similar to the work you
are doing now, or was it a different
sort of work?

    Similar   1 -> QA.17.(but 'home-
                  workers' GO TO QA.15.)

    Different 2 -> QA.12.(a)

QA.12.(a) (IF CODE 2 AT QA.12.)

In what ways was the work different?
Could you describe what you actually
did in your job? (n.b. Take most
recent full-time job before marriage/
children - part-time if no full-time
job)
....
....
.... | 29

ALL THOSE IN OUTSIDE PAID EMPLOYMENT,
GO TO QA.17. 'HOME-WORKERS' GO TO QA.15

ASK ALL THOSE NOT IN PAID EMPLOYMENT
(CODE 3 AT QA.1.)

QA.13. Were you employed before you were
married or had children?

    Yes   ->QA.13.(a) & (b)
    No   3 ->QA.15.

QA.13.(a) (IF 'YES' TO QA.13.) | 27

Was this full-time or part-time?

    Full-time   1 -> QA.13.(b)
    Part-time   2

QA.13.(b) Where exactly did you work
in your last full-time job before you
were married or before you had children? (Or in your last part-time job,
if no previous full-time job)
(n.b. Obtain name of factory, firm,

6

etc. and <u>address</u> of workplace (street, suburb))................................	28

IF CODE 1 OR 2 AT QA.13., CONTINUE:

QA.14 What sort of work did you do? Could you describe what you <u>actually did</u> in your job? (n.b. Take <u>most recent</u> full-time job, where applicable. OR <u>most recent</u> part-time job, if <u>no</u> previous <u>full-time</u> employment)
....
....
....

	29

ASK ALL THOSE <u>NOT</u> IN PAID EMPLOYMENT - AND '<u>HOME-WORKERS</u>'

QA.15 If you could have someone to take care of things here at home, would you like to take an outside job right now, or are you happy enough to be at home?

Outside job	1	
Happy at home	2	30
D.K.	3	

'HOME-WORKERS', GO TO QA.17.

ASK ALL THOSE NOT IN PAID EMPLOYMENT, <u>ONLY</u>

QA.16 Women have different reasons for not working. What would be <u>your</u> main reasons for not working? (n.b. Code 1, 2 and 3 CAREFULLY)

RING <u>NO MORE</u> THAN <u>3</u> CODES

'Duty' to children/bad for children to be away from them	1	31
<u>Desire</u> to be with children when <u>young</u>	2	32
Lack of suitable child care facilities	3	33
Difficulty of school hours/holidays	4	
No time/too many other (social) commitments	5	
Housework/problems of combining work with housework	6	
No suitable jobs available (<u>type</u> of work)	7	

7

No suitable jobs available (<u>hours</u> of work)	8
Don't need money/not worth it	9
Husband doesn't allow	10
Don't want/prefer not to	*11

(* n.b. Don't code this no. until after <u>probing</u> for specific reasons)

Other (specify).....................	12
D.K.	X

<u>ASK ALL RESPONDENTS</u>

QA.17. Do you intend to go out to work when all your children are at school all day?

    Yes   1 -> QA.18.
    No   -> QA.17.(a)
    D.K. 3 -> QA.22.

☐ 34

QA.17.(a) (IF 'NO' TO QA.17)

Do you intend to do paid work at home?

    Yes   2 -> QA.19.

    No   5⌉
    D.K. 4⌋ -> QA.22.

IF CODE 1 AT QA.17. <u>ONLY</u>, CONTINUE:

QA.18. Whereabouts do you think you will probably work? (SHOW CARD A:2)
Do you think it is <u>most likely</u> you will be working locally, or in another centre in this part of London, or up in town, or where?

    Local   1⌉
    Surrounding area 2
    C. London   3⌈-> QA.19.
  ..Other (specify) 4
    D.K.   5⌋

☐ 35

(TAKE BACK CARD A:2)

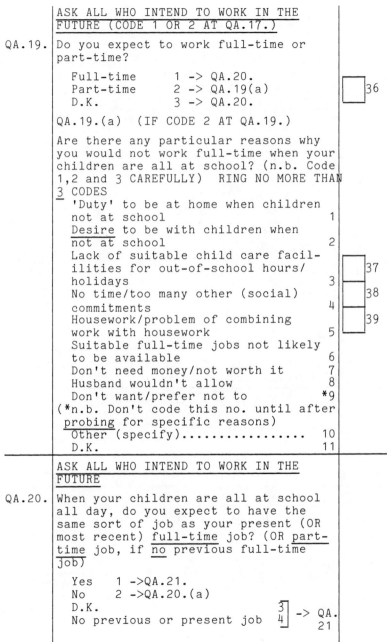

ASK ALL WHO INTEND TO WORK IN THE
FUTURE (CODE 1 OR 2 AT QA.17.)

QA.19. Do you expect to work full-time or
part-time?

    Full-time   1 -> QA.20.
    Part-time   2 -> QA.19(a)   36
    D.K.   3 -> QA.20.

QA.19.(a)   (IF CODE 2 AT QA.19.)

Are there any particular reasons why
you would not work full-time when your
children are all at school? (n.b. Code
1,2 and 3 CAREFULLY) RING NO MORE THAN
3 CODES
    'Duty' to be at home when children
    not at school   1
    Desire to be with children when
    not at school   2
    Lack of suitable child care facil-
    ilities for out-of-school hours/   37
    holidays   3
    No time/too many other (social)   38
    commitments   4
    Housework/problem of combining   39
    work with housework   5
    Suitable full-time jobs not likely
    to be available   6
    Don't need money/not worth it   7
    Husband wouldn't allow   8
    Don't want/prefer not to   *9
    (*n.b. Don't code this no. until after
     probing for specific reasons)
    Other (specify).................   10
    D.K.   11

ASK ALL WHO INTEND TO WORK IN THE
FUTURE

QA.20. When your children are all at school
all day, do you expect to have the
same sort of job as your present (OR
most recent) full-time job? (OR part-
time job, if no previous full-time
job)

    Yes   1 ->QA.21.
    No   2 ->QA.20.(a)
    D.K.   3] -> QA.
    No previous or present job 4]   21

297

9

QA.20(a)   (IF CODE 2 AT QA.20.)

In what ways do you expect your job to be different from what you have done before?.............................
....
....

□ 40

ASK ALL WHO INTEND TO WORK IN THE FUTURE

QA.21.   Do you expect to have to make any preparations for your future job - in the way of further education, or training, or re-training, for example?

     Yes   -> QA.21(a) & (b)

     No   6⌉ -> QA.22
     D.K.   7⌋

QA.21(a) (IF 'YES' TO QA.21.)

What sort of preparations do you expect to make?

Further education
(exams/college/private study)   1⌉
Job training (practical/'on
the job')   2⌋
Re-training (exams.etc.)   3 -> QA.
Re-training (practical)   4 21(b)
Other (specify)............. 5⌋

QA.21.(b) [IF CODES 1-5 AT QA.21.(a)]

Are you already making such preparations?

     Yes   1⌉-> QA.22.
     No   2⌋

□ 41

□ 42

□ 43

ASK ALL RESPONDENTS

QA.22.   Leaving your family circumstances aside, on the whole, would you prefer to stay at home or go out to work?

     Stay at home   1
     Go out to work 2
     D.K.   3

□ 44

10

QA.23. I am going to read you some of the
things people say about women and their
work and I would like you to tell me
how much you agree or disagree with
each one. (SHOW CARD A:3)
(n.b. If 'no opinion at all' ring the
QUESTION NO.)

	Agree very much	Agree a little	Neither agree nor di- sagree	Disa- gree a litt- le	Dis- agree very much	
1.Having her own job is the best way a woman can become a complete and independent person.	1	2	3	4	5	45 46 47
2.Husbands rather than wives should have the final voice in family matters	1	2	3	4	5	48 49 50
3.A woman needs a job of her own.	1	2	3	4	5	
4.A job is all right but for a woman real fulfilment lies in a home and children	1	2	3	4	5	
5.A woman and her family will all benefit if she does a job	1	2	3	4	5	
6.A woman's place is in the home	1	2	3	4	5	

(TAKE BACK CARD A:3)

299

SECTION B - SHOPPING

<table>
<tr>
<td>QB.1.</td>
<td>

ASK ALL RESPONDENTS

The next section of the survey is about weekday shopping trips. How often, on weekdays during the day-time, do you go out to buy food or general items? Do you go out every day, 2 or 3 times a week, about once a week, or less often?

Daily	1
2 or 3 times a week	2
Once a week	3 -> QB.2.
Less often	4
Never	5 -> QB.4.

</td>
<td>51</td>
</tr>
<tr>
<td>QB.2.</td>
<td>

IF CODE 1-4 AT QB.1., CONTINUE:

Could you tell me where you mainly go for your everyday food shopping? (n.b. Obtain as precise a location as possible - i.e. name of shopping centre, or name of shopping street or parade if local shops used).

....
....

</td>
<td>52</td>
</tr>
<tr>
<td>QB.3.</td>
<td>

Would you describe the shops you normally use, on weekdays, as local shops - that is, are they within ordinary walking distance of your home?

   Yes -> QB.3.(a)
   No   -> QB.3.(b)

QB.3.(a) (IF 'YES' TO QB.3.)

Some women prefer to get their weekday shopping at bigger shopping centres. Can you make any comments about why you don't choose to go further afield? (n.b. Probe for 'any other reasons') RING NO MORE THAN 3 CODES

Too much trouble	1
Journey too difficult/inconvenient	2
Difficult to take child(ren)	3
Expense of fares	4
Take too long/insufficient time available	5

</td>
<td></td>
</tr>
</table>

12

Prefer to use local shops	6
Larger centre too impersonal/enjoy stopping to chat while out shopping	7
Not necessary/do most of shopping on main trip	8
Local centre is district centre	9
Other (specify)....................	10
D.K.	11

53
54
55

QB.3.(b) (IF 'NO' TO QB.3.)

Some women prefer to get their weekday shopping at local shops. Can you make any comments about why you don't choose to go to your local shops? (n.b. probe for 'any other reasons')
RING NO MORE THAN 3 CODES

Local shops too expensive	1
Limited range of goods	2
Combine shopping with other activity elsewhere	3
Car available	4
Good public transport to bigger centre	5
Plenty of time available	6
Prefer to shop where not known by shopkeepers/assistants/other shoppers	7
No 'local' shops	8
Other (specify)....................	9
D.K.	10

56
57
58

ASK ALL RESPONDENTS

QB.4. Do you go on a main shopping trip at any time, as well as, or instead of your weekday shopping? (e.g. evening/weekend)

59

Yes   1 -> QB.5.
No   2 -> QC.1.

IF CODE 1 AT QB.4. CONTINUE:

QB.5. Do you go on this main food shopping trip at any particular time - for example, do you go when there is some-one else to help you, or to look after your child(ren) so you can go alone, or when there is a car available for you to go in?

13

Accompanied by husband	1
Accompanied by other relative	2
Accompanied by friend	3
Go alone while child(ren) cared for	4
Go with someone else while child(ren) cared for	5
When car available	6
Other (specify).....................	
....	7
D.K.	8

60

61

QB.6. Where do you <u>normally</u> go for <u>main</u> food shopping trips? (n.b. Obtain as precise a location as possible - i.e. name of shopping centre, or name of shopping street or parade if local shops used).........................
....

62

SECTION C - LEISURE, RECREATION AND PARK USE

ASK ALL RESPONDENTS

QC.1. Now I'd like to ask you about your everyday leisure activities. Firstly about visiting parks - How often, on average, do you visit a park or children's playground with your child(ren), on <u>weekdays</u> during the <u>daytime</u> - I mean, when the weather <u>is fine</u>? (SHOW CARD C:1)

> Daily   1
> 2 or 3 times a week   2
> Once a week   3
> 2 or 3 times a month 4 -> QC.1.(a)
> Once a month   5
> Less often   6
>
> Never   7 -> QC.5.

63

(TAKE BACK CARD C:1)

QC.1.(a) (IF CODE 1-6 AT QC.1.)

What is the <u>name</u> of the park (or playground) you <u>normally</u> go to, and where exactly is it? (Obtain as precise a location as possible - adjoining street, suburb)
....
....

64

APPENDIX A - COPY OF THE QUESTIONNAIRE

14

IF CODE 1-6 AT QC.1., CONTINUE:

QC.2. How long does it take you to get to the park or playground which you would normally visit? (CODE HIGHER FIGURE WHEN INTERMEDIATE TIME GIVEN)

```
5 minutes                          1
10 minutes                         2
15 minutes                         3     [ ] 65
20 minutes                         4
more than 20 minutes               5
D.K./Location varies greatly       6
```

QC.3. Do you <u>normally</u> get to this park by walking, or by car, or what?

```
Walk                               1
Car (drive or driven)              2
Bus                                3     [ ] 66
Train/tube                         4
Other (specify)..............      5
Varies greatly                     6
```

QC.4. How do you <u>normally</u> spend <u>your</u> time when you <u>are with</u> your child(ren) in the park or playground?

```
Only supervising play/playing            [ ] 67
with child                         1
Own Activities (e.g. reading,            [ ] 68
walking)                           2
Meet friends/stop and chat         3
Other (specify)..............      4
```

ASK ALL RESPONDENTS

QC.5. Do you have a garden?

```
Yes    -> QC.5.(a)
No     3 -> QC.6.                        [ ] 69
```

QC.5.(a) (IF 'YES' TO QC.5.)

Does your child/do your children play in it?

```
Yes    1 ]-> QC.6.
No     2
```

303

15

QC.6.	And now, a few questions about visiting other people. First of all, do you have any close relatives living in the local area - that is, near enough for you to be able to walk to their homes?	

Yes   -> QC.6.(a)
No   Ring code 8 on table, and
       GO TO QC.7.

QC.6.(a) (IF 'YES' TO QC.6.)

How often would you normally see them, either at your home or theirs, on weekdays during the daytime? □ 70
(SHOW CARD C:1)

Frequency	Local Relatives QC.6.(a)	Non-local Relatives QC.7.	Local Friends QC.8.	Non local friends QC.9.
Every day	1	1	1	1
2 or 3 times/ week	2	2	2	2
Once a week	3	3	3	3
2 or 3 times/ month	4	4	4	4
Once a month	5	5	5	5
Less often	6	6	6	6
Never	7	7	7	7
N/A (no relatives/ friends)	8	8	8	8

ASK ALL RESPONDENTS

QC.7.	How often would you normally see relatives who live outside the local area, either at your home or theirs, on weekdays during the daytime? (ANSWER ON TABLE ABOVE)	□ 71

QC.8.	How often would you normally visit friends' homes in the local area, during the daytime on weekdays, or have friends visit you? (ANSWER ON TABLE ABOVE)	□ 72

16

QC.9.	And, finally, how often would you <u>normally</u> see friends who live outside the local area, either at your home or theirs, on <u>weekdays</u> during the <u>daytime?</u>	73
	(ANSWER ON TABLE ABOVE) (TAKE BACK CARD C:1)	

ASK ALL RESPONDENTS

QC.10. What sort of things do you have in common with the friends you visit, or chat to on the street? (n.b. if respondent only mentions: 'young children in common', ask: Do you have any other things in common with them?)

RING <u>NO MORE</u> THAN <u>3</u> CODES

Young children in common	1
Age-group (of women)	2
At school together	3
At work together/same occupation	4
Similar educational/'class' background	5
Similar interests/activities	6
Nothing special (includes 'neighbours')	7
Other (specify).................	8
No friends at all	9
D.K.	10

74
75
76

QC.11 Now - a general question about <u>weekday</u> leisure and social activities. Are there any particular things which you do on a regular basis - at least 2 or 3 times a month? For example, do you do any of these things on <u>weekdays</u> during the <u>daytime?</u> (SHOW CARD C:2) Or is there anything else that you do?

(FILL IN DETAILS IN COLUMNS 1-5 ON THE TABLE OPPOSITE - PAGE 17)

Do you take your child(ren) with you when you go?

(CODE IN COLUMN 6 OPPOSITE - YES 1, NO 2, VARIES 3)

APPENDIX A - COPY OF THE QUESTIONNAIRE

17

QC.11. Regular weekday leisure and social activities

Activity 1	Time of week 2	Location (address) 3	Travel mode 4	Journey time 5	Child? 6

18

QC.12.	Are there any activities, such as those listed on the card (CARD C:2), which you would <u>like</u> to do, on <u>week-days</u> during the <u>daytime</u>, but don't at present do?
	
	    Yes -> QC.12.(a) & (b)
	    No 11 ->QC.13.	

QC.12.(a) (IF 'YES' TO QC.12.)

What sort of things would you like to do?

....
....
....

☐ 77
☐ 78
☐ 79

QC.12.(b) (IF 'YES' TO QC.12.)

What mainly keeps you from doing these things at present? (n.b. If CODE 1 is given, ASK: Are there any other reasons?)

RING <u>NO MORE</u> THAN <u>3</u> CODES

Family commitments/children to look after   1
Access difficult/no car/too far, etc.2
No money   3
Health reasons   4
Work reasons   5
No one to go with   6
No time available   7
Too lazy, etc.   8
Facilities in area are poor/non existent   9
Other (Specify)................... 10

☐ 6
☐ 7
☐ 8

         (TAKE BACK CARD C:2)

<u>ASK ALL RESPONDENTS</u>

QC.13. We've been thinking quite a bit about different sorts of activities - work, shopping, recreation, home visiting, and social activities, for example. Now, I'd like you to think back to <u>yesterday</u>, and tell me all the things you did, outside of your home (and garden), and the approximate times when you left home and came back home.

<u>GO TO PAGE 20</u>

19

QC.13.   Yesterday's out-of-home activities

Activity	Time Out	Time Home	Location (address)	Travel Mode	Journey Time	Child?
1	2	3	4	5	6	7

20

(PROMPT: Starting at about 9 0'clock,
did you do anything in the morning?
..........What about the afternoon now?
NOT EVENING ACTIVITIES

(FILL IN DETAILS IN COLUMNS 1-6 ON THE
TABLE OPPOSITE - PAGE 19)

Did you take your (pre-school)
child(ren) with you?

(Code in column 7 OPPOSITE - Yes 1
                             No 2)

QC.14. Did a friend or relative visit you in
your home at all yesterday, during the
daytime?

    Yes   -> QC.14.(a)
    No   -> QC.15.

QC.14.(a) (IF 'YES' TO QC.14.)

Who came to visit you? At about what
time did they arrive and leave?

Visitor	Time Arrived	Time Left
....	....	....
....	....	....
....	....	....
....	....	....

ASK ALL RESPONDENTS

QC.15. Now, I would like you to fill in some
answers by yourself. Here are some
words and phrases which we would like
you to use to describe how you feel
about your present life. (GIVE SELF-
COMPLETION SHEET TO RESPONDENT). To
show you how to fill it in, look at
the example on this card (SHOW CARD
C:3)

For example, if you feel your life is
extremely exciting you would tick this
box on the right (point to box)
If you think your life is extremely
dull you would tick this box on the
left (point to box).
If you think your life is neither dull
nor exciting you would tick the box in

APPENDIX A - COPY OF THE QUESTIONNAIRE

Please put a tick   in whichever box applies to each
line.

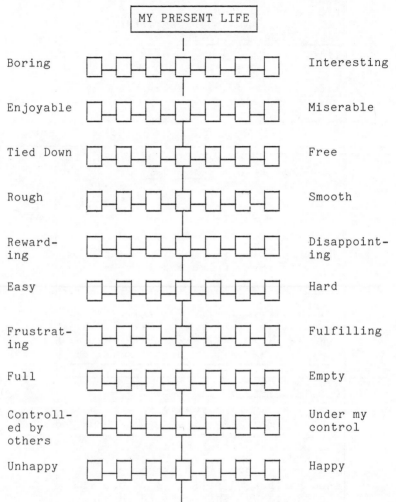

MY PRESENT LIFE	
Boring	Interesting
Enjoyable	Miserable
Tied Down	Free
Rough	Smooth
Reward-ing	Disappoint-ing
Easy	Hard
Frustrat-ing	Fulfilling
Full	Empty
Controll-ed by others	Under my control
Unhappy	Happy

21

the middle (point to box).
The other boxes stand for <u>fairly</u>
<u>exciting</u> (point to boxes) and <u>fairly</u>
<u>dull</u> (point to boxes).
Remember, the nearer the box you tick
is to the end of the line, the more
you think each word applies to your
<u>present</u> life. (TAKE BACK CARD C:3)

TAKE BACK SELF-COMPLETION SHEET

SECTION D - LOCAL AREA AND MOBILITY

ASK ALL RESPONDENTS

QD.1 | Now I have some questions about this local area.
First, thinking about the kinds of things you would like to have near where you live - places you go to fairly often - how convenient would you say this local area is: is it <u>very</u> <u>convenient</u>, <u>convenient enough</u>, <u>not very</u> <u>convenient</u>, or <u>not convenient at all</u>?

Very convenient	1
Convenient enough	2
Not very convenient	3
Not convenient at all	4
D.K./No opinion	5

9

QD.2. | How long have you yourself lived in this local area?

.... years

10

QD.3. | Did you grow up in this area - that is, were you living here when you were about 12 to 15 years old?

Yes 1 -> QD.4.
No   -> QD.3.(a)

QD.3(a) (IF 'NO' TO QD.3.)

Where did you live at that time?
(n.b. Obtain as precise a location as possible)..........................
....

11

22

QD.4. How friendly would you say this local area is? (SHOW CARD D:1)

Very friendly	1
Quite friendly	2
Neither friendly nor unfriendly	3
Quite unfriendly	4
Very unfriendly	5
D.K./No opinion	6

☐ 12

(TAKE BACK CARD D:1)

QD.5. How good is the public transport service for people who live around here? (SHOW CARD D:2)

Very good	1
Fairly good	2
Neither good nor bad	3
Not very good	4
Not good at all	5
D.K./No opinion	6

☐ 13

(TAKE BACK CARD D:2)

QD.6. On average, how often do you travel by bus with your child(ren) during weekdays? (SHOW CARD C:1)

☐ 14

Frequency	Bus (QD.6)	Train/ tube (QD.7.)	Out of area (QD.8.)
Every day	1	1	1
2 or 3 times per week	2	2	2
Once a week	3	3	3
2 or 3 times per month	4	4	4
Once a month	5	5	5
Less often	6	6	6
Never	7	7	7

QD.7. And how often do you travel by train or tube with your child(ren) during weekdays? (ANSWER ABOVE)

☐ 15

23

QD.8.	Could you tell me how often, on average, you would travel out of the local area, during the daytime on a weekday? (ANSWER ABOVE) (TAKE BACK CARD C:1)	☐ 16

IF RESPONDENT NEVER TRAVELS BY BUS (CODE 7 AT QD.6.), GO TO QD.10.

IF RESPONDENT EVER TRAVELS BY BUS (CODE 1-6 AT QD.6.) CONTINUE:

QD.9. Do you find there are any problems with using buses, on weekdays when you have your child(ren) with you? (n.b. if CODE 1 - also PROBE for specific problems)

RING NO MORE THAN 3 CODES

Difficulties/effort with children	1
Nowhere to put pushchair/pram/ shopping	2
No help on or off bus	3
Controlling child(ren)/danger	4
Expense - fares	5
Unreliable services	6
Infrequent services	7
Other (specify)...................	8
No problems	9

☐ 17
☐ 18
☐ 19

IF RESPONDENT NEVER TRAVELS BY TRAIN/ TUBE (CODE 7 AT QD.7.), GO TO QD.11.

IF RESPONDENT EVER TRAVELS BY TRAIN/ TUBE (CODE 1-6 AT QD.7.), CONTINUE:

QD.10. What about trains - do you find there are any problems with using them, on weekdays when you have your child(ren) with you? (n.b. If CODE 1 - also PROBE for specific problems)

RING NO MORE THAN 3 CODES

Difficulties/effort with children	1
No help up or down stairs	2
Difficulty on escalators	3
Controlling child(ren)/danger	4
Expense - fares	5
Unreliable services	6
Infrequent services	7

☐ 20
☐ 21
☐ 22

24

Other (specify).................... 8
No problems   9

	ASK ALL RESPONDENTS	
QD.11.	Do you have a car in this household? (IF 'YES') Is that one, or more than one?	
	Two + 1⌉ -> QD.12. One 2⌋ No car 3 -> QD.13.	[ ] 23
	IF HOUSEHOLD HAS CAR (CODE 1 OR 2 AT QD.11.), CONTINUE:	
QD.12.	Is there a car available for you to use during the daytime on weekdays - that is, is there normally one here, not on special occasions? Yes 1 No 2	[ ] 24
	ASK ALL RESPONDENTS	
QD.13.	Do you hold a current driving licence? Yes 1 No 2	[ ] 25
QD.14.	Most women find that walking is the main way they get around on weekdays. Do you find any particular difficulties with walking to various places with your child(ren)?.................	[ ] 26 [ ] 27 [ ] 28

SECTION E - CHILD CARE

	ASK ALL RESPONDENTS	
QE.1.	The next few questions are about your child(ren) in particular. Firstly could you tell me if your child/any of your children normally has a sleep during the daytime? Yes 1 No 2	[ ] 29

QE.2. | Does your child/Do any of your children go to a nursery school or supervised playgroup? (n.b. not a 'mother and toddler' club)

   Yes -> QE.2.(a) & (b) & (c)
   No   9 -> QE.3.

QE.2.(a) (IF 'YES' TO QE.2.)

What hours do they go? (n.b. if hours vary between children, consider only youngest child)

5 full days (morning
  & afternoon)   1
1-4 full days per week   2
5 mornings per week   3
1-4 mornings per week   4
5 afternoons per week   5
1-4 afternoons per
  week   6   ->QE.2.(b) & (c)
Other regular hours
  (specify)..........   7
Variable hours each
  week   8

☐ 30

QE.2.(b) Can you tell me where it is? (Street name and suburb).............
....

☐ 31

QE.2.(c) How long does it take you to get there from home?
................minutes (1 way trip)

☐ 32

RESPONDENTS WITH CHILDREN AT NURSERY SCHOOL, GO TO QE.5.

IF NO CHILD AT NURSERY SCHOOL (CODE 9 AT QE.2.), CONTINUE:

QE.3. | Would you like your child(ren) to go to a nursery school or supervised playgroup, before they go to school full-time?

   Yes -> QE.3.(a)
   No   3 -> QE.4.

QE.3.(a) (IF 'YES' TO QE.3.)

Have you put their name(s) down for a nursery school or supervised playgroup?

☐ 33

26

Yes -> QE.3.(b) & (c)
No   2 -> QE.4.

QE.3.(b) (IF CODE 1 AT QE.3.(a))

Can you tell me where it is?
(Street name and suburb)............
....

↑
31

QE.3.(c) How long would it take you
to get to the nursery school or playgroup from home?
...............minutes (1 way trip)->
                              QE.5.

↑
32

QE.4.

IF CODE 2 OR 3 AT QE.3., CONTINUE:

Is there any particular reason for
this?
....
....
....
....

34

35

IF CODE 2 AT QE.3., GO TO QE.5.; IF
CODE 3 AT QE.3., GO TO QE.6.

QE.5.

ASK ALL RESPONDENTS, EXCEPT CODE 3 AT
QE.3.

Some women say that the most important
reason they send their children to
nursery school is to have some free
time to do things on their own. While
others say that the benefit to their
children of nursery school is as important, or even more important, than the
free time they themselves get as a
result. Which of these statements
comes closest to your own view?

(SHOW CARD E:1 AND READ OUT:)

(a) Having some free time myself is
    the most important reason for
    sending my children to nursery
    school   1
(b) Having some free time myself is
    important, but the benefit to my
    children of nursery school is
    equally important too.   2
(c) The benefit to my children of
    nursery school is the most

36

27

important reason for sending them
them there.   3

(TAKE BACK CARD E:1)

ASK ALL RESPONDENTS

QE.6. | It's often difficult, or impossible to take children with you to various places - to work, or to social meetings, or on main shopping trips, for instance. Do you ever leave your child(ren) with anyone else, during the daytime on weekdays, so that you can do these sorts of things on your own?

Yes   -> QE.6.(a) & (b)
No   10 -> QE.9.

QE.6(a) (IF 'YES' TO QE.6.)

Who do you mainly leave your child(ren) with? (ONE code only) (n.b. If 'Friend', ASK: Do you pay your friend or does she look after them for nothing? IF 'PAID', RING CODE 5 INSTEAD OF CODE 4)

Husband (shift-worker)	1
Mother/mother-in-law	2
Other relative	3
Friend	4
Paid child-minder	5
Day nursery (not at work)	6
Nursery school/play-group	7
Nursery run by employer	8
Someone else (specify).	9

-> QE.6.(b)

37

QE.6.(b) And how far is that from your home? (n.b. Obtain location where child(ren) left - street name and suburb)............................
....

38

317

28

	IF CHILDREN EVER LEFT (CODE 1-9 AT QE.6.), CONTINUE:
QE.7.	How often on weekdays would you leave them with someone else, on average? (SHOW CARD C:1)

Every day   1 ⎤
2 or 3 times per week   2 ⎥
Once a week   3 ⎥ ->QE.8.   ☐ 39
2 or 3 times per month 4 ⎥
Once a month   5 ⎥
Less often   6 ⎦

(TAKE BACK CARD C:1)

QE.8.	And for how long each time?

Full day   1 ⎤
Full morning   2 ⎥
Full afternoon   3 ⎥ -> QE.10.   ☐ 40
1-2 hours   4 ⎥
Less than 1 hour   5 ⎥
Varies greatly   6 ⎦

	IF CHILDREN NEVER LEFT (CODE 10 AT QE.6. ONLY), CONTINUE:
QE.9.	Are there any particular reasons why you don't leave them with anyone else? ....

☐ 41

☐ 42

	ASK ALL RESPONDENTS
QE.10.	Would you say that in your case, being a mother has always been enjoyable, that it has nearly always been enjoyable, that it has usually been enjoyable, that it has sometimes been enjoyable, or that being a mother has hardly ever been enjoyable? (SHOW CARD E:2)

☐ 43

Always   1
Nearly always   2
Usually   3
Sometimes   4
Hardly ever   5

(TAKE BACK CARD E:2)

29

QE.11.	Have you ever wished that you could be free from the responsibilities of being a mother?

Yes -> QE.11.(a)
No   3

QE.11.(a) (IF 'YES' TO QE.11.)

Have you felt this way <u>often</u>, or just sometimes?

Often   1
Sometimes 2

☐ 44

SECTION F - HUSBANDS (N.B. OMIT WHOLE SECTION IF NO HUSBAND LIVING IN HOUSEHOLD - GO TO SECTION G)

<u>ASK ONLY THOSE WITH HUSBANDS LIVING IN HOUSEHOLD - SEE Q.1.</u>

QF.1. Now, there are some questions about your husband's work and attitudes. Firstly, what job does he do? Could you describe what he actually does at work? ....

☐ 45

IF UNEMPLOYED' OR 'STUDENT' - GO TO QF.7.

<u>ASK ALL THOSE WITH HUSBANDS IN PAID EMPLOYMENT ONLY</u>

QF.2. What is his <u>main</u> means of travel to work?   ↓
(n.b. Code ONE only: for travel mode covering the greatest DISTANCE)

Walking	1
Cycling	2
Public Bus	3
Firm's Bus	4
Train/Tube	5
Lift in car/Motor bike	6
Own car/motor bike	7
Other (specify)..................	8

☐ 46

319

30

QF.3.	Where exactly does he work? (n.b. Obtain <u>name</u> of factory, firm, etc. and <u>address of</u> workplace (street and suburb)).............................. 47
QF.4.	About how long does it usually take him to get from home to work (the main place he works), door to door? ....minutes (1 way trip) 48

QF.5.	Does he work shiftwork of any kind?
	
	   Yes -> QF.6.
	   No -> QF.5.(a)
	
	   QF.5.(a) (IF 'NO' TO QF.5.)
	
	At what time does he normally <u>start</u> and <u>finish</u> at work?
	
	(USE 24 HOUR CLOCK) <u>Start</u>...<u>Finish</u>...
	      -> QF.7. 49

	<u>IF HUSBAND WORKS SHIFTS ('YES' TO QF.5</u>)
QF.6.	What kind of shifts does he work? Permanent early mornings 1 Permanent evenings 2 Permanent nights 3 'Double-day' shifts 4 Alternating days and nights 5 Rolling 3 - shift system 6 Others (specify)................ 7 D.K. 8 50
	<u>ASK ALL RESPONDENTS</u>
QF.7.	Does your husband actively encourage <u>you</u> to go out to work, does he discourage you in any way, or does he leave it entirely up to you? Encourages 1 Leaves it up to me 2 Discourages 3 D.K. 4 51

31

QF.8.	Do you feel that the amount of house-work your husband does is too much, about right and fair, or not really enough? Too much 1 About right and fair 2 Not really enough 3 D.K. 4	☐ 52
QF.9.	And how do you feel about the amount of day-to-day care of the children that your husband does? Is it too much, about right and fair, or not really enough? Too much 1 About right and fair 2 Not really enough 3 D.K. 4	☐ 53

QF.10.	At what age did your husband finish his full-time education?
	(IGNORE GAPS)
	14- 15 16 17 18 19 20 21 22 23+ Still DK/
	                            at NA
	                          Coll-
	                          ege
	1 2 3 4 5 6 7 8 9 10 11 12
		☐ 54

QF.11.	And how old was he on his last birth-day? ....years	☐ 55

SECTION G - PERSONAL DETAILS

QG.1.	ASK ALL RESPONDENTS Finally we would like a little back-ground information about yourself. Do you have any particular problems with your health? Yes -> QG.1.(a) No 4 -> QG.2. QG.1.(a) (IF 'YES' TO QG.1.) Would you say that these problems keep you from doing a lot of things you wish you could do, just certain things or can you do almost anything you wish?

32

lot of things 1	
Certain things 2	56
Almost anything 3	

ASK ALL RESPONDENTS

QG.2. Apart from your child(ren), is there anyone else who depends on you to provide some daily service for them? I mean, helping to look after someone like a sick or elderly relative or friend?

Yes   -> QG.2.(a)
No   6 -> QG.3.

QG.2.(a) (IF 'YES' TO QG.2.)

Who is this person?

Parent/parent-in-law 1	
Other relative 2	
Friend 3	57
Neighbour 4	
Other person (specify)..........5	

ASK ALL RESPONDENTS

QG.3. Thinking back to when you were a young child, say less than about ten years old - did <u>your</u> mother have a job outside the home?

Yes 1	
No 2	
D.K. 3	58
Mother not at home deceased,etc.4	

QG.4. And what was your father's main occupation when you were a bit older, say between the ages of 12 and 15? What exactly did he do?

....
....   59

(n.b. if NO FATHER, obtain 'head of households' occupation at that time)

QG.5. At what age did you finish your full-time education? (IGNORE GAPS)

14-	15	16	17	18	19	20	21	22	23+	Still at College	DK/ NA	
1	2	3	4	5	6	7	8	9	10	11	12	60

33

QG.6.	And how old were you on your last birthday? ....years	☐ 61

QG.7. Do you own this house/flat, are you buying it on a mortgage or loan, renting it from the council or a private landlord, or what?

☐ 62

```
Own outright              1 ⌉
Buying on mortgage/loan   2 |  -> QG.8.
Council rent              3 ⌋
Private rent              -> QG.7.(a)
Free with job             6 ⌉
Lodger/living with
   relatives              7 |  -> QG.8.
Other (specify)..........8 ⌋
```

QG.7.(a) (IF 'PRIVATE RENT' AT QG.7.)

Is it rented furnished or unfurnished?

```
Private furnished     5 ⌉
Private unfurnished   4 ⌋  -> QG.8.
```

☐ 63

ASK ALL RESPONDENTS

QG.8. Taking into account all the money that comes into your household, including all the wages and salaries of all those who are working, pensions, benefits and any other money from any other sources, which group on this card, (SHOW CARD C:1) comes nearest to the total income of your household nowadays before any deductions are made?

Income Group

1 2 3 4 5 6 7 8

D.K.   9
Refused 10

(IF RESPONDENT KNOWS ONLY NET INCOME - write in details here:

☐ 64

....

(TAKE BACK CARD C:1)

Thank you very much for your help.

34

INTERVIEWER OBSERVATION - TO BE COMPLETED AFTER LEAVING HOUSE/FLAT

1. Is dwelling.........Detached   1
                        Semi-detached   2   □ 65
                        Terraced   3
                        Flat/Maisonette   4

2. If dwelling is a FLAT or MAISONETTE, how
    many floors are there in the block?   □ 66

    ....

3. If dwelling is a FLAT or MAISONETTE,
    enter on which floor level the entrance   □ 67
    is:

                        Basement   X
                        Ground   O

    Floor No: Write in ....

CLASSIFICATION

1. Address of dwelling (No. and Road name)
                                                 □ 68
    ....

2. Interviewer's Name ....

3. Day of week.........Tuesday   1
                        Wednesday   2   □ 69
                        Thursday   3
                        Friday   4

4. Week of interview... 13-16th Sept.   1
                         20-23rd Sept.   2   □ 70
                         27-30th Sept.   3

5. Weather on previous day (LEAVE BLANK)   □ 71

APPENDIX B

THE SAMPLING PROCEDURE

Women with young children form one population sub-
group which it is very difficult physically to locate. In an attempt to ensure a random sample, it
would have been possible (given unlimited time and
resources) to use electoral registers for the purpose of sampling women, who could then have been app-
roached and only interviewed if they had at least
one child under the age of full-time schooling.
Since there was a strict time limit imposed on the
survey period, this method of sampling was rejected
as impractical. Small-area data from the 1971
Census were obviously of very little relevance to
the location of the population under study (since
any children under five years of age at that time
would no longer be, in 1977) but they were of some
use in indicating the approximate number of households with children under five which might be expected to exist in any enumeration district (e.d.).
Although numbers varied widely between different
e.d.s, it seemed that e.d.s with about 100 households would contain at least four households with
children under five.
     Other possible methods of locating the popula-
tion under study, in order to sample from it, were
considered but these all suffered from various forms
of bias. The use of playgroup registers would
obviously have biased the sample in favour of women
who were more involved in outside activities. Primary school lists of future pupils would be more
likely to contain the names of children whose
mothers were more interested in education or those
with brothers and sisters already at the school,
since the registration of children on school waiting
lists is not compulsory. Similar problems of sample
bias in favour of more actively involved women would
arise with the use of club membership, adult

education class or other activity-oriented lists.

The most comprehensive data source from which a sample of women with young children could possibly be derived is the complete record of births within the borough which is held by the local authority. This is not a perfect source of information since it does not record migrations either into or out of the borough, nor does it record changes of address within the borough but it does represent the best source of location data on the particular population sub-group under study. This information is not, however, available to outside researchers, both because it is considered to be classified information and because, in any case, the logistical problem of transcribing some 8,000 names and addresses from the register is too great for the local authority to consider under-taking (outside researchers not being permitted direct access to the records).

One further source of information concerning the location of women with young children was explored in the hope of obtaining a fairly accurate picture of the population from which a sample could be drawn. This was the registration lists at child health clinics. Medical records lodged with General Practitioners have been used in the past by resear-chers as a means of locating respondents (for example, Gavron, 1966; Bott, 1957) but only in studies where the total number of respondents requi-red was low and where there was no real attempt to sample randomly or perform data analytic techniques on the results obtained from the questionnaires. General practitioners' records are biased to the extent that residents of the borough do not have to register with a doctor within the borough. In fact, since the reorganisation of health services in 1974, the borough of Merton has been combined with the boroughs of Wandsworth and Sutton into one Area Health Authority, the sub-areas of which do not co-incide with the borough boundaries. Community clinics have been set up in the different sub-areas and registrations with doctors are now far less likely necessarily to occur in the borough of residence.

However, child health clinics are still distri-buted widely within the borough of Merton (14 of these are in existence at the present time) and it is most likely that women with babies would take them for health care services to the nearest clinic to their home. Clinic records could be considered fairly complete in terms of the population under study since almost all mothers would attend a clinic at least once with a new-born child and, therefore, would be listed on the register. (Dowling (1977) found that 91% of children in the 1970 British Birth Cohort study attended a child health clinic at some time up to the end of the third year of life.) All children attaining the age of five are automatically removed from the clinic register and at least some (known) out-migrants would also be removed from the lists. Bias would still exist of course; one would expect the children of in-migrants to be under-represented on the registers, especially those moving into the area after the period of babyhood. Herbert and Williams (1964, 114) have suggested that child health clinic attendance can be correlated with low socio-economic class but there was no apparent evidence to support this suggestion in the case of Merton. However, in the event, information from clinic records was refused on the grounds of confidentiality, even though it was stressed that no information was required beyond simple addresses.

Having explored all possible avenues of know-ledge, it was necessary to accept the fact that a true distribution of the group under study (namely, women with young children) could not be readily obtained. An entirely different approach to the problem of sampling, therefore, had to be used. It was decided firstly to sample enumeration districts (e.d.s) within the borough and then to attempt to interview four respondents in each selected e.d.

The total size of the sample was set at 400. This number was chosen as the largest possible sample which could be handled by the interviewing resources available, during the limited three week interviewing period. In this type of survey, where primarily nominal-level data is obtained, the most important influence on the required sample size is the necessity to disaggregate the data in order to control for different variables in the analysis procedure. The limitations in the use of the chi-square statistic dictate that the total sample size must be fairly large (not more than 20 per cent of cells in a table may contain less than an expected frequency of five and no cell may contain less than one). A sample size of 400 was considered adequate to cope with this problem. Since four respondents were to be interviewed in each e.d., it was necess-ary to select 100 e.d.s (out of a total of 375 in the borough of Merton).

The selection of e.d.s could have been quite simply achieved by a random sampling process. How-ever, in the case of Merton (according to the 1971

Census), the total number of private households in
any e.d. might range from under 50 to over 250.
Since it was likely that e.d.s containing fewer than
100 households probably would not provide the required number of potential respondents (i.e. four), it
was decided to sample the e.d.s in such a way that
the probability of a particular e.d. being selected
was proportional to the number of households contained within it. This lessened the chance of selection for an e.d. containing relatively few households.
In the event, only five of the chosen e.d.s contained fewer than 100 households and only one had fewer
than 50 households.

In addition to the question of potential respondent numbers, a further decision was made explicitly to stratify the sample in order to secure a
reasonable cross-section of the population in terms
of social class. All the e.d.s in the borough were
ranked on the basis of the percentage of heads of
households in professional and managerial occupations at the 1971 Census Registrar General's socio-
economic groups 1,2,3,4 and 13). From this ranked
list 100 e.d.s were selected, the probability of
selection being determined by the number of households contained within each e.d. (as mentioned
above). The resulting sample included the e.d. with
the highest percentage of professional and managerial
heads of households in the borough (90.9 per cent)
and, at the opposite extreme, it included two e.d.s
with no heads of households in these socio-economic
groups. The distribution of sample e.d.s is shown
as background information on all maps.

As a method of stratifying the eventual sample
of women with young children, this stratification of
the e.d. sample, of course, left much to be desired.
In the first place, the use of the presence or absence of heads of households in professional and managerial occupations as the determining factor could
not give an accurate picture of the mix of different
socio-economic groups within each e.d. - both
because other groups were excluded from consideration in the ranking procedure and because the socio-
economic group data of the 1971 Census itself represented only a 10 per cent sample of the population.
A second problem related to the period since the 1971
Census and the possibility of subsequent changes having occurred in socio-economic structure (in one
notable case an e.d. was selected in which all the
privately-owned or rented housing had been replaced
by high-rise council flats in the intervening
period). However, perhaps the most impor tant problem

connected with the method of stratification outlined above was the danger of assuming that respondents would 'represent' the socio-economic mix of an e.d. No attempt was made in the interviewing procedure to select respondents from professional and managerial groups, in proportion to their occurrence in the population of the relevant e.d. However, it was hoped that, by stratifying the e.d.s in the manner described above and by sampling from the stratified list, a sufficient number of respondents in each major social class grouping would be interviewed to ensure the possibility of testing for the importance of social class differences in the resulting activity analyses.

Having selected the sample of 100 e.d.s within the borough, it was decided to use a simple 'snow-balling' method to locate actual questionnaire respondents. The first respondent in an e.d. would be 'found' by questioning residents concerning the location of women with children under school-age. Having interviewed one respondent, the second would be found by asking the first respondent to indicate the home of another woman in a similar situation to herself and so on. Undoubtedly this method was open to bias, since friends and immediate neighbours were often named but the overall bias in the sample was minimised by the fact that only four respondents were interviewed in each e.d. It is also true that, in very many cases, potential respondents were indicated who were not known at all by the previous respondent and who, therefore, would be expected to have quite different activity patterns from the informant. The snow-balling method worked well in practice, although in some areas containing very few women with young children, it was necessary to knock on every door in order to obtain four interviews. In only three e.d.s was there an insufficient number of potential respondents. In these cases the interviewers concerned were instructed to search for the remaining respondents in the immediately adjacent e.d. closest to the selected e.d. on the class-ranked list.

VARIABLES IN DICHOTOMISED FORM

Variable	Code 1	Code 0
Number of children under 5	2 or more	1
Age of youngest child	2 or more years	Under 2 years
Attitude to motherhood	No desire to be free from responsibility	Some desire to be free from responsibility
Socio-economic group of husband	Non-manual	Manual
Family income	£3000 or more p.a.	Below £3000 p.a.
Terminal education age	17 or older	16 or younger
Tenure of household	Owner-occupiers	Other tenure type
Flat dwelling	Lives in a flat	Lives in a house
Car availability	Car available	Car not available
Length of residence	1 year or longer	Less than 1 year
Employment status	In paid employment	Not in employment
Socio-economic group of respondent (last full-time employment)	Non-manual	Manual
Reasons for working	Money most important	Other
Work location	Out at work	Work at home
Attitude to present employment	Firstly a worker	Firstly a housewife

APPENDIX C - VARIABLES IN DICHOTOMISED FORM

Variable	Code 1	Code 0
Present job 'status' in relation to previous job	Same job or 'status' level	Lower 'status' job
Regular/casual working	Regular worker	Casual worker
Employment status preference (housewives)	Prefer to work	Other
Husband's attitude to wife working	Positive or neutral	Negative
Childhood experience	Mother out at work	Mother not out at work

SUPPLEMENTARY TABLES

Table D1 Cross-tabulation of employment status with 'work 2' statement: 'A woman needs a job of her own' (Percentages in brackets)

	Disagree	Neutral	Agree	Total
Not in employ-ment	102 (83.6)	45 (68.2)	139 (65.6)	286 (71.5)
In paid employ-ment	20 (16.4)	21 (31.8)	73 (34.4)	114 (28.5)
Total	122 (100.0)	66 (100.0)	212 (100.0)	400 (100.0)

Gamma = .32

Table D2 Cross-tabulation of employment status with husband's attitude, 'Does your husband enc-ourage you to go out to work, does he dis-courage you in any way or does he leave it entirely up to you?' (Percentages in brackets)

	Discour-ages	Neutral	Encour-ages	Total
Not in employ-ment	55 (83.3)	183 (70.7)	33 (63.5)	271 (71.9)
In paid employment	11 (16.7)	76 (29.3)	19 (36.6)	106 (28.1)
Total	66 (100.0)	259 (100.0)	52 (100.0)	377 (100.0)

Gamma = .28   (23 missing cases)

Table D3 Cross-tabulation of employment status with age of the youngest child (Percentages in brackets)

	0	1	2	3	4	Total
Not in employment	84 (83.2)	75 (78.1)	56 (62.2)	42 (63.6)	29 (61.7)	286 (71.5)
In paid employ-	17 (16.8)	21 (21.9)	34 (37.8)	24 (36.4)	18 (38.3)	114 (28.5)
Total	101 (100.0)	96 (100.0)	90 (100.0)	66 (100.0)	47 (100.0)	400 (100.0)

Gamma = .30

Table D4 Cross-tabulation of working days with work location (Percentages in brackets)

	Out at work	Work at home	Total
Mon-Friday weekdays	15 (19.5)	9 (24.3)	24 (21.1)
Weekdays but not every day	19 (24.7)	19 (51.4)	38 (33.3)
Evening/weekend only	43 (55.8)	9 (24.3)	52 (45.6)
Total	77 (100.0)	37 (100.0)	114 (100.0)

chi-square = 11.06 (p = 004)(286 missing cases)

Table D5 Cross-tabulation of present job 'status' in relation to former 'status', with work location (Percentages in brackets)

	Out at work	Work at home	Total
Same type of job held	22 (28.9)	12 (32.4)	34 (30.1)
Different job but similar 'status'	24 (31.6)	4 (10.8)	28 (24.8)
Lower 'status' job held	30 (39.5)	21 (56.8)	51 (45.1)
Total	76 (100.0)	37 (100.0)	113 (100.0)

chi-square = 6.08 (p=.05) (287 missing cases)

Table D6   Cross-tabulation of present job 'status' in relation to former 'status', with 'work 1' statement: 'Having her own job is the best way a woman can become a complete and independent person' (Percentages in brackets)

	Disagree	Neutral	Agree	Total
Same type of job held	10 (29.4)	1 (2.9)	23 (67.6)	34 (100.0)
Different job but similar 'status'	10 (35.7)	4 (14.3)	14 (50.0)	28 (100.0)
Lower 'status' held	12 (23.5)	7 (13.7)	32 (62.7)	51 (100.0)
Total	32 (28.3)	12 (10.6)	69 (61.0)	113 (100.0)

chi-square = 4.50 (p=.34) (287 missing cases)

Table D7   Cross-tabulation of 'satisfaction with employment status', with 'attitude to work' (categorised) (Percentages in brackets)

	'Tradit-ional'	'Neutral'	'Progress-ive'	Total
1) Satisfied worker	5 (9.3)	18 (33.3)	31 (57.4)	54 (100.0)
2) Dissatisfied worker	8 (34.8)	6 (26.1)	9 (39.1)	23 (100.0)
3) Satisfied housewife	54 (58.1)	22 (23.7)	17 (18.3)	93 (100.0)
4) Dissatisfied house-wife	57 (29.5)	62 (32.1)	74 (38.3)	193 (100.0)
Total	124 (34.2)	108 (29.8)	131 (36.1)	363 (100.0)

chi-square = 43.74 (p=.001) (37 missing cases)

Table D8 Cross-tabulation of 'satisfaction with employment status', with 'attitude to the
position of women' (categorised)
(Percentages in brackets)

	'Tradit-ional'	'Neutral'	'Progress-ive'	Total
1) Satis-fied worker	11 (20.4)	15 (27.8)	28 (51.9)	54 (100.0)
2) Dissatis-fied worker	6 (26.1)	7 (30.4)	10 (43.5)	23 (100.0)
3) Satisfied housewife	43 (46.2)	20 (21.5)	30 (32.3)	93 (100.0)
4) Dissatis-fied housewife	48 24.9)	63 (32.6)	82 (42.5)	193 (100.0)
Total	108 (29.8)	105 (28.9)	150 (41.3)	363 (100.0)

chi-square = 17.86 (p=.007) (37 missing cases)

Table D9 Cross-tabulation of 'satisfaction with
employment status', with 'attitude to moth-
motherhood responsibilities'
(Percentages in brackets)

	Some desire to be free from responsibil-ities	No desire to be free from responsibil-ities	Total
1) Satis-fied worker	33 (61.1)	21 (38.9)	54 (100.0)
2) Dissatis-fied worker	12 (52.2)	11 (47.8)	23 (100.0)
3) Satisfied housewife	35 (37.6)	58 (62.4)	93 (100.0)
4) Dissatis-housewife	101 (52.3)	92 (47.7)	193 (100.0)
Total	181 (49.9)	182 (50.1)	363 (100.0)

chi-square = 8.82 (p=.03) (37 missing cases)

APPENDIX D - SUPPLEMENTARY TABLES

Table D10   Cross-tabulation of 'satisfaction with
            employment status', with age of youngest
            child in the family
            (Percentages in brackets)

	Under 2 years	2 or more years	Total
1) Satisfied worker	15 (27.8)	39 (72.2)	54 (100.0)
2) Dissatis-fied worker	7 (30.4)	16 (69.6)	23 (100.0)
3) Satisfied housewife	51 (54.8)	42 (45.2)	93 (100.0)
4) Dissatis-fied housewife	108 (56.0)	85 (44.0)	193 (100.0)
Total	181 (49.9)	182 (50.1)	363 (100.0)

chi-square = 17.80 (p=.001) (37 missing cases)

Table D11   Cross-tabulation of 'satisfaction with
            employment status', with number of children
            under 5 years   (Percentages in brackets)

	1 child	2+ children	Total
1) Satisfied worker	35 (64.8)	19 (35.2)	54 (100.0)
2) Dissatis-fied worker	20 (87.0)	3 (13.0)	23 (100.0)
3) Satisfied housewife	63 (67.7)	30 (32.3)	93 (100.0)
4) Dissatis-fied housewife	122 (63.2)	71 (36.8)	193 (100.0)
Total	240 (66.1)	123 (33.9)	363 (100.0)

chi-square = 5.34 (p=.15) (37 missing cases)

Table D12   Cross-tabulation of 'satisfaction with work status', with reason for working (Percentages in brackets)

	Money most important	Money and other reasons	Other reasons more important	Total
1) Satisfied worker	18 (33.3)	27 (50.0)	9 (16.7)	54 (100.0)
2) Dissatisfied worker	10 (43.5)	13 (56.5)	0	23 (100.0)
Total	28 (36.4)	40 (51.9)	9 (11.7)	77 (100.0)

gamma = -.34   (323 missing cases)

Table D13   Cross-tabulation of 'satisfaction with employment status', with family income (Percentages in brackets)

	Under £3000	£3000-£4999	£5000-£6999	£7000+	Total
1) Satisfied worker	6 (13.6	23 (52.3)	11 (25.0)	4 (9.1)	44 (100.0)
2) Dissatisfied worker	3 (16.7)	6 (33.3)	5 (27.8)	4 (22.2)	18 (100.0)
3) Satisfied housewife	13 (17.6)	30 (40.5)	16 (21.6)	15 (20.3)	74 (100.0)
4) Dissatis- housewife	27 (16.7)	75 (46.3)	43 (26.5)	17 (10.5)	162 (100.0)
Total	49 (16.4)	134 (45.0)	75 (25.2)	40 (13.4)	298 (100.0)

chi-square = 7.54   (p=.58)   (102 missing cases)

Table D14   Cross-tabulation of 'satisfaction with
             employment status', with socio-economic
             group of husband (Percentages in brackets)

	Manager-ial and profess-ional	Other non-manual	Skilled manual	Partly-skilled & un-skilled	Total
1)Satisf-ied worker	9 (18.4)	12 (24.5)	23 (46.9)	5 (10.2)	49 (100.0)
2)Dissat-isfied worker	8 (42.1)	3 (15.8)	6 (31.6)	2 (10.5)	19 (100.0)
3)Satisf-ied house-wife	39 (44.8)	11 (12.6)	32 (36.8)	5 (5.7)	87 (100.0)
4)Dissatis-fied house-wife	53 (29.0)	47 (25.7)	65 (35.5)	18 (9.8)	183 (100.0)
Total	109 (32.2)	73 (21.6)	126 (37.3)	30 (8.9)	338 (100.0)

chi-square = 16.37   (p=.05)   (62 missing cases)

Table D15   Cross-tabulation of frequency of weekday
             shopping,with socio-economic group of
             husband   (Percentages in brackets)

	Profess-ional & Manager-ial	Other non-manual	Skilled manual	Partly-skilled & Un-skilled	Total
Every day	27 (23.1)	30 (40.0)	61 (46.2)	12 (38.7)	130 (36.6)
2 or 3 times per week	68 (58.1)	33 (44.0)	56 (42.4)	15 (48.4)	172 (48.5)
Once a week or less	22 (18.8)	12 (16.0)	15 (11.4)	4 (12.9)	53 (14.9)
Total	117 (100.0)	75 (100.0)	132 (100.0)	31 (100.0)	355 (100.0)

gamma = -.23   (45 missing cases)

APPENDIX D - SUPPLEMENTARY TABLES

Table D16   Cross-tabulation of frequency of weekday
            shopping,with family income (Per annum)
            (Percentages in brackets)

	Up to £3000	£3-5000	£5-7000	£7000 or more	Total
Every day	22 (45.8)	53 (36.6)	24 (32.0)	11 (24.4)	110 (35.1)
2 or 3 times per week	19 (39.6)	70 (48.3)	35 (46.7)	28 (62.2)	152 (48.6)
Once a week or less often	7 (14.6)	22 (15.2)	16 (21.3)	6 (13.3)	51 (16.3)
Total	48 (100.0)	145 (100.0)	75 (100.0)	45 (100.0)	313 (100.0)

gamma = .14   (87 missing cases)

Table D17   Cross-tabulation of frequency of weekday
            shopping,with employment status (and work
            location) (Percentages in brackets)

	Out at work	Work at home	Not in employment	Total
Every day	28 (38.9)	13 (35.1)	101 (37.3)	142 (37.4)
2 or 3 times per week	30 (41.7)	19 (51.4)	134 (49.4)	183 (48.2)
Once a week or less often	14 (19.4)	5 (13.5)	36 (13.3)	55 (14.5)
Total	72 (100.0)	37 (100.0)	271 (100.0)	380 (100.0)

chi-square = 2.41   (p=.66) (20 missing cases)

APPENDIX D - SUPPLEMENTARY TABLES

Table D18   Cross-tabulation of frequency of weekday shopping, with number of children under 5 years (Percentages in brackets)

	One	Two or More	Total
Every day	100 (40.3)	42 (31.8)	142 (37.4)
2 or 3 times per week	116 (46.8)	67 (50.8)	183 (48.2)
Once a week or less often	32 (12.9)	23 (17.4)	55 (14.5)
Total	248 (100.0)	132 (100.0)	380 (100.0)

gamma = .17   (20 missing cases)

Table D19   Cross-tabulation of whether shops used for weekday shopping are the closest to home, with grade of shopping centre used for weekday shopping (Percentages in brackets)

	1	2	3	4	5	6	7	Total
Yes	9 (90.0)	63 (98.4)	45 (100.0)	7 (100.0)	103 (52.8)	13 (39.4)	0	240 (63.2)
No	1 (10.0)	1 (1.6)	0	0	92 (47.2)	20 (60.6)	26 (100)	140 (36.8)
Total	10 (100)	64 (100)	45 (100)	7 (100)	195 (100)	33 (100)	26 (100)	380 (100)

chi-square = 129.20 (p=.001)(20 missing cases)

Table D20 Cross-tabulation of frequency of weekday shopping, with perceived proximity of shopping centre used for weekday shopping (Percentages in brackets)

	Local	Non-local	Total
Every day	138 (41.3)	4 (8.7)	142 (37.4)
2 or 3 times per week	160 (47.9)	23 (50.0)	183 (48.2)
Once a week or less often	36 (10.8)	19 (41.3)	55 (14.5)
Total	334 (100.0)	46 (100.0)	380 (100.0)

gamma = .69   (20 missing cases)

Table D21 Cross-tabulation of use of main shopping trip, with employment status (and work location) (Percentages in brackets)

	Out at work	Work at home	Not in employment	Total
Yes	52 (67.5)	30 (81.1)	215 (75.2)	297 (74.3)
No	25 (32.5)	7 (18.9)	71 (24.8)	103 (25.7)
Total	77 (100.0)	37 (100.0)	286 (100.0)	400 (100.0)

chi-square = 2.85 (p=.24)

Table D22 Cross-tabulation of whether voluntary work is undertaken, with terminal education age (Percentages in brackets)

	15 or less	16	17-18	19 or more	Total
No	138 (95.2)	98 (95.1)	78 (92.9)	57 (83.8)	371 (92.7)
Yes	7 (4.8)	5 (4.9)	6 (7.1)	11 (16.2)	29 (7.3)
Total	145 (100.0)	103 (100.0)	84 (100.0)	68 (100.0)	400 (100.0)

gamma = .35

APPENDIX D - SUPPLEMENTARY TABLES

Table D23 Cross-tabulation of whether voluntary
work is undertaken,with employment status
(and work location)
(Percentages in brackets)

	Out at work	Work at home	Not in employment	Total
No	71 (92.2)	29 (78.4)	271 (94.8)	371 (92.7)
Yes	6 (7.8)	8 (21.6)	15 (5.2)	29 (7.3)
Total	77 (100.0)	37 (100.0)	286 (100.0)	400 (100.0)

chi-square = 13.11   (p=.001)

Table D24 Cross-tabulation of frequency of park
visiting,with socio-economic group of
husband (Percentages in brackets)

	Profess-ional & Manager-ial	Other non-manual	Skilled Manual	Partly-skilled & Un-skilled	Total
More than once a week	50 (40.7)	40 (50.6)	56 (40.6)	9 (28.1)	155 (41.7)
Once a week or less often	57 (46.3)	34 (43.0)	58 (42.0)	17 (53.1)	166 (44.6)
Never	16 (13.0)	5 (6.3)	24 (17.4)	6 (18.8)	51 (13.7)
Total	123 (100.0)	79 (100.0)	138 (100.0)	32 (100.0)	372 (100.0)

gamma = .09   (28 missing cases)

APPENDIX D - SUPPLEMENTARY TABLES

Table D25 Cross-tabulation of frequency of park visiting, with terminal education age (Percentages in brackets)

	Below 16 years	16 years	17-18 years	19 years or older	Total
More than once a week	51 (35.2)	38 (36.9)	44 (52.4)	27 (39.7)	160 (40.0)
Once a week or less often	70 (48.3)	44 (42.7)	30 (35.7)	36 (52.9)	180 (45.0)
Never	24 (16.6)	21 (20.4)	10 (11.9)	5 (7.4)	60 (15.0)
Total	145 (100.0)	103 (100.0)	84 (100.0)	68 (100.0)	400 (100.0)

gamma = -.13

Table D26 Cross-tabulation of frequency of park visiting, with age of the youngest child (Percentages in brackets)

	0	1	2	3	4	Total
More than once a week	41 (40.6)	42 (43.8)	36 (40.0)	21 (31.8)	20 (42.6)	160 (40.0)
Once a week or less often	35 (34.7)	40 (41.7)	47 (52.2)	40 (60.6)	18 (38.3)	180 (45.0)
Never	25 (24.8)	14 (14.6)	7 (7.8)	5 (7.6)	9 (19.1)	60 (15.0)
Total	101 (100.0)	96 (100.0)	90 (100.0)	66 (100.0)	47 (100.0)	400 (100.0)

gamma = -.03

Table D27 Cross-tabulation of frequency of park visiting,with journey time to park or playground normally visited (Percentages in brackets)

	5 mins or less	6-10 mins	More than 10 mins	Total
Every day	42 (25.9)	16 (14.8)	9 (12.9)	67 (19.7)
2 or 3 times per week	46 (28.4)	31 (28.7)	16 (22.9)	93 (27.4)
Once a week or less	74 (45.7)	61 (56.5)	45 (64.3)	180 (53.0)
Total	162 (100.0)	108 (100.0)	70 (100.0)	340 (100.0)

gamma = .25   (60 missing cases)

Table D28 Cross-tabulation of frequency of park visiting,with Grade of park normally visited (Percentages in brackets)

	1	2	3	4	Total
Every day	7 (14.3)	47 (21.0)	9 (25.0)	4 (16.0)	67 (20.1)
2 or 3 times per week	15 (30.6)	59 (26.3)	7 (19.4)	11 (44.0)	92 (27.5)
Once a week or less often	27 (55.1)	118 (52.6)	20 (55.6)	10 (40.0)	175 (52.3)
Total	49 (100.0)	224 (100.0)	36 (100.0)	25 (100.0)	334 (100.0)

gamma = .07   (66 missing cases)

APPENDIX D - SUPPLEMENTARY TABLES

Table D29   Cross-tabulation of frequency of family visiting, with terminal education age
(Percentages in brackets)

	Below 16 years	16 years	17-18 years	19 years or older	Total
At least twice a week	58 (40.0)	30 (29.1)	21 (25.0)	8 (11.8)	117 (29.2)
Once a week or less often (includes never)	87 (60.0)	73 (70.9)	63 (75.0)	60 (88.2)	283 (70.8)
Total	145 (100.0)	103 (100.0)	84 (100.0)	68 (100.0)	400 (100.0)

gamma = .36

Table D30   Cross-tabulation of frequency of visiting local friends (those respondents without local friends being excluded), with mode of household tenure
(Percentages in brackets)

	Owner-occupied housing	Council-rented housing	Other housing (mainly privately rented)	Total
Every day	69 (26.6)	15 (25.4)	24 (43.6)	108 (29.0)
2 or 3 times a week	99 (38.2)	16 (27.1)	14 (25.5)	129 (34.6)
Once a week or less often	79 (30.5)	18 (30.5)	13 (23.6)	110 (29.5)
Never	12 (4.6)	10 (16.9)	4 (7.3)	26 (7.0)
Total	259 (100.0)	59 (100.0)	55 (100.0)	373 (100.0)

chi-square = 19.31 (p=.004)   (27 missing cases)

Table D31   Cross-tabulation of weekday use of trains, with opinion on public transport (Percentages in brackets)

	Very good or fairly good	Neither good nor bad	Not very good or not good at all	Total
Once a week or more often	30 (14.3)	4 (12.1)	6 (5.0)	40 (11.0)
Less often than once a week	83 (39.5)	13 (39.4)	42 (34.7)	138 (37.9)
Never	97 (46.2)	16 (48.5)	73 (60.3)	186 (51.1)
Total	210 (100.0)	33 (100.0)	121 (100.0)	364 (100.0)

gamma = .24   (36 missing cases)

Table D32   Cross-tabulation of weekday use of buses, with location of area where respondent grew up   (Percentages in brackets)

	Local area	Elsewhere S.W. London	Outside S.W. London	Total
Once a week or more often	49 (37.1)	17 (20.7)	35 (19.2)	101 (25.5)
Less often than once a week	37 (28.0)	35 (42.7)	44 (24.2)	116 (29.3)
Never	46 (34.8)	30 (36.6)	103 (56.6)	179 (45.2)
Total	132 (100.0)	82 (100.0)	182 (100.0)	396 (100.0)

gamma = .30   (4 missing cases)

APPENDIX D - SUPPLEMENTARY TABLES

Table D33   Cross-tabulation of weekday use of trains,
with distance from a station (British
Rail or Underground)
(Percentages in brackets)

	Within $\frac{1}{4}$ mile	$\frac{1}{4}$ - $\frac{1}{2}$ mile	Over $\frac{1}{2}$ mile	Total
Once a week or more often	28 (18.9)	10 (8.3)	2 (1.5)	40 (10.0)
Less often than once a week	56 (37.8)	48 (40.0)	40 (30.3)	144 (36.0)
Never	64 (43.2)	62 (51.7)	90 (68.2)	216 (54.0)
Total	148 (100.0)	120 (100.0)	132 (100.0)	400 (100.0)

gamma = .21

Table D34   Cross-tabulation of weekday use of trains,
with car availability
(Percentages in brackets)

	Car available	Car not available	Total
Once a week or more often	7 (5.4)	33 (12.2)	40 (10.0)
Less often than once a week	43 (33.3)	101 (37.3)	144 (36.0)
Never	79 (61.2)	137 (50.6)	216 (54.0)
Total:	129 (100.0)	271 (100.0)	400 (100.0)

gamma = -.23

Table D35   Cross-tabulation of public transport mode used, with car availability (Percentages in brackets)

	Car available	Car not available	Total
Buses and trains used	23 (17.8)	114 (42.1)	137 (34.2)
Buses used only	9 (7.0)	72 (26.6)	81 (20.2)
Trains used only	27 (20.9)	20 (7.4)	47 (11.7)
Neither buses nor trains used	70 (54.3)	65 (24.0)	135 (33.7)
Total	129 (100.0)	271 (100.0)	400 (100.0)

chi-square = 68.95   (p=.001)

Table D36   Cross-tabulation of perceived convenience of local area, with opinion on public transport (Percentages in brackets)

	Very Good	Fairly Good	Neutral/ Not very Good	Not Good at all	Total
Very convenient	41 (63.1)	57 (40.4)	28 (27.5)	10 (19.6)	136 (37.9)
Convenient enough	18 (27.7)	56 (39.7)	46 (45.1)	18 (35.3)	138 (38.4)
Not very convenient	5 (7.7)	22 (15.6)	22 (21.6)	16 (31.4)	65 (18.1)
Not convenient at	1 (1.5)	6 (4.3)	6 (5.9)	7 (13.7)	20 (5.6)
Total	65 (100.0)	141 (100.0)	102 (100.0)	51 (100.0)	359 (100.0)

gamma = .39   (41 missing cases)

APPENDIX D - SUPPLEMENTARY TABLES

Table D37   Cross-tabulation of type of pre-school
facility used, with distance to the
nearest private playgroup/nursery school
(Percentages in brackets)

	Under ¼ mile	¼ - ½ mile	Over ½ mile	Total
State	71 (41.0)	39 (60.0)	12 (54.5)	122 (46.9)
Private	102 (59.0)	26 (40.0)	10 (45.5)	138 (53.1)
Total	173 (100.0)	65 (100.0)	22 (100.0)	260 (100.0)

gamma = -.30   (140 missing cases)

Table D38   Cross-tabulation of distance to the
nearest state nursery school/class, with
socio-economic group of husband
(Percentages in brackets)

	Profess-ional & Manager-ial	Other Non-manual	Skilled Manual	Partly-skilled & un-skilled	Total
Under ¼ mile	34 (27.6)	25 (31.6)	55 (39.9)	12 (37.5)	126 (33.9)
¼-½ mile	34 (27.6)	27 (34.2)	53 (38.4)	12 (37.5)	126 (33.9)
Over ½ mile	55 (44.7)	27 (34.2)	30 (21.7)	8 (25.0)	120 (32.3)
Total	123 (100.0)	79 (100.0)	138 (100.0)	32 (100.0)	372 (100.0)

gamma = -.22   (28 missing cases)

Table D39   Cross-tabulation of number of different
            types of activity on previous day, with
            age of the youngest child
            (Percentages in brackets)

Age of the youngest child

No. of activities	0	1	2	3	4	Total
0	8 (7.9)	6 (6.3)	2 (2.2)	1 (1.5)	4 (8.5)	21 (5.3)
1	38 (37.6)	22 (22.9)	17 (18.9)	9 (13.6)	11 (23.4)	97 (24.3)
2	26 (25.7)	39 (40.6)	36 (40.0)	21 (31.8)	13 (27.7)	135 (33.7)
3	22 (21.8)	21 (21.9)	28 (31.1)	25 (37.9)	13 (27.7)	109 (27.2)
4 or more	7 (6.9)	8 (8.3)	7 (7.8)	10 (15.2)	6 (12.8)	38 (9.5)
Total	101 (100.0)	96 (100.0)	90 (100.0)	66 (100.0)	47 (100.0)	400 (100.0)

gamma = .20

Fig.E1 'Satisfaction with Life' : Results from the 1973 national survey

Please put a tick in whichever box applies to each line (n=98. Percentages below boxes).

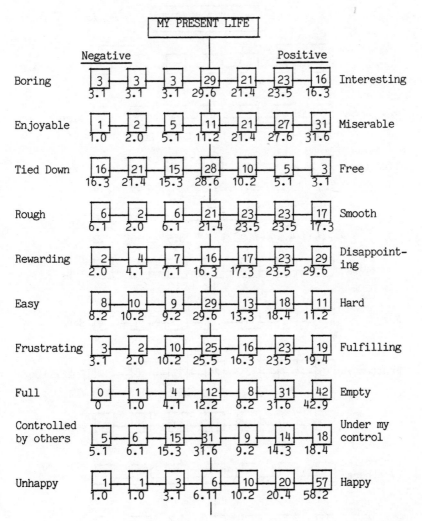

Fig.E2   'Satisfaction with Life' : Results from the 1975
          national survey

Please put a tick   in whichever box applies to each line
(n =84.   Percentages below boxes)

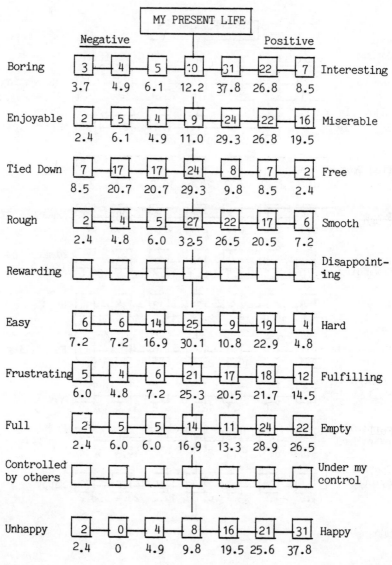

	Negative			MY PRESENT LIFE		Positive	
Boring	3	4	5	10	31	22	7	Interesting
	3.7	4.9	6.1	12.2	37.8	26.8	8.5	
Enjoyable	2	5	4	9	24	22	16	Miserable
	2.4	6.1	4.9	11.0	29.3	26.8	19.5	
Tied Down	7	17	17	24	8	7	2	Free
	8.5	20.7	20.7	29.3	9.8	8.5	2.4	
Rough	2	4	5	27	22	17	6	Smooth
	2.4	4.8	6.0	32.5	26.5	20.5	7.2	
Rewarding								Disappointing
Easy	6	6	14	25	9	19	4	Hard
	7.2	7.2	16.9	30.1	10.8	22.9	4.8	
Frustrating	5	4	6	21	17	18	12	Fulfilling
	6.0	4.8	7.2	25.3	20.5	21.7	14.5	
Full	2	5	5	14	11	24	22	Empty
	2.4	6.0	6.0	16.9	13.3	28.9	26.5	
Controlled by others								Under my control
Unhappy	2	0	4	8	16	21	31	Happy
	2.4	0	4.9	9.8	19.5	25.6	37.8	

APPENDIX E - SUPPLEMENTARY TABLES

Fig. E3 'Satisfaction with Life' : Results from the Merton Survey

Please put a tick in whichever box applies to each line
(n = 400. Percentages below boxes)

	MY PRESENT LIFE	
Negative		Positive

Boring	15	6	36	119	103	63	57	Interesting
	3.7	1.5	9.0	29.8	25.7	15.8	14.2	
Enjoyable	6	3	18	72	92	99	109	Miserable
	1.5	0.7	4.5	18.0	23.0	24.7	27.2	
Tied Down	67	57	73	122	36	26	18	Free
	16.7	14.2	18.2	30.5	9.0	6.5	4.5	
Rough	15	6	24	139	72	69	74	Smooth
	3.7	1.5	6.0	34.7	18.0	17.2	18.5	
Rewarding	9	6	10	67	66	101	140	Disappointing
	2.3	1.5	2.5	16.7	16.5	25.3	35.0	
Easy	36	33	59	139	44	43	45	Hard
	9.0	8.2	14.8	34.7	11.0	10.8	11.2	
Frustrating	23	25	41	115	57	70	68	Fulfilling
	5.7	6.3	10.2	28.8	14.2	17.5	17.0	
Full	10	3	8	63	67	77	171	Empty
	2.5	0.7	2.0	15.8	16.7	19.3	42.7	
Controlled by others	34	27	39	107	53	54	85	Under my control
	8.5	6.8	9.7	26.7	13.2	13.5	21.2	
Unhappy	3	2	4	51	49	104	186	Happy
	0.7	0.5	1.0	12.7	12.2	26.0	46.5	
Total Score (Grouped)	6	6	41	156	133	56	1	
	1.5	1.5	10.2	39.0	33.3	14.0	0.2	